THEY
LOOKED LIKE THIS

THEY
LOOKED LIKE THIS

An Assembly
of Authentic Word-Portraits
of Men and Women in
English History and Literature
over 1900 years

COMPILED BY
GRANT UDEN

OXFORD
BASIL BLACKWELL

Printed in Great Britain
in the City of Oxford
AT THE ALDEN PRESS
and bound by
The Kemp Hall Bindery, Oxford

As a beauty I'm not a great star,
Others are handsomer far;
But my face—I don't mind it
Because I'm behind it;
It's the folk out in front that I jar.

—Anthony Euwer

Whoever would wish to study the topography of the human countenance in its declivities and concavities, in its mountain ridges or its ravines cut by the course of time, let him pause here and take his lesson. The result is marvellous. We can scarcely add, agreeable.

—*Art Journal,* 1864

INTRODUCTION

Though I have been reading history in one form or another, in ways either dedicated or desultory, for nearly half a century, it was not, I think, till I read the Director of the National Portrait Gallery's brilliant book on the English face* that I first realised how little accurate knowledge I had of the way characters in history and literature looked to their contemporaries. Hazy memories from school-days were mingled with impressions gathered from painters, engravers and caricaturists; biographers had blurred the none-too-clear outlines by reading into those portraits qualities that were never there, and historical novelists had sinned even more heinously; the film-maker had erred most of all, with a contemptuous disregard of fact that, even when it was known, still left its legacy in the memory.

Superficially, it would appear that the most reliable source for accurate information about a character's appearance is the contemporary painting or drawing. But it is many centuries before portraits begin to appear, and to survive, in any number. Even when they do, one has to contend with strong tendencies—which have by no means disappeared in our own day—to stylise, to glamorise, and even to deliberately falsify out of respect for the wishes—and the purse—of the sitter. It is remarkable how different half-a-dozen portraits of the same person by as many different artists can be, according to the complexities of mind and character that each saw, or thought he saw, behind the mere features of the sitter. Neither must it be forgotten that many distinguished artists have loudly lamented their inability to capture the real likeness of some of their subjects.

It might be thought that, with the coming of the camera and the photographer, all these problems would be at an end. But there is often nothing so peculiarly lifeless as a photograph from life. Certainly no-one would rely on the average passport photograph to preserve a true likeness for posterity.

So that we are left with the written and printed word, the

* David Piper, The English Face, Thames and Hudson, 1957.

impressions recorded either on the spot or in retrospect by those who knew and watched the characters of history; or who talked with men and women who knew and watched them. Here, surely, is the greatest hope for clarity and accuracy, making some allowance for the natural bias of friend and foe and for the vagaries of memory.

This, therefore, has been my object in collecting this gallery of word-portraits over a period of close on two thousand years of English life. I have tried to include only the testimony of eye-witnesses; or, failing that, the evidence of people who talked with eye-witnesses. Only occasionally, as in the case of Boadicea or Robert Bruce, have I allowed a greater gap of time because of the lack of other evidence, and because there seemed a good chance of authentic tradition having been preserved. I have not been concerned with character, only with physical appearance, though sometimes the two are inextricably interwoven. There are many gaps, either because no reliable description has survived or, what is more likely, it has eluded my discovery. Sometimes the silence of history has surprised me. Where, among all the spate of words that have been written about him, is there an accurate description of the appearance of King John?

I am greatly indebted to a number of friends who have aided my search, supplied my wants and remedied my ignorance; especially to Mrs. Tim Pedley, Alan Atkinson, Richard Cooper, Christopher Pelly, and Christopher Lloyd. Of the librarians who have sustained me, I am particularly grateful to Marion Hewitt, Marian Hetherington and Richard Mainwood. The sources to which I owe my information are, I hope, usually sufficiently clear in the text; but I must single out several which are not specifically mentioned. The compilers of Basil Blackwell's 'They Saw It Happen' volumes put me on the track of a great deal of valuable material; and I gratefully acknowledge a special debt to Hugh Macdonald, whose 'Portraits in Prose' (George Routledge & Sons, 1946), though they are not concerned exclusively with physical appearance, gave me much information I should not otherwise have come by.

G.U.

ACKNOWLEDGEMENTS

The author and publisher wish to thank the following for permission to reproduce copyright material from the sources shown:

THE NONESUCH PRESS LTD for the extract from *A Journal by Monsieur de Maisse*, 1931

COLUMBIA UNIVERSITY PRESS for the extract from *Chaucer's World* by Rickert

CHATTO & WINDUS LTD for the extracts from *The Chronicle of Jocelyn of Brakelond*, 1907 and from *Stars and Markets*, 1957 by Sir Charles Tennyson

CONSTABLE PUBLISHERS for the extract from *The Early Lives of Milton* by Helen Darbyshire

W. & R. CHAMBERS LTD for the extract on Mary Russell Mitford from *Cyclopaedia of English Literature*, 1901

HAMISH HAMILTON LTD for the extracts from *Cockerell* by Wilfred Blunt

PHAIDON PRESS LTD for the extracts quoted from *Erasmus of Rotterdam* by Johan Huizinga, with a selection of the letters of Erasmus, translated from the Latin by Barbara Flower, London, 1952

JONATHAN CAPE LTD for the extract from *The Pre-eminent Victorian* by Joanna Richardson

GEORGE ALLEN & UNWIN LTD for the extracts from *A History of Cricket*, 1962 by H. S. Altham and *Reminiscences of Oxford*, 1907 by Rev. W. Tuckwell

METHUEN & CO LTD for the extracts from *Memories of Victorian Oxford* by Sir Charles Oman

ENCYCLOPAEDIA BRITANNICA LTD for the extracts from the article on De Quincey, 1952 printing

ODHAMS BOOKS LTD for the extract from *Great Contemporaries* by Winston S. Churchill

MACMILLAN & CO LTD for the extracts from *The Journals of Mrs Arbuthnott* by Francis Bamford

LONGMANS, GREEN & CO LTD for the extracts from *Journal of James Yonge* by F. N. L. Poynter and from *Joseph Conrad* by Oliver Warner

ACKNOWLEDGEMENTS

CHAPMAN & HALL LTD for the extracts from *Brighton, its History, its Foibles and Fashions* by Lewis Melville

ANGUS & ROBERTSON LTD, SYDNEY for the extract from *Now Came Still Evening On* by Julian Ashton

J. W. ARROWSMITH LTD for the extract from *Home Life with Herbert Spencer*, 1906

ESSEX RECORD OFFICE for the extract from Round MSS., D/Drg 3/6. from *English History from Essex Sources, Vol. I*

M. B. YEATS, ESQ AND MACMILLAN & CO LTD for the extracts from *Autobiographies* by W. B. Yeats

ERNEST BENN LTD for the extracts from *Three Early 19th Century Diaries* by Lord Macaulay, edited by A. Aspinall and from *Life of Richard Cobden*, 1903 by John Morley

THE CLARENDON PRESS for the extracts from *The Dictionary of National Biography* and *Brief Lives*, 1898 by John Aubrey

THE TRUSTEES OF THE LONDON MUSEUM for the extracts from *Catalogue No. 5 (Costume)*, 1935

THE HONOURABLE SOCIETY OF CYMMRODORION for the extract from *De Nugis Curialium* by M. R. James

THE COUNCIL OF THE NAVY RECORDS SOCIETY for the extract from *The Life of Sir John Leake*, 1920

THE CONTROLLER OF H.M. STATIONERY OFFICE for the extracts from Crown Copyright material in the Public Record Office

THE CRESSET PRESS for the extracts from *Historia Novorum in Anglia*, 1964, translated by Geoffrey Bosanquet

WILLIAM HEINEMANN LTD for the extracts from *The Richmond Papers*, 1926 by Mrs. Stirling; from *Extraordinary People* by Hesketh Pearson; and *Portraits and Sketches* by Edmund Gosse

THE COUNCIL OF THE EARLY ENGLISH TEXT SOCIETY for the extract from *The Life and Death of Sir Thomas Moore*, 1932 by Nicholas Harpsfield. Ed. by E. V. Hitchcock and R. W. Chambers

MRS MARY BENNETT for the extracts from *An Unfinished Autobiography*, 1940 by H. A. L. Fisher

THOMAS NELSON & SONS LTD for the extract from *The Life of King Edward the Confessor* by Frank Barlow

HOUGHTON MIFFLIN COMPANY, BOSTON for the extract from *Dickens Days in Boston* by E. F. Payne

CASSELL AND COMPANY LTD for the extract from *Memoirs of Forty Years*, 1914 by Princess Radziwill

EYRE & SPOTTISWOODE LTD for the extracts from *Ancestors and*

ACKNOWLEDGEMENTS

Friends, 1962 by John Lehmann and from *English Historical Documents*, *Vol. II* edited by Professor David C. Douglas and G. W. Greenaway

THE PRESIDENT AND COUNCIL OF THE HAKLUYT SOCIETY and the CAMBRIDGE UNIVERSITY PRESS for the extracts from *Further English Voyages to South America*, 1951 edited and translated by Irene Wright

JOHN MURRAY LTD for the extracts from *Robert Adam and His Circle*, 1962 by John Fleming; from *Parliamentary Reminiscences and Reflections*, 1917 by Lord George Hamilton; from *Lady Bessborough and her Family Circle*, 1940 by the Earl of Bessborough; from *Sixty Years in the Wilderness*, 1909 by Henry Lucy and from *Henry George Liddell, a Memoir*, 1899 by the Rev. Henry Thompson

THE BODLEY HEAD LTD for the extract from *Albert the Good*, 1932 by Hector Bolitho

ARCHON BOOKS, HAMDEN, CONNECTICUT, for the extract from *The Journal of James Yonge*, 1963 by F. N. L. Poynter

ROUTLEDGE AND KEGAN PAUL LTD for the extract from *Memoirs of the Comte de Gramont*, 1932 by Peter Quennell

MICHAEL MACCARTHY, ESQ for the extracts from *Criticisms, Remnants and Portraits* by Sir Desmond MacCarthy

The author and publisher have made every effort to clear all copyright material, but in spite of their efforts, it has been impossible to trace the holders of some of the extracts. In the event of any unforeseen infringements, they express their regrets, and would welcome any information which would remedy such oversight in future editions.

THEY
LOOKED LIKE THIS

A BECKET, THOMAS (1118?–1170), Archbishop of Canterbury; murdered in the cathedral on December 29th.

Thomas was handsome and pleasing of countenance, tall of stature, with a prominent and slightly aquiline nose, nimble and active in his movements, gifted with eloquence of speech and an acute intelligence, high-spirited, ever pursuing the path of highest virtue, amiable to all men. . . .

In his consecration as archbishop he was anointed with the visible unction of God's mercy. Putting off the secular man, he now put on Jesus Christ. . . . Clad in a hair shirt of the roughest kind, which reached to his knees and swarmed with vermin, he mortified his flesh with the sparest diet, and his accustomed drink was water used for cooking of hay . . . He often exposed his naked back to the lash of discipline. Immediately over his hair-shirt he wore the habit of a monk, as being abbot of the monks of Canterbury; above this he wore the garb of a canon so as to conform to the custom of clerks. But the stole, the emblem of the sweet yoke of Christ, was ever day and night about his neck. His outward visage was like to that of ordinary men, but within all was different.

SOURCE: William Fitz-Stephen, *Materials for the History of Thomas Becket, Archbishop of Canterbury*, 1878; included in Douglas and Greenaway, *English Historical Documents*, Vol. II, 1042–1189, Eyre and Spottiswoode, 1953.

ADAM, ROBERT (1728–1792), architect; with his brothers, built the Adelphi, London, and a number of important country mansions.

Would you like to know the appearance of your once plain friend? Read the description and you have him. A most

Frenchified head of hair, loaded with powder, ornaments his top; a complete suit of cut velvet of two colours, his body—which is set off by a white satin lining; white silk stockings and embroidered silk gushets, his legs; Mariguin pumps with red heels, his feet; stone-buckles like diamonds shine on his knees and shoes. A gold-handled sword, with white and gold handle knot, ornaments his side; Brussels lace, his breast and hands; a solitaire ribbon, his neck; a smous hat his oxter. In the mornings he honours his head with a large hat and white feather, his side with a gold belt and hanger, and in cold weather his whole body is wrapt in a white freeze cloak with black velvet neck and sleeves, which is the mode amongst the Seigneurs of this kingdom. In short, were I to enumerate the collection of curiosities which at first adorned my body and made me laugh but are now as familiar to me as my garter, I should both divert and surprise you ... I often burst out a-laughing upon this single thought—of what you would all say were I for a moment to show myself in the drawing room thus metamorphosed!

AGED 26.

SOURCE: Robert Adam, in a letter from Paris to his mother; quoted in John Fleming, *Robert Adam and His Circle*, John Murray, 1962.

ADDISON, JOSEPH (1672–1719), essayist, poet and statesman.

He would get up so early as between two and three o'clock in the height of summer, and lay in bed till between eleven and twelve in the depth of winter. He was untalkative whilst here, and often thoughtful; and sometimes so lost in thought, that I have come into his room, and staid five minutes there before he has known anything of it.

SOURCE: Abbé Philippeaux in Rev. Joseph Spence, *Observations and Characters of Books and Men*, edit. S. W. Singer, 1820.

Of his habits, or external manners, nothing is so often mentioned as that timorous or sullen taciturnity, which his friends called modesty by too mild a name. Steele mentioned with great tenderness, 'that remarkable bashfulness, which is a cloak that hides and muffles merit;' ... Chesterfield affirms, that 'Addison was the most timorous and awkward man that he ever saw'.

SOURCE: Doctor Samuel Johnson, *The Lives of the Most Eminent English Poets*, Vol. II, 1781.

ADELAIDE, QUEEN OF WILLIAM IV (1792–1849).

... a little insignificant person as I ever saw. She was dressed, as perhaps you will see by the papers, 'exceeding plain' in bombazine with a little shabby muslin collar, dyed leghorn hat, and leather shoes.

SOURCE: Letter from an onlooker, on a visit by the Queen to the Tower of London; quoted in Mary Hopkirk's *Queen Adelaide*, John Murray, 1946.

AGED 38.

The Queen came to Lady Bathurst's to see the review and hold a sort of drawing room ... She is very ugly, with a horrid complexion, but has good manners, and did all this (which she hated) very well. She said the part as if she was acting and wished the green curtain to drop.

SOURCE: *The Greville Memoirs*.

ALBERT FRANCIS CHARLES AUGUSTUS EMMANUEL, husband of Queen Victoria and Prince-Consort of England (1819–1861).

Albert is a fine young fellow, well grown for his age, with agreeable and valuable qualities; and who, if things go well, may, in a few years, turn out a strong, handsome man, of a kindly, simple, yet dignified demeanour. Externally, therefore, he possesses all that pleases the sex, and at all times and in all countries must please. It may prove, too, a lucky circumstance that even now he has something of an English look.

AGED 16.

SOURCE: King Leopold of the Belgians; letter preserved in the papers of Baron Stockmar; quoted in Hector Bolitho's *Albert the Good*, Cobden-Sanderson, 1932.

ALFRED or **AELFRED** (849–901), king of the West Saxons; called 'the Great'.

As he advanced through the years of infancy and youth, his form appeared more comely than that of his brothers; in look, in speech and in manner, he was more graceful than they.

Though established in royal power, the king was wounded by the nails of many tribulations. From his twentieth to his forty-fifth year (in which he now is) he has been troubled incessantly by the severe visitation of an unknown disease; never an hour passes but he either suffers from it, or is nearly desperate from fear of it.

SOURCE: Asser, Bishop of Sherborne's *Life of Aelfred*.

ALLEN, VISCOUNT (?–1843), known as 'King' Allen; fought with distinction at Talavera; club-man and dandy.

'King' Allen was a well-known character in London for many years. He was a tall, stout, and pompous-looking personage, remarkably well got up, with an invariably new-looking hat and well-polished boots. His only exercise and usual walk was from White's to Crockford's, and from Crockford's to White's.

Who, in this ponderous old man, would have recognised the gallant youth who, as Ensign in the Guards, led his men on with incredible energy and activity across the ravine at Talavera; where if the great Duke had not sent the 48th Regiment to their assistance, very little more would have been heard of 'King' Allen and his merry men?

Lord Allen greatly resembled in later life an ancient grey parrot, both in the aquiline outline of his features, and his peculiar mode of walking, with one foot crossed over the other in a slow and wary manner.

SOURCE: Captain R. H. Gronow, *Reminiscences*.

ALVANEY, LORD (1789–1849), soldier, wit and man of fashion.

He was one of the rare examples (particularly rare in the days of the dandies, who were generally sour and spiteful) of a man combining brilliant wit and repartee with the most perfect good nature. His manner, above all, was irresistible; and the slight lisp, which might have been considered as a blemish, only added piquancy and zest to his sayings.

In appearance, he was about the middle height, and well and strongly built, though he latterly became somewhat corpulent . . . His face had somewhat of the round form and smiling expression which characterise the jolly friars one meets with in Italy. His hair and eyes were dark, and he had a very small nose, to which, after deep potations, his copious pinches of snuff had some difficulty in finding their way, and were in consequence rather lavishly bestowed upon his florid cheek . . .

Alvaney had a delightful recklessness and *laisser aller* in all things. His manner of putting out his light at night was not a very pleasant one for his host for the time being. He always read in bed, and when he wanted to go to sleep, he either extinguished his candle by throwing it on the floor in the middle of the room, and taking a shot at it with the pillow, or else quietly placed it, when still lighted, under the bolster. At Badminton, and other country houses, his habits in this respect were so well known, that a servant was ordered to sit up in the passage to keep watch over him . . .

In his latter years Lord Alvaney was a martyr to the gout . . .

SOURCE: Captain R. H. Gronow, *Reminiscences*.

AMHERST, JEFFREY, Baron Amherst (1717–1797), field marshal; commanded expedition to North America, 1758; governor general of British North America.

With Lord Amherst I was well acquainted. In his person he

B

was tall and thin, with an aquiline nose, and an intelligent countenance . . . The constitutional tranquillity of his temper secured him . . . from being ruffled at any indications of popular dissatisfaction. I have scarcely ever known a man who possessed more stoical apathy or command over himself. Naturally taciturn and reserved, he rarely disclosed his sentiment on any subject of a political nature. Even at the Cabinet Dinners, which were held weekly, I have heard Lord Sacville say that, though he usually gave his decided affirmative or negative to the specific measure proposed, yet he always did it in few words, often by a monosyllable: but never could without great difficulty be induced to assign the reasons, or to state the ground of his opinion.

SOURCE: Sir N. William Wraxall, *Historical Memoirs of My Own Life*, 1815.

ANNE (1665–1714), queen of Great Britain.

Her majesty was labouring under a fit of the gout, and in extreme pain and agony, and on this occasion everything about her was much in the same disorder as about the meanest of her subjects. Her face, which was red and spotted, was rendered something frightful by her negligent dress . . .

AGED 42.

SOURCE: Sir John Clerk, *Memoirs*.

Queen Anne had a person and appearance not at all ungraceful, till she grew exceeding gross and corpulent. There was something of majesty in her look, but mixed with a sullen and constant frown, that plainly betrayed a gloominess of soul and a cloudiness of disposition within.

SOURCE: *Private Correspondence of Sarah, Duchess of Marlborough*, 1838.

Her person was middle-sized and well-made, but after she bare children, corpulent; her hair dark brown, her complexion sanguine and ruddy; her features strong but regular; and the only blemish in her face was owing to the difluxion she had in her infancy on the eyes, which left a contraction in the upper lids, that gave a cloudy air to her countenance ... What was most remarkable in her personal accomplishments was a clear harmonious voice, particularly conspicuous in her graceful delivery of her speeches to Parliament.

SOURCE: Abel Boyer, *History of the Life and Reign of Queen Anne.*

ANNE BOLEYN (1507–1536), second queen of Henry VIII.

... a beauty not so whitely as clear and fresh above all we may esteem, which appeared much more excellent by her favour passing sweet and cheerful. There was found, indeed, upon the side of her nail upon one of her fingers some little show of a nail, which yet was so small, by the report of those that have seen her, as the work-master seemed to leave it an occasion of greater grace to her hand, which, with the tip of one of her other fingers, might be and was usually by her hidden, without any least blemish to it.

AGED 15.

SOURCE: George Wyatt, *Life of Anne Boleyn*, ed. Singer; and quoted by J. S. Brewer in *The Reign of Henry VIII*, John Murray, 1884.

Not one of the handsomest women in the world ... Of middling stature, swarthy complexion, long neck, wide mouth, bosom not much raised, and in fact has nothing but ... her eyes, which are black and beautiful.

SOURCE: The Venetian Ambassador; quoted in David Piper, *The English Face*, Thames and Hudson, 1957.

ANNE, PRINCESS ROYAL (1709–1759) eldest daughter of George II.

The Princess Royal's personal beauties were a lively clean look and a very fine complexion, though she was marked a good deal with the small-pox. The faults of her person were that of being very ill made, though not crooked, and a great propensity to fat . . . She rose very early, was many hours alone and never unemployed. She had more command of her passions than people generally have whose passions are so strong . . . She was the proudest of all her proud family . . .

AGED 24.

SOURCE: Lord Hervey, *Memoirs of the Reign of George II.*

ANSELM, SAINT (1033–1109), Archbishop of Canterbury.
No detailed account of Anselm's appearance is known to me, but the following passage, describing his reluctant appointment to the See of Canterbury at the hands of the sick William II, gives a vivid picture of his physical reactions on one occasion.

Then the King, perceiving that the efforts of all of them were being spent in vain, bade them all kneel at Anselm's feet, in the hope that possibly in that way he might be induced to consent. But what then? Why, when they kneeled down, Anselm himself kneeled down too and still refused to be moved from his original decision. Growing angry with him and blaming themselves for weakness in suffering the delay which they had in heeding his objections, they cried, 'Fetch the pastoral staff, the pastoral staff!' Then seizing hold of his right arm they began, some dragging him against his will, some pushing behind, to bring him to the King's bedside. But when the King held out the staff to him, he closed his hand and utterly refused to take it. Then the Bishops tried to raise his fingers, which were tightly clenched against his palm, then even so the staff should be put into his hand. But when in this they had for some time laboured in vain and he himself uttered groans of anguish for the pain which he suffered, at last they lifted his forefinger, which he immediately closed again, and so the staff was placed in his closed hand and staff and hand together were pressed and held fast by the hands of the Bishops. Then, while the crowd cried, 'Long live the Bishop; long may he live', the Bishops and clergy began with uplifted voices to chant the *Te Deum*; and so the Archbishop elect was carried, rather than led, into the neighbouring church, all the time resisting to the utmost of his power . . .

SOURCE: Eadmer, monk of Canterbury; *Historia Novorum in Anglia*, translated by Geoffrey Bosanquet, Cresset Press, 1964.

ARLINGTON, first Earl of (1618–1685), member of Charles II's Cabal ministry.

He had a scar across the bridge of his nose which he covered with a long patch or, to speak more accurately, with a little lozenge-shaped plaster. Scars upon the face usually give a certain air of truculence and bellicosity which is not unbecoming. In his case, however, it had quite the contrary effect; and this remarkable plaster had so accommodated itself to the secretive and mysterious air of his visage, that it seemed to add to it a kind of importance and capability.

Behind the shelter of this countenance, composed of an overwhelming anxiety to thrust himself forward, which passed for industry, and of an impenetrable stupidity which passed for power to keep a secret, Arlington had given himself out as a politician on the grand scale. Since nobody had the leisure to go into his pretensions, they had taken his word for it, and he had been made Minister and Secretary of State simply on his face value.

SOURCE: Anthony Hamilton, *Memoirs of the Comte de Gramont*, translated by Peter Quennell, George Routledge & Sons, 1930.
Arlington received the gash across his nose fighting on the Royalist side in the Civil War, and the black plaster was perhaps intended to emphasise rather than hide it.

ARNOLD, MATTHEW (1822–1888), educationist and writer.

The face, strong and rugged, the large mouth, the broad lined brow, and vigorous coal-black hair, bore no resemblance, except for that fugitive yet vigorous something which we call 'family likeness', to either his father or his mother—still less to the brother so near to him in age. But the Celtic trace is there, though derived, I have sometimes thought, rather from an Irish than a Cornish source. Arnold's mother . . . was partly of Irish blood . . . And I have seen in Ireland faces belonging to the 'black Celt' type—faces full of power, and humour, and softness, visibly moulded out of the good common earth by the nimble spirit within, which have reminded me of my uncle. Nothing indeed at first sight could have been less romantic or dreamy than his outward aspect . . . He stood four-square—a courteous, competent man of affairs, an admirable inspector of schools, a delightful companion, a guest whom everybody wanted, and no one could bind for long; one of the sanest, most independent, most cheerful and loveable of mortals.

SOURCE: Mrs. Humphrey Ward, *A Writer's Recollections*, 1918.

ARUNDEL, EARL OF (1586–1646).
See Howard, Thomas, second Earl of Arundel and Surrey.

AUGUSTA OF SAXE-GOTHA, PRINCESS OF WALES (1719–1772), wife of Frederick Lewis, Prince of Wales, eldest son of George II.

The Princess was rather tall, and had health and youth enough . . . joined to a modest and good-natured face, to make her countenance not disagreeable; but her person, from being very ill-made, a good deal awry, and her motions awkward, had, in spite of all the finery of jewels and brocade, an ordinary air, which no trappings could ever cover or exalt.

AGED 17.

SOURCE: Lord Hervey, *Memoirs of the Reign of George II*.

AUSTEN, JANE (1775–1817), novelist.

. . . a friend of mine, who visits her now, says that she has stiffened into the most perpendicular, precise, taciturn piece of single-blessedness that ever existed, and that, till *Pride and Prejudice* showed what a precious gem was hidden in that unbending case, she was no more regarded in society than a poker or a fire-screen . . . She is still a poker—but a poker of whom everyone is afraid.

AGED 40.

SOURCE: Mary Russell Mitford; *Life of Mary Russell Mitford Related in a Selection from her Letters to her Friends*, edit. A. G. L'Estrange, 1870.

In person she was very attractive; her figure was rather tall and slender, her step light and firm, and her whole appearance of health and animation. In complexion she was a clear brunette with a rich colour; she had full round cheeks with a mouth and nose small but well-formed, bright hazel eyes and brown hair forming natural curls round her face. If not so regularly handsome as her sister yet her countenance had a peculiar charm of its own to the eyes of most beholders. She was never seen morning or evening without a cap. I believe that she and her sister were generally thought to have taken to the garb of middle age earlier than their looks or years required, and that though remarkably neat in their dress as in all their ways, they were scarcely sufficiently regardful of the fashionable or the becoming.

SOURCE: James Edward Austen-Leigh, *Memoir of Jane Austen*, 1869.

BACON, FRANCIS, first Baron Verulam and Viscount St. Albans (1561–1626), Lord Chancellor and writer.

He was of middling stature, his countenance had indented with age before he was old; his presence grave and comely; of a high-flying and lively wit, striving in some things to be rather admired than understood, yet so quick and easy where he would express himself, and his memory so strong and active, that he appeared the master of a large and plenteous store-house of knowledge . . .

SOURCE: Arthur Wilson, *History of Great Britain, being the Life and Reign of James I.*

He had a delicate, lively hazel eye; Doctor Harvey told me it was like the eye of a viper.

SOURCE: John Aubrey, *Brief Lives*, edit. Andrew Clark, 1898.

BACON, SIR NICHOLAS (1509–1579), Lord Keeper of the Great Seal; father of Francis Bacon.

For he was loaden with a corpulent body, especially in his old age, so that he would be not only out of breath, but also almost out of life, with going from Westminster Hall to the Star Chamber; insomuch, when sitting down in his place, it was some time before he could recover himself; and therefore it was usual in that court that no lawyer should begin to speak till the lord keeper held up his staff as a signal to him to begin.

SOURCE: Thomas Fuller, *The Worthies of England.*

BARBAULD, ANNA LETITIA (1743–1825), writer.

She was possessed of great beauty, distinct traces of which she retained to the latest of her life. Her person was slender, her complexion exquisitely fair with the bloom of perfect health; her features regular and elegant, and her dark blue eyes beamed with the light of wit and fancy.

SOURCE: Archibald Hamilton Rowan, *Autobiography;* quoted in Betsy Rodgers's *Georgian Chronicle*, Methuen, 1958.

Mrs. Barbauld bore the remains of great personal beauty. She had a brilliant complexion, light hair, blue eyes, a small elegant figure, and her manners were very agreeable, with something of the generation then departing.

AGED 62.

SOURCE: Henry Crabb Robinson, *Diary, Reminiscences and Correspondence;* quoted in Betsy Rodgers's *Georgian Chronicle*, Methuen, 1958.

BARRÉ, ISAAC (1726–1802), soldier and politician; treasurer of the Navy.

Of an athletic frame and mould, endowed with extraordinary powers of voice, Barré, as a speaker, roughly enforced, rather than solicited or attracted attention. Severe, and sometimes coarse in his censures or accusations, he nevertheless always sustained his charges against Ministers, however strong, with considerable force of argument and language. Slow, measured, and dictatorial in his manner of enunciation, he was not carried away by those beautiful digressions of genius or fancy with which Burke captivated and entertained his audience . . . Deprived already of one eye, and menaced with a privation of both; advanced in years, grey-headed, and of a savage aspect, he reminded the beholders when he rose, of Belisarius rather than of Tully.

SOURCE: Sir N. William Wraxall, *Historical Memoirs of My Own Life*, 1815.

BARROW, ISAAC (1630–1677), divine, mathematician and classical scholar; tutor of Isaac Newton.

He was in person of the lesser size and lean, of extraordinary strength, of a fair and calm complexion, a thin skin, very sensible of the cold; his eyes grey, clear and somewhat short-sighted, his hair of a light auburn, very fine and curling . . .

One morning, going out of a friend's house before which a huge and fierce mastiff was chained up (as he used to be all day) the dog flew at him, and he had that present courage to take the dog by the throat, and after much struggling bore him to the ground, and held him there till the people could rise and part them, without any other hurt than the straining of his hands, which he felt some days after.

Some would excuse me for noting that he seem'd intemperate in the love of fruit, but it was to him physick as well as food . . . and he was very free too in the use of tobacco, believing it did help to regulate his thinking.

SOURCE: Abraham Hill, *Life*, 1683.

He was by no means a spruce man, but most negligent in his dress ... He was a strong man, but pale as the candle he studied by.

SOURCE: John Aubrey, *Brief Lives*, edit. Andrew Clark, 1898.

BEACONSFIELD, FIRST EARL OF (1804–1881). See Disraeli, Benjamin, first Earl of Beaconsfield.

BEATTIE, JAMES (1735–1803), Scottish poet.

In person he was of the middle size, of a broad, square make, which seemed to indicate a more robust constitution than he really possessed. In his gait there was something of a slouch. During his later years he grew corpulent and unwieldy; but a few months before his death his bulk was greatly diminished. His features were very regular; his complexion somewhat dark. His eyes were black, brilliant, full of a tender and melancholy expression, and, in the course of conversation with his friends, became extremely animated.

SOURCE: Alexander Dyce, *Memoir*, prefaced to Aldine Edition of Beattie's poetical works, 1831.

BELDHAM, WILLIAM (1766–1863), Hambledon cricketer, nicknamed 'Silver Billy'.

It was a study for Phidias to see Beldham rise to strike, the grandeur of the attitude, the settled composure of the look, the piercing lightning of the eye, the rapid glance of the bat, were electrical. Men's hearts throbbed within them, their cheeks turned pale and red. Michaelangelo should have painted him. Beldham was great in every hit, but his peculiar glory was the cut. Here he stood with no man beside him, the laurel was all his own; it was like the cut of a racket. His wrist seemed to turn on springs of the finest steel. He took the ball, as Burke did the House of Commons, between wind and water; not a moment too soon. Beldham still survives. He lives near Farnham, and in his kitchen, black with age, hangs the trophy of his victories, the delight of his youth, the exercise of his manhood, and the glory of his age—his BAT.

AGED ABOUT 90.

SOURCE: Rev. John Mitford, Review of *The Young Cricketer's Tutor* in the *Gentleman's Magazine,* July and September, 1833.

Upon turning to . . . William, we come to the finest batter of his own, or perhaps of any age. William Beldham was a close-set active man, standing about five feet eight inches and a half. He had light-coloured hair, a fair complexion, and handsome as well as intelligent features. We used to call him 'Silver Billy'. No-one within my recollection could stop a ball better, or make more brilliant hits all over the ground. Wherever the ball was bowled, there she was hit away, and in the most severe, venomous style . . . but when he could cut them at the point of the bat, he was in his glory; and, upon my life, their speed was as the speed of thought. One of the most beautiful sights that can be imagined, and which would have delighted an artist, was to see him make himself up to hit a ball. It was the *beau ideal* of grace, animation, and concentrated energy.

SOURCE: John Nyren, *The Young Cricketer's Tutor,* 1833.

BENTLEY, DOCTOR RICHARD (1662–1742), scholar and critic; Master of Trinity College, Cambridge.

As for the *hat*, I must acknowledge it was of formidable dimensions, yet I was accustomed to treat it with great familiarity, and if it had ever been further from the hand of its owner than the peg upon the back of his great armchair, I might have been dispatched to fetch it, for he was disabled by the palsy in his latter days; but the hat never strayed from its place . . .

I have broken in upon him many times in his hours of study, when he would put his book aside, ring his hand-bell for his servant, and be led to his shelves to take down a picture-book for my amusement. I do not say his good-nature always gained its object, as the pictures which his books generally supplied me with were anatomical drawings of dissected bodies, very little calculated to communicate delight; but he had nothing better to produce; and surely such an effort on his part, however unsuccessful, was no feature of a cynic; a cynic *should be made of sterner stuff* . . .

His ordinary style of conversation was naturally lofty, and his frequent use of *thou* and *thee* with his familiars carried with it a kind of dictatorial tone, that savoured more of the closet than the court; this is readily admitted, and this on first approaches might mislead a stranger; but the native candour and inherent tenderness of his heart could not long be veiled from observation, for his feelings and affections were at once too impulsive to be long repressed, and he too careless of concealment to attempt at qualifying them.

SOURCE: Richard Cumberland (his grandson), *Memoirs of Richard Cumberland*, 1806.

BETTY, WILLIAM HENRY WEST (1791–1874), actor; known as 'The Infant Roscius'.

A very extraordinary phenomenon has lately burst upon the theatrical world. A boy of the name of Beatie (sic), not exceeding twelve years of age, reads and enacts all the principal of Shakespeare's characters, in a style of superiority that astonishes the most experienced actors. He has performed in Ireland, and is now exciting general astonishment at Edinburgh. Off the stage his manners are puerile, as he is often seen playing marbles in a morning, and Richard the Third in the evening. He is rather short of his age, slight made, but has great expression of countenance. The moment he begins to converse upon stage business, he appears an inspired being.

SOURCE: *Morning Herald*, August 6, 1804; quoted in John Ashton, *The Dawn of the XIXth Century in England*, 1895.

BLAKE, ROBERT (1599–1657), Admiral and General at Sea.

Admiral Blake, as to his person, was of a middle stature, about five feet and a half, a little inclining to corpulence; he was of a fresh, sanguine complexion, his hair was of the frizzled kind, and, as was then much the mode, he wore whiskers, which he curled when he was in any ways provoked. He was commonly very plain in his dress, but when he was abroad and appeared as General was always as became his rank, with a reserve of moderation.

SOURCE: John Oldmixon, *The History and Life of Admiral Blake*, 1746. (Oldmixon, though sometimes unreliable, made use of authentic information and traditions from Blake's family).

BLAKE, WILLIAM (1757–1827), poet and artist.

I found him in a small room which seemed to be both a working room and a bedroom. Nothing could exceed the squalid air both of the apartment and his dress; yet there is diffused over him an air of natural gentility.

SOURCE: Henry Crabb Robinson, *Diary, Reminiscences and Correspondence*.

I used constantly to go to see Mr. and Mrs. Blake when they lived near Blackfriars Bridge, and never have I known an artist so spiritual, so devoted, so single-minded, or so full of vivid imagination as he. Before Blake began a picture he used to fall on his knees and pray that his work might be successful. The room was squalid and untidy. And once Mrs. Blake, in excuse for the general lack of soap and water, remarked to me: 'You see, Mr. Blake's skin don't dirt!'

SOURCE: George Richmond; quoted in *The Richmond Papers*, Heinemann, 1926.

His eye was the finest I ever saw: brilliant, not roving, clear and intent; yet susceptible; it flashed with genius or melted with tenderness. It could also be terrible. Cunning and falsehood quailed under it, but it was never busy with them. It pierced them and turned away. Nor was the mouth less expressive; the lips flexible and quivering with feeling. I yet recall it when, on one occasion, dwelling upon the exquisite parable of the

Prodigal, he began to repeat a part of it; but at the words: 'When he was yet a great way off, his father saw him', could go no further; his voice faltered and he was in tears.

SOURCE: Letter written in 1855 to Alexander Gilchrist by Samuel Palmer; included in Gilchrist's *The Life of William Blake*, 1863.

Richmond made a pencil-drawing of his friend and mentor which was considered by his contemporaries to be the best likeness of Blake ever achieved, and from it a cast was subsequently made. Once, showing this cast to a visitor long years afterwards, Richmond drew attention to the position of the ears, which are low down, away from the face, near the back of the neck, exhibiting an unusual height of head above them. 'I have noticed this particular position of the ear finely characterized in three men,' he remarked. 'Cardinal Newman, Henry Hallam, and Mr. Blake; and I once told Mr. Gladstone that I never understood what a great man he was till I sat behind him in church and saw his bulwark of a neck.'

SOURCE: A. M. W. Stirling, *The Richmond Papers*, Heinemann, 1926.

BOADICEA or **BOUDICCA** (?–62), Queen of the Iceni of Norfolk and Suffolk; led revolt against the Ninth Legion.

She was very tall, in appearance terrifying, in the glance of her eyes most fierce, and her voice was harsh; a great mass of the tawniest hair fell to her hips; around her neck she wore a large golden necklace; and she wore a tunic of divers colours over which a thick mantle was fastened with a brooch. This was her invariable attire.

SOURCE: Dio Cassius; quoted by Leonard Cottrell in *The Great Invasion*, Evans Bros., 1960. Dio Cassius, the Greek historian, was writing about 125 years after Boadicea's death; but his words have the ring of authenticity and he may well have drawn on the accounts of those who actually saw her.

BOLEYN, ANNE (1507–1536), second queen of Henry VIII. See Anne Boleyn.

BOSWELL, JAMES (1740–1795), biographer of Doctor Johnson.

He spoke the Scotch accent strongly, though by no means so as to affect, even slightly, his intelligibility to an English ear. He had an odd mock solemnity of manner, that he had acquired imperceptibly from constant thinking of and imitating Dr. Johnson; whose own solemnity, nevertheless, far from mock, was the result of pensive rumination. There was, also, something slouching in the gait and dress of Mr. Boswell, that wore an air, ridiculously enough, of purporting to personify the same model. His clothes were always too large for him; his hair, or wig, was constantly in a state of negligence; and he never for a moment sat still or upright upon a chair. Every look and movement displayed either intentional or involuntary imitation. Yet certainly it was not meant as caricature; for his heart, almost even to idolatry, was in his reverence of Dr. Johnson.

AGED 39.

SOURCE: Fanny Burney, *Diary and Letters*.

BOYER, REV. JAMES (1736–1814), Upper Master at Christ's Hospital, and schoolmaster to Lamb, Coleridge and Hunt.

... a short stout man, inclining to paunchiness, with large face and hands, an aquiline nose, long upper lip, and a sharp mouth. His eye was close and cruel. The spectacles he wore threw a balm over it. Being a clergyman, he dressed in black, with a powdered wig. His clothes were cut short; his hands hung out of his sleeves, with tight wristbands, as if ready for execution; and as he generally wore grey worsted stockings, very tight, with a little balustrade leg, his whole appearance presented something formidably succinct, hard and mechanical. In fact, his weak side, and undoubtedly his natural destination, lay in carpentry; and he accordingly carried, in a side-pocket made on purpose, a carpenter's rule.

SOURCE: Leigh Hunt, *Autobiography*.

He had two wigs, both pedantic, but of differing omen. The one serene, smiling, fresh-powdered, betokened a smiling day. The other, an old, discoloured, unkempt, angry caxon, denoting frequent and bloody execution. Woe to the school when he made his morning appearance in his . . . passionate wig.

SOURCE: Charles Lamb, *Christ's Hospital Five and Thirty Years Ago*.

BOYLE, HON. ROBERT (1627–1691), chemist and natural philosopher.

When a boy at Eton [was] very sickly and pale. He is very tall (about six foot high) and straight.

SOURCE: John Aubrey, *Brief Lives*, edit. Andrew Clark, 1898.

Glasses, pots, chemical and mathematical instruments, books and bundles of papers, did so fill and crowd his bed-chamber, that there was but just room for a few chairs . . .

In his diet (as in habit) he was extremely temperate and plain; nor could I ever discern in him the least passion, transport or censoriousness, whatever discourse or the times suggested. All was tranquil, easy, serious, discreet and profitable . . .

He was rather tall and slender of stature, for most part valetudinary, pale and much emaciated . . . In his first addresses, being to speak or answer, he did sometimes a little hesitate, rather than stammer, or repeat the same word; imputable to an infirmity, which, since my remembrance, he had exceedingly overcome. This, as it made him somewhat slow and deliberate, so after the first effort he proceeded without the least interruption in his discourse. And I impute this impediment much to the frequent attacks of palsies, contracted I fear not a little by his often attendance on chemical operations. It has plainly astonish'd me to have seen him so often recover when he has not been able to move, or bring his hand to his mouth; and indeed the contexture of his body, during the best of his health, appeared to me so delicate, that I have frequently compar'd him to a crystal or Venice glass; which tho' wrought never so thin and fine, being carefully set up, would outlast the hardier metals of daily use.

SOURCE: letter from John Evelyn to Wotton, March 30th, 1696; from *Memoirs Illustrative of . . . John Evelyn and a Selection of his Familiar Letters.*

He entertained me with free discourse above an hour in his chamber. He is a thin man, weak in his hands and feet . . . soft voice, pleasant though pale countenance, somewhat long-faced, and a long straight nose somewhat sharp.

AGED 60.

SOURCE: *Journal of James Yonge* (1647–1712), *Plymouth Surgeon,* edit. G. N. L. Poynter, Longmans, 1963.

BRADLAUGH, CHARLES (1833–1891), politician and free-thinker; several times unseated, ejected and expelled from the House.

I was cross-examined by Bradlaugh. Bradlaugh was a very big man, and he had enormous feet, which were encased in a gigantic pair of Wellington boots. They attracted my attention, as he was examining me, and after a few questions I saw that I could always ascertain what the effect of my answer upon him was by the wriggling and convulsive motion of these two gigantic boots. So I kept my eyes fastened upon his boots rather than on his face, and the boots soon told me that he was nonplussed and could make nothing of his brief.

On another occasion I had a most amusing encounter with Mr. Bradlaugh at Tottenham. Bradlaugh lived there and was a considerable power amongst the extremists. He had been heavily defeated in a Parliamentary contest at Northampton a day or two before our meeting. This defeat did not improve his temper or that of his followers. As soon as I had spoken, he came from the far end of the hall, where his followers were concentrated, close up to the platform, and he began in a loud and hectoring manner to put to me the catch Radical catechism. Suddenly a man, as much bigger than Bradlaugh as Bradlaugh was than myself, got up with a huge club and said: 'Give me the signal, my lord, and I will crack this infernal scoundrel's skull.' A perfect pandemonium ensued. Bradlaugh's people tried to come to their hero's rescue, my people keeping them back. Bradlaugh and the big man both remained immovable, but Bradlaugh was furtively watching out of the corner of his eye the big club over his head, and the holder of it was watching intently for me to give the signal for an onslaught. The tension was broken by a big Irish parson who was Rector of Tottenham, and who had had many an encounter with Bradlaugh. He jumped up and began to exorcise Bradlaugh with tongue and fists as if he were a devil. I was afraid he would strike Bradlaugh, so I got hold of one end of the very long tails of the orthodox parson's frock-coat. One of my uncles seized the end of the other tail, and the result of our combined effort was that the coat split up right to the neck, leaving us each with a coat-tail in our hands.

SOURCE: Lord George Hamilton, *Parliamentary Reminiscences and Reflections*, 1868–1885, John Murray, 1917.

BRAXFIELD, LORD (1722–1799). See Macqueen, Robert, Lord Braxfield.

BRIGHT, JOHN (1811–1889), statesman and orator.

Mr. Bright had all the resources of passion alive within his breast. He was carried along by vehement political anger, and, deeper than that, there glowed a wrath as stern as that of an ancient prophet . . . His invective was not the expression of mere irritation, but a profound and menacing passion. Hence he dominated his audience from a height, while his companion [Richard Cobden] rather drew them along after him as friends and equals.

SOURCE: John Morley, *Life of Richard Cobden*, Fisher Unwin, 1903.

BRONTË, ANNE (1820–1849), authoress.

Anne was quite different in appearance from the others ... Her hair was a very pretty, light brown, and fell on her neck in graceful curls. She had lovely violet-blue eyes, fine pencilled eyebrows, and clear, almost transparent complexion.

AGED 13.

SOURCE: Ellen Nussey, *Reminiscences of Charlotte Brontë;* quoted in Winifred Gérin's *Anne Brontë*, Thos. Nelson & Son, 1959.

This was the only occasion on which I saw Anne Brontë. She was a gentle, quiet, rather subdued person, by no means pretty, yet of pleasing appearance ... Her manner was curiously expressive of a wish for protection and encouragement, a kind of constant appeal, which invited sympathy.

AGED 28.

SOURCE: George Smith, *Cornhill Magazine*, December, 1900; quoted in Winifred Gérin's *Anne Brontë*, Thos. Nelson & Son, 1959.

BRONTË, CHARLOTTE (1816–1855), novelist.

In 1831, she was a quiet, thoughtful girl, of nearly fifteen years of age, very small in figure—'stunted' was the word she applied to herself—but as her limbs and head were in just proportion to the slight, fragile body, no word in ever so slight a degree suggestive of deformity could properly be applied to her; with soft, thick hair, and peculiar eyes, of which I find it difficult to give a description, as they appeared to me in her later life. They were large and well shaped; their colour a reddish-brown; but if the iris was closely examined, it appeared to be composed of a great variety of tints. The usual expression was of quiet, listening intelligence; but now and then, on some just occasion for vivid interest or wholesome imagination, a light would shine out, as if some spiritual lamp had been kindled, which glowed behind those expressive orbs. I never saw the like in any other human creature. As for the rest of her features, they were plain, large, and ill set; but, unless you began to catalogue them, you were hardly aware of the fact, for the eyes and power of the countenance over-balanced every physical defect; the crooked mouth and the large nose were forgotten, and the whole face arrested the attention, and presently attracted all those whom she herself would have cared to attract. Her hands and feet were the smallest I ever saw; when one of the former was placed in mine, it was like the soft touch of a bird in the middle of my palm. The delicate long fingers had a peculiar fineness of sensation, which was one reason why all her handi-work, of whatever kind—writing, sewing, knitting—was so clear in its minuteness. She was remarkably neat in her whole personal attire; but she was dainty as to the fit of her shoes and gloves.

I can well imagine that the grave serious composure, which, when I knew her, gave her face the dignity of an old Venetian portrait, was no acquisition of later years, but dated from that early age when she found herself in the position of an elder sister to motherless children. But in a girl only just entered in her teens, such an expression would be called (to use a country phrase) 'old-fashioned'; and in 1831, the period of which I now write, we must think of her as a little, set, antiquated girl, very quiet in manners and very quaint in dress; for besides the influence exerted by her father's ideas concerning the simplicity of attire befitting the wife and daughters of a country clergyman, her aunt, on whom the duty of dressing her nieces principally devolved, had never been in society since she left Penzance, eight or nine years before, and the Penzance fashions of that year were still dear to her heart.

AGED 14.

SOURCE: Mrs. Gaskell, *The Life of Charlotte Brontë*.

I first saw her coming out of a covered cart, in very old-fashioned clothes, and looking very cold and miserable. She was coming to school at Miss Wooler's. When she appeared in the school-room, her dress was changed, but just as old. She looked a little old woman, so short-sighted that she always appeared to be seeking something, and moving her head from side to side to catch a sight of it. She was very shy and nervous, and spoke with a strong Irish accent. When a book was given her, she dropped her head over it until her nose nearly touched it, and when she was told to hold her head up, up went the book after it, still close to her nose, so that it was not possible to help laughing.

AGED 14.

SOURCE: Mary Taylor; quoted in *The Life of Charlotte Brontë*.

Charlotte's appearance did not strike me at first as it did others . . . She never seemed to me the unattractive little person others designated her, but certainly she was at this time anything but *pretty*; even her good points were lost. Her naturally beautiful hair of soft silky brown being then dry and frizzy-looking, screwed up in tight little curls, showing features that were all the plainer from her exceeding thinness and want of complexion . . . A dark, rusty-green dress of old-fashioned make detracted still more from her appearance; but let her wear that she might, or do what she would, she had ever the demeanour of a born gentlewoman.

AGED 14.

SOURCE: Ellen Nussey, *Reminiscences of Charlotte Brontë*, Scribner's Magazine, May 1871; reprinted in Brontë Society Transactions, 1899.
Ellen Nussey was a new girl at Miss Wooler's school at Roe Head at the same time as Charlotte. It was she who found Charlotte crying behind the schoolroom curtains on the first day.

I must confess that my first impression of Charlotte Brontë's appearance was that it was interesting rather than attractive . . . She was very small, and had a quaint, old-fashioned look. Her head seemed too large for her body. She had fine eyes, but her face was marred by the shape of the mouth and by the complexion . . . There was but little feminine charm about her and of this fact she was uneasily and perpetually conscious . . . I believe she would have given all her genius and all her fame to be beautiful. Perhaps few women ever existed more anxious to be pretty than she, or more angrily conscious of the circumstance that she was *not* pretty.

AGED 32.

SOURCE: George Smith, her publisher, *In the Early Forties*, The Critic, January, 1901.

The news of the wedding* had slipt abroad before the little party came out of church, and many old and humble friends were there, seeing her look 'like a snow-drop', as they say. Her dress was white embroidered muslin, with a lace mantle, and white bonnet trimmed with green leaves, which perhaps might suggest the resemblance to the pale wintry flower.

AGED 38.

SOURCE: Mrs. Gaskell, *The Life of Charlotte Brontë.*

Among other tales of his sitters, Richmond used to relate one of Charlotte Brontë. When, on June 13 1850, she arrived to sit for her portrait, he noticed with perplexity that, after she had removed her hat, on the top of her head there reposed a small square of brown merino! Whether it was employed to prop up her hat, or what was its use, he could not imagine, but at last he observed deferentially: 'Miss Brontë, you have a little pad of brown merino on the top of your head—I wonder if I might ask you to remove it?' To his dismay, Charlotte Brontë, nervous and hypersensitive, burst into tears of confusion.

SOURCE: A. M. W. Stirling, *The Richmond Papers*, Heinemann, 1926.

BRONTË, EMILY (1818–1848), authoress.

Emily had by this time acquired a lithesome, graceful figure. She was the tallest person in the house, except her father. Her hair, which was naturally as beautiful as Charlotte's, was in the

* Charlotte's wedding to the Rev. Arthur Bell Nicholls, formerly curate at Haworth.

same unbecoming tight curl and frizz, and there was the same want of complexion. She had very beautiful eyes—kind, kindling, liquid eyes; but she did not often look at you: she was too reserved. Their colour might be said to be dark grey, at other times dark blue, they varied so. She talked very little.

SOURCE: Ellen Nussey, *Reminiscences of Charlotte Brontë*, Scribner's Magazine, May 1871; reprinted in Brontë Society Transactions, 1899 and quoted in Winifred Gérin's *Anne Brontë*, Thos. Nelson & Son, 1959.

BRONTË, REVEREND PATRICK (1777–1861), author; father of Charlotte, Emily and Anne Brontë.

He was nearly blind. He could grope his way about, and recognise the figures of those he knew well, when they were placed against a strong light; but he could no longer see to read; and thus his eager appetite for knowledge and information of all kinds was severely balked. He continued to preach. I have heard that he was led up into the pulpit, and that his sermons were never so effective as when he stood there, a grey sightless old man, his blind eyes looking out straight before him, while the words that came from his lips had all the vigour and force of his best days.

AGED 69.

SOURCE: Mrs. Gaskell, *The Life of Charlotte Brontë*.

BRONTË, PATRICK BRANWELL (1817–1848), brother of Charlotte and Emily Brontë.

He and his sister Charlotte were both slight and small of stature ... I have seen Branwell's profile; it is what would be generally esteemed very handsome; the forehead is massive, the eye well set and the expression of it fine and intellectual; the nose too is good; but there are coarse lines about the mouth, and the lips, though of handsome shape, are loose and thick, indicating self-indulgence, while the slightly retreating chin conveys an air of weakness of will. His hair and complexion were sandy. He had enough of Irish blood in him to make his manners frank and genial, with a kind of natural gallantry about them.

SOURCE: Mrs. Gaskell, *Life of Charlotte Brontë*.

... in stature a little below middle height; slim and agile in figure, and with a clear and ruddy complexion and a voice of ringing sweetness, whose utterance and use of English was perfect.

SOURCE: F. A. Leyland, *The Brontë Family, with Special Reference to Patrick Branwell Brontë*.

BROUGHAM, HENRY PETER, Baron Brougham and Vaux (1778–1868), Lord Chancellor.

... I have often wondered at the *want* of sense, discretion, judgment and common sense that we see so frequently accompany the most brilliant talents, but damn me if I ever saw such an instance as I have just witnessed in ... Brougham. By Heaven! he has uttered a speech which, for power of *speaking*, surpassed anything you ever heard ... He could not have roared louder if a file of soldiers had come in and pushed the Speaker out of his chair. Where the devil a fellow could get such lungs and such a flow of jaw upon such an occasion as this surpasses my imagination.

AGED 38.

SOURCE: Thomas Creevey, *Creevey Papers*.

One of the young ladies said, 'We have seen a good deal of Mr. Brougham lately, he went to the play with us 3 or 4 times, and you never saw such a figure as he is. He wears a black stock or collar round his neck, it is so wide that you can see a dirty coloured handkerchief under tied right round his neck. You never saw such an object, or anything half so dirty.'

AGED 49.

SOURCE: *Creevey Papers*.

Brougham's hand was full of papers, and his whole appearance was restless, harassed, eager, spare, keen, sarcastic and nervous ... Brougham never shakes hands, but he held out his two fingers ... inside and outside the whole appearance told of hurry-scurry, harass, fag, late hours, long speeches and vast occupation. Since I saw him last he seems grown ten years older—looks more nervous and harassed a great deal.

AGED 50.

The Chancellor sat today. His eye is as fine as an eye I ever saw. It is like a lion's, watching for prey. It is a clear grey, the light vibrating at the bottom of the iris, and the cornea shining, silvery and tense. I never before had the opportunity of examining Brougham's face with the scrutiny of a painter, and I am astonished at that extraordinary eye.

AGED 55.

SOURCE: Benjamin Haydon's *Autobiography*.

BROWNING, ELIZABETH BARRETT (1806–1861), poetess.

A slight, girlish figure, very delicate, with exquisite hands and feet; a round face with a most noble forehead; a large mouth, beautifully formed and full of expression, lips like parted coral, teeth large, regular and glittering with healthy whiteness, large dark eyes with such eyelashes; a dark complexion, literally as bright as the dark China rose; a profusion of silky dark curls; and a look of youth and modesty hardly to be expressed.

AGED 30.

SOURCE: *Letters of Mary Russell Mitford*, edit. Henry F. Chorley, 1872.

At her own fireside she struck me as very pleasing and exceedingly sympathetic. Her physique was peculiar: curls like the pendant ears of a water-spaniel and poor little hands—so thin that when she welcomed you she gave you something like the foot of a young bird.

AGED 49.

SOURCE: Frederick Locker, *My Confidences*, London, 1896.

I am 'little and black' like Sappho . . . five feet one high . . . eyes of various colours as the sun shines—called blue, black, without being accidentally black and blue—affidavit-ed for grey—sworn at for hazel—and set down by myself (according to my 'private view' in the glass) as dark-green-brown—grounded with brown and green otherwise; what is called 'invisible green' in invisible garden fences . . . Not much nose of any kind; certes no superfluity of nose; but to make for it, a mouth suitable to a larger personality—oh, and a very, very little voice . . . Dark hair and complexion—small face and sundries.

SOURCE: self-portrait, written to Benjamin Haydon; quoted in Dorothy Hewlett's *Elizabeth Barrett Browning*, Cassell & Co., 1953.

BROWNING, ROBERT (1812–1889), poet.

. . . slim and dark, and very handsome; and—may I hint it—just a trifle of a dandy, addicted to lemon-coloured kid-gloves and such things . . . But full of ambition, eager for success, eager for fame . . .

AGED 25.

SOURCE: quoted by G. K. Chesterton, in Robert Browning (English Men of Letters), Macmillan, 1903.

He had the happy knack of making even a small boy feel that it gave him real pleasure to shake that small boy by the hand or to pat him on the back and talk to him about the little interests of his life . . . His dress was simple, his manner was genial, and his appearance, although he was by no means a tall man, was in the highest degree manly and impressive. His massive, noble head was splendidly set on a strong neck; his shoulders were solid, and his chest was deep, a fit generator for the resonant voice with which he held you in conversation . . . I can still feel the grip of his hand and see the kind light in his eyes as he looked into mine.

AGED ABOUT 52.

SOURCE: Rudolph Lehmann; quoted in John Lehmann, *Ancestors and Friends*, Eyre and Spottiswoode, 1962.

In person, Browning was below the middle height, but broadly built and of great muscular strength, which he retained through life in spite of his indifference to all athletic exercises. His hair was dark brown, and in early life exceedingly full and lustrous; in middle life it faded, and in old age turned white, remaining copious to the last.

SOURCE: Edmund Gosse, *Dictionary of National Biography*, 1901.

BRUCE, ROBERT, Earl of Carrick and **KING ROBERT I** of Scotland (1274–1329).

His figure was graceful and athletic, with broad shoulders; his features were handsome; he had the yellow hair of the northern race, with blue and sparkling eyes. His intellect was quick, and he had a gift of fluent speech in the vernacular, delightful to listen to.

SOURCE: John Mair (Major), *Historia Majoris Britanniae*, 1521 (Paris); republished Edinburgh, 1740. Though the description is not contemporary, Mair was a careful historian and was probably making use of authentic tradition.

BRUMMELL, GEORGE BRYAN (1778–1840), commonly called 'Beau Brummell', leader of fashion.

No scents, but plenty of clean linen, country bleached ... Correct morning dress, hessians and pantaloons, or top-boots and buckskins, with a blue coat, and a light or buff-coloured waistcoat. In the evening, black pantaloons, buttoning tight to the ankle, striped silk stockings, an opera hat, a blue coat and a white waistcoat.

SOURCE: Brummell's prescription, which he himself followed, for the well-dressed man.

Unluckily, Brummell, soon after joining his regiment, was thrown from his horse at a grand review at Brighton, when he broke his classical Roman nose. This misfortune, however, did not affect the fame of the beau; and although his nasal organ had undergone a slight transformation, it was forgiven by his admirers, since the rest of his person remained intact . . .

He was remarkable for his dress, which was generally conceived by himself; the execution of his sublime imagination being carried out by that superior genius, Mr. Weston, tailor, of Old Bond Street . . .

His house in Chapel Street corresponded with his personal 'get up'; the furniture was in excellent taste, and the library contained the best works of the best authors of every period and of every country. His canes, his snuff-boxes, his Sèvres china, were exquisite; his horses and carriage were conspicuous for their excellence and, in fact, the superior taste of a Brummell were discoverable in everything that belonged to him.

SOURCE: Captain R. H. Gronow, *Reminiscences*.

Keen grows the wind, and piercing is the cold;
My pins are weak and I am growing old;
Around my shoulders this worn cloak I spread,
With an umbrella to protect my head,
Which once had wit enough to astound the world,
But now possesses naught but wig well curl'd.
Alas, alas, while wind and rain do beat,
That great Beau Brummell thus should walk the street.

SOURCE: Newspaper verses, published during Brummell's poverty-stricken years in Caen (1830–1840).

BUCKINGHAM, DUKE OF. See Villiers, George, first and second Dukes (1592–1628) and (1628–1687).

BURKE, EDMUND (1729–1797), statesman.

He is tall, his figure is noble, his air commanding, his address graceful, his voice is clear, penetrating, sonorous and powerful; his language is copious various and eloquent, his manners are attractive, his conversation is delightful.

SOURCE: Fanny Burney, *Diary and Letters*.

In dress and exterior he was not less negligent than Fox; but, the spirit of party did not blend with the colour of his apparel; and he rarely or never came to the House in Blue and Buff... Burke constantly wore spectacles. His enunciation was vehement, rapid, and never checked by any embarrassment; for his ideas outran his powers of utterance, and he drew from an exhaustless source. But his Irish accent, which was as strong as if he had never quitted the banks of the Shannon, diminished to the ear the enchanting effect of his eloquence on the mind . . . In brilliancy of wit, Lord North alone could compete with Burke; for Sheridan had not then appeared . . . Throughout his general manner and deportment in Parliament, there was something petulant, impatient, and at times almost intractable, which greatly obscured the lustre of his talents. His very features, and the undulating motions of his head, were eloquently expressive of this irritability, which on some occasions seemed to approach towards alienation of mind. Even his friends could not always induce him to listen to reason and remonstrance, though they sometimes held him down in his seat, by the skirts of his coat, in order to prevent the ebullitions of his anger or indignation.

AGED 52.

SOURCE: Sir N. William Wraxall, *Historical Memoirs of My Own Life*, 1815.

BUNYAN, JOHN (1628–1688), preacher and writer.

He appeared in countenance to be of a stern and rough temper, but in his conversation mild and affable, not given to loquacity or much discourse in company, unless some urgent occasion required it, observing never to boast of himself . . . but rather seem low in his own eyes . . .

As for his person, he was tall of stature, strong-boned though not corpulent, somewhat of a ruddy face with sparkling eyes, wearing his hair on the upper lip after the old British fashion, his hair reddish, but in his latter days sprinkled with grey; his nose well-set, but not declining or bending, and his mouth moderately large, his forehead something high, and his habit always plain and modest.

SOURCE: George Cokayne, *A Continuation of Mr. Bunyan's life* . . . added to the 1692 edition of Bunyan's *Grace Abounding*, first published in 1666.

BURLEIGH, LORD (1520–1528). See Cecil, William, Baron Burleigh.

BURNET, GILBERT (1643–1715), bishop of Salisbury; theologian and historian.

> A portly prince, and goodly to the sight,
> He seem'd a son of Anak for his height:
> Like those whom stature did to crowns prefer;
> Black-brow'd, and bluff, like Homer's Jupiter;
> Broad-back'd, and brawny-built for love's delight,
> A prophet form'd to make a female proselyte.
> A theologue more by need than genial bent;
> By breeding sharp, by nature confident.

SOURCE: John Dryden, *The Hind and the Panther*, 1687.

BURNS, ROBERT (1759–1796), poet.

I was a lad of 15 when he came to Edinburgh, but had sense enough to be interested in his poetry, and would have given the world to know him. I saw him one day with several gentlemen of literary reputation, among whom I remember the celebrated Dugald Stewart. Of course, we youngsters sat silent, looked and listened . . .

His person was robust, his manners rustic, not clownish . . . His countenance was more massive than it looks in any of his portraits. There was a strong expression of shrewdness in his lineaments; the eye alone indicated the poetic character and temperament. It was large and of a dark cast, and literally glowed when he spoke with feeling or interest. I never saw such

another eye in a human head. His conversation expressed
perfect self-confidence, without the least obtrusive forwardness.

SOURCE: letter from Sir Walter Scott, quoted in J. G. Lockhart's
Life of Burns.

BUTE, EARL OF (1713–1792). See Stuart, John, third Earl of
Bute.

BUTLER, SAMUEL (1612–1680), satirical writer; author of
Hudibras.

He is of a middle stature, strong set, high coloured, a head of
sorrel hair; a severe and sound judgment . . . He has been much
troubled with the gout, and particularly 1629, he stirred not
out of his chamber from October till Easter.

SOURCE: John Aubrey, *Brief Lives*, edit. Andrew Clark, 1898.

. . . I saw the famous old Mr. Butler, the author of *Hudibras*, an
old paralytic claret drinker, a morose surly man, except
elevated with claret, when he becomes very brisk and incom-
parable company.

AGED 66.

SOURCE: *Journal of James Yonge* (1647–1712), *Plymouth Surgeon*,
edit. G. N. L. Poynter, Longmans, 1963.

BUTLER, SAMUEL (1835–1902), writer; author of *The Way of
All Flesh, Erewhon Revisited*, etc.

In stature he was a small man, but you hardly noticed that. His
slightly-built frame was disguised in clothes of enviable bagginess
and of a clumsy conventional cut, and he wore prodigiously
roomy boots. But it was the hirsute, masculine vigour of his head
which prevented you from thinking him a small man. Indeed, it
was a surprise to me to hear afterwards that he had coxed at Cambridge the St. John's boat: I had remembered him, it seemed,
as a rather heavy man. His company manner was that of a kind
old gentleman, prepared to be a little shocked by any disregard

of the proprieties; the sort of old gentleman who is very mild in
reproof, but whose quiet insistence that everybody should
behave is most soothing to elderly ladies of limited means. He
spoke softly and slowly, often with his head a little down, looking gravely over his spectacles and pouting his lips, and with a
deliberate demureness so disarming that he was able to utter
the most subversive sentiments without exciting more than a
moment's astonishment . . . It was comic to anyone who knew
what a bull in a china shop he really was. And though he was a
great adept at poking gentle fun at people, he never snubbed
them or scored off them . . .

I have spoken of the extreme demureness of his manner in
company. It was apt to be interrupted in a rather startling
manner. When he laughed the change in his expression was
extraordinary. His laughter was mostly silent. The corners of
his mouth went up in a wide semicircle beneath his beard, his
eyes sparkled with mockery, and suddenly before you, instead
of the face of a quaintly staid, elderly gentleman mindful of
the P's and Q's, was the wild laughing face of an old faun, to
whom the fear of giving himself away was obviously a sensation
unknown.

SOURCE: Desmond MacCarthy, *Criticism*, Putnam, 1932; and
Remnants, 1918.

BYNG, JOHN (1704–1757), admiral.

The man I never saw but in the street, or in the House of
Commons, and there I thought his carriage haughty and
disgusting. From report, I had formed a mean opinion of his
understanding; and from the clamours of the world, I was
carried away with the multitude in believing he had not done
his duty; and in thinking his behaviour under *his* circumstances
weak and arrogant. I never interested myself enough about
him to enquire whether this opinion was well or ill founded.
When his pamphlet appeared, I read it, and found he had been
cruelly and scandalously treated . . .

The fatal morning arrived, but was by no means met by the

Admiral with reluctance. The whole tenor of his behaviour had been cheerful, steady, dignified, sensible. While he felt like a victim, he acted like a hero . . . He took an easy leave of his friends, detained the officers not a moment, went directly to the deck, and placed himself in a chair with neither ceremony nor tightness. Some of the more humane officers represented to him, that his face being uncovered might throw reluctance into the executioners, and besought him to suffer a handkerchief. He replied with the same unconcern, 'If it will frighten *them*, let it be done: they would not frighten me.' His eyes were bound; they shot, and he fell at once.

AGED 53.

SOURCE: Horace Walpole, *Memoirs*, published 1822–1845.

BYRON, GEORGE GORDON, sixth Baron (1788–1824), poet.

I entered his house as in a certain degree familiarised to the appearance of its master, but great was my astonishment, though prepared to make a fair allowance to artists, to see before me a being bearing as little resemblance to the pretended facsimile as I to Apollo . . . I had certainly been taught to expect one thing I found—a long oval face with a handsome nose, and a kind of rapt expression of thoughtfulness, blended with a cynical hint amounting to 'don't think me thoughtful for want of thought'; but instead of . . . the absent, unsociable and supercilious deportment I had been prepared to meet, we were presented with the personification of frankness itself; his countenance was enlivened with smiles, and his whole manner the very reverse of anything like abstraction, not to say misanthropy . . .

Lord B. is, as near as I can judge, about five feet nine inches in height, and of an athletic make, which is most apparent from the loins downwards, the breast having suffered from the attitude acquired through his lameness* . . . His face is pale,

* This does not agree with descriptions by Doctor Julius Millingen and John Cam Hobhouse, both of whom said the upper part of Byron's body was well-developed.

D

and from the angle of one jaw to the other unusually broad. The forehead is remarkably striking and fine . . . the hair receding at the temples; its surface as smooth as alabaster, except when a moment of abstraction leaves it with lines of thought.

His eyes are strikingly expressive . . . somewhat between a light blue and grey. His eyelashes are long and thick; eyebrows distinct and finely arched, both nearly the colour of his hair. His nose, so far from aquiline and thin, as represented in plates I have seen, rather inclines to turn up at the point; it is of moderate length, rather broad between the alae . . . much of that style which is found among athletic, full-faced highlanders of a fair complexion. The upper lip is rather short than otherwise; the mouth well-proportioned, the lips round and plump without being thick, with a pleasing curl or curve outwards which, on their being separated in speaking or smiling, display to great advantage a beautifully white, regular set of teeth. His chin is dimpled . . .

His hair is parted all over his head into innumerable small spiral curls, about three inches long, which is somewhat surprising, as it is as fine as silk . . . Its colour light auburn, or perhaps it may be more properly described as light brown, inclining to auburn . . . His beard is shaved all over his face, except the upper lip, but his *moustache* is certainly no ornament, as it is of a flaxen whiteness . . . complexion is fair and florid.

His hands are exquisitely formed, very white and the nails beautiful. Of the feet I cannot judge, as he wore boots; that on the sound foot was clumsily made, with the view, I suppose, of rendering the shapelessness of the other less apparent . . . though not so deformed as many as I have known, yet it is sufficiently so to occasion a considerable limp in his walk.

He wore a deep green hussar jacket, with a black woollen shag collar and cuffs, with a profusion of cording, braid and frogs, a plain black waistcoat, blue trowsers with a broad scarlet stripe on the sides, and a blue foraging cap with a scarlet border and leathern shade . . .

He had a slight burr in uttering words in which the letter 'r' occurred . . . and it was far from disagreeable. His voice was sweet and sonorous, his prevailing mode of expression deliberate, though slow, and I thought I detected a slight touch of a Scottish accent, which, however, I could not satisfy myself existed.

AGED 36.

SOURCE: Letters written by Surgeon James Forester, quoted originally by Thomas Medwin, without indication of their origin, in 1834. Forrester visited the poet at Missolonghi in January, 1824.

Lord Byron at that time wore a very narrow cravat of white sarsnet, with the shirt-collar falling over it; a black coat and waistcoat, and very broad white trousers to hide his lame foot—these were of Russian duck in the morning, and jean in the evening. His watch-chain had a number of small gold seals appended to it, and was looped up to a button of his waistcoat. His face was void of colour; he wore no whiskers. His eyes were grey, fringed with long black lashes; and his air was imposing, but rather supercilious.

SOURCE: John Timbs, *A Century of Anecdote, 1760–1860.*

CALLINGS, MRS. (c. 1827), a Westmorland clergyman's wife.

... the Clergyman of the parish dined with us, and his Wife ... such a devil for ugliness as you never beheld—a regular strolling player in a barn, a cap bolt upright of a yard's length, her hair behind nearly pulled up to the roots to be got into the cap, and in the front an amethyst star half mast high; so I did nothing but rave about her, and at our Whist, Lady Augusta entertained, 'Well, I believe after all that Mrs. Callings is a very good kind woman at bottom.' 'So,' says I, 'I know nothing of her bottom, but she is a deuced comical one at top ...'

SOURCE: Thomas Creevey, *The Creevey Papers.*

CAMBRIDGE, DUKE OF (1819–1904). See George William Frederick Charles, second Duke.

CAMPBELL, THOMAS (1777–1844), poet.

They who knew Mr. Campbell only as the author of *Gertrude of Wyoming* and the *Pleasures of Hope*, would not have suspected him to be a merry companion, overflowing with humour and anecdote, and anything but fastidious ... He was one of the few men whom I could at any time have walked half a dozen miles through the snow to spend an evening with ...

When I first saw this eminent person, he gave me the idea of a French Virgil. Not that he was like a Frenchman ... But he seemed to me to embody a Frenchman's ideal notion of the Latin poet; something a little more cut and dry than I had looked for; compact and elegant, critical and acute, with a consciousness of authorship upon him ... His skull was sharply cut and fine; with plenty, according to the phrenologists, both of the reflective and amative organs; and his poetry will bear them out ... His face and person were rather on a small scale; his features regular; his eye lively and penetrating; and when he spoke, dimples played about his mouth, which, nevertheless, had something restrained and close in it. Some gentle puritan seemed to have crossed the breed, and to have left a stamp on his face, such as we often see in the female Scotch face rather than the male.

SOURCE: Leigh Hunt, *Autobiography*.

CANNING, GEORGE (1770–1827), statesman.

Canning had nothing of the stiffness, arrogance, or ordinary person of Pitt. He exhibited no extremes. His evening dress was in the plainer fashion of the time. There seemed to me about him, too, something of the character of his eloquence, classical, tasteful, candid, and conscious of innate power. A handsome man in feature, compact in person; moulded between activity and strength, although I fancied even then he exhibited marks of what care and ambition had done for him. His countenance indicated firmness of character, with a good-natured cast over all. He was bald as 'the first Caesar' ...

His gait as he paced the drawing-room I even now see, his

well-fitted blue ribbed silk stockings and breeches with knee buckles fitting well-turned limbs.

SOURCE: Redding, *Fifty Years' Recollections*.

CARLYLE, THOMAS (1795–1881), essayist and historian.

. . . Carlyle running his chin out . . . and his eyes glowing till they looked like the eyes and beak of a bird of prey . . .

Carlyle allows no one a chance, but bears down all opposition, not only by his wits, and onset of words, resistless as so many bayonets, but by actual physical superiority, raising his voice, and rushing on his opponent with a torment of sound.

SOURCE: Margaret Fuller, *Autobiography*.

Carlyle soon appeared and looked as if he felt a well-dressed London crowd scarcely the arena for him to figure in as a popular lecturer. He is a tall, robust-looking man; rugged simplicity and indomitable strength are in his face and such a glow of genius in it—not always smouldering there but flashing from his beautiful grey eye, from the remoteness of their deep setting under that massive brow. His manner is very quiet but he speaks like one who is tremendously convinced of what he utters and who had much—very much—in him that was quite unutterable, quite unfit to be uttered to the uninitiated ear; and when the Englishman's sense of beauty or truth exhibited itself in vociferous cheers, he would impatiently, almost contemptuously, wave his hand as if that were not the sort of homage which Truth demanded. He began in a rather low nervous voice with a broad Scotch accent but it soon grew firm and shrank not abashed from its great task.

AGED 45.

SOURCE: Caroline Fox, *Journal*.

His appearance is fine, without being ostentatiously singular—his hair dark—his cheek tinged with a healthy red—his eye, the truest index of his genius, flashing out, at times, a wild and mystic fire from its dark and quiet surface. He is above the middle size, stoops slightly, dresses carefully, but without any approach to foppery. His address, somewhat high and distant at first, softens into simplicity and cordial kindness. His conversation is abundant, inartificial, flowing on, and warbling as it flows . . . rendered racy by the accompaniment of the purest Annandale accent, and coming to its climaxes, ever and anon, in long, deep, chest-shaking bursts of laughter.

AGED 50.

SOURCE: George Gilfillan, *A Third Gallery of Literary Portraits*, 1845.

CAROLINE AMELIA ELIZABETH (1768–1821), queen of George IV.

Pretty face—not expressive of softness—her figure not graceful—fine eyes, good hands, tolerable teeth, but going—fair hair and light eyebrows, good bust—short, with what the French call *des épaules impertinentes*.

AGED 27.

SOURCE: Lord Malmesbury; quoted in Mary Hopkirk's *Queen Adelaide*, John Murray, 1946.

The first thing I saw in the room was a short, very fat elderly woman, with an extremely red face (owing, I suppose, to the heat) in a Girl's white . . . dress, but with shoulder, back and neck quite low (disgustingly so) down to the middle of her stomach; very black hair and eyebrows, which gave her a fierce look, and a wreathe of light pink roses on her head. She was dancing and at the end of the dance a pretty little English boy ran up and kiss'd her. I was staring at the oddity of her appearance when suddenly she nodded and smil'd at me, and not recollecting her, I was convinc'd she was mad, till William push'd me, saying: 'Do you not see the Princess of Wales nodding to you?' It is so long since I have seen her near . . . she is so much fatter and redder, that added to her black hair and eyebrows, extraordinary deep, I had not the least recollection of her.

AGED 47.

SOURCE: Earl of Bessborough, *Lady Bessborough and her Family Circle*, John Murray, 1940; quoted in John Fisher's *Eighteen Fifteen*, Cassell, 1963.

A fat woman of fifty years of age, short, plump and high-coloured. She wore a pink hat with seven or eight pink feathers floating in the wind, a pink bodice cut very low, and a short white skirt which hardly came below her knees, showing two stout legs with pink top-boots; a rose coloured sash, which she was continuously draping, completed the costume.

AGED ABOUT 50.

SOURCE: Comtesse de Boigne, *Memoirs, 1781–1814*.

CARR, ROBERT, Earl of Somerset (d. 1645), favourite of James I.

I tell you, good knight, this fellow is straight-limbed, well-favoured, strong-shouldered and smooth-faced, with some sort of cunning and show of modesty; tho', God wot, he knoweth well when to show his impudence.

SOURCE: Lord Thomas Howard, in a letter to Sir John Harington; quoted in G. P. V. Akrigg's *Jacobean Pageant*, Hamish Hamilton, 1962.

CARROLL, LEWIS (1832–1898). See Dodgson, Charles Lutwidge.

CARTERET, JOHN, Earl Granville (1690–1763), politician.

His person was handsome, open, and engaging; his eloquence at once rapid and pompous, and by the mixture, a little bombast. He was an extensive scholar, master of classic criticism, and of all modern politics. He was precipitate in his manner, and rash in all his projects ... He would profess amply, provoke indiscriminately, oblige seldom. It is difficult to say whether he was oftener intoxicated by wine or ambition; in fits of the former, he showed contempt for everybody; in rants of the latter, for truth.

AGED 61.

SOURCE: Horace Walpole, *Memoirs*, published 1822–1845.

CASTLEREAGH, VISCOUNT (1769–1822). See Stewart, Robert, Viscount Castlereagh.

CATHERINE OF BRAGANZA (1638–1705), queen of Charles II.

... her face is not so exact as to be called beauty though her eyes are excellent good, and not anything in her face that in the last degree can shock one; on the contrary she hath as much agreeableness in her looks altogether as ever I saw, and if I have any skill in physiognomy which I think I have she must be as good a woman as ever was born, her conversation as much as I can perceive is very good for she has wit enough and a most agreeable voice.

AGED 24.

SOURCE: Charles II, in a letter to the Earl of Clarendon.

Meeting Mr. Pierce, the chyryrgeon, he took me into Somerset House; and there carried me into the Queen-Mother's presence-chamber, where she was, with our Queen sitting on her left hand, whom I never did see before; and though she be not very charming, yet she hath a good, modest and innocent look, which is pleasing.

AGED 24.

SOURCE: Samuel Pepys, *Diary*.

By and by the King and Queen, who looked in this dress, a white laced waistcoat and a crimson short petticoat, and her hair dressed *à la négligence*, mighty pretty; and the King rode hand in hand with her.

AGED 25.

SOURCE: Samuel Pepys, *Diary*.

She was yet of the handsomest countenance of all the rest and though low of stature, prettily shaped, languishing and excellent eyes, her teeth wronging her mouth by sticking out a little too far; for the rest, lovely enough.

SOURCE: John Evelyn, *Diary*.

After this, the sun almost set, her Majesty the Queen, etc. being in the park, Mr. Pearse carried us at a postern gate that led through a terrace walk into the park, to see the court return . . . At length we saw the Queen come waddling like a duck; she is much altered from what she was when I saw her in Portugal, and was plainly clad.

AGED 43.

SOURCE: *Journal of James Yonge* (1647–1712), *Plymouth Surgeon*, edit. G. N. L. Poynter, Longmans, 1963.

CAVENDISH, MARGARET, Duchess of Newcastle (1624?–1674), writer.

Met my Lady Newcastle going with her coachmen and footmen all in velvet; herself, whom I never saw before, as I have often heard her described, for all the town-talk is now-a-days of her extravagancies, with her velvet cap, her hair about her ears; many black patches, because of pimples about her mouth; naked-necked, without anything about it, and a black *just-au-corps*. She seemed to be a very comely woman . . .

AGED 43.

SOURCE: Samuel Pepys, *Diary*.

CAVENDISH, WILLIAM, Duke of Newcastle (1592–1676), governor of Charles, Prince of Wales; royalist commander and writer.

His shape is neat, and exactly proportioned; his stature of a middle size, and his complexion sanguine.

His behaviour is such that it might be a pattern for all gentlemen; for it is courtly, civil, easy and free, without formality, or constraint; and yet hath something in it of grandeur, that causes an awful respect towards him . . .

He accoutres his person according to the fashion, if it be one that is not troublesome and uneasy for men of heroic exercises and actions. He is neat and cleanly; which makes him to be somewhat long in dressing, though not so long as many effeminate persons are. He shifts ordinarily once a day, and every time when he uses exercise, or his temper is more hot than ordinary.

In his diet he is so sparing and temperate, that he never eats nor drinks beyond his set proportion, so as to satisfy only his natural appetite. He makes but one meal a day, at which he drinks two good glasses of small-beer, one about the beginning, the other at the end thereof, and a little glass of sack in the middle of his dinner; which glass of sack he also uses in the morning, for his breakfast, with a morsel of bread. His supper consists of an egg, and a small draught of beer. And by his temperance he finds himself very healthful, and may live many years, he being now of the age of seventy-three, which I pray God from my soul to grant him.

AGED 73.

SOURCE: Margaret, Duchess of Newcastle, *The Life of William Cavendish, Duke of Newcastle,* 1667.

CECIL, WILLIAM, Baron Burleigh (1520–1598), statesman.

He was rather well-proportioned than tall, being of the middle size, very straight and upright of body and legs, and until age and his infirmity of the gout surprised him, very active and nimble of body.

SOURCE: quoted in Rev. Francis Wrangham's *The British Plutarch*, new edit., 1816.

For if he might ride privately in his garden, upon his little mule, or lie a day or two at his little lodge at Theobald's, retired from great business or too much company, he thought it his greatest greatness. . . . He hated idleness and loved no idle persons . . . and it was notable to see his continual agitation both of body and mind, for he was ever more weary of a little idleness than of great labour. If he had nothing of necessity to do, he would yet busy himself, either in reading, writing or meditation, and was never less idle than when he had most leisure to be idle.

SOURCE: an anonymous member of his household; Francis Peck, *Desiderata Curiosa*, 1732–1735.

The chief men of her [Elizabeth's] council also were there, that is to say, the Lord Treasurer, who is carried in a chair and is very old and white . . . he is very deaf and I have to shout quite loud.

AGED 77.

SOURCE: Journal of André Horault, Sieur de Maisse; quoted in Conyers Read's *Lord Burghley and Queen Elizabeth*. Jonathan Cape, 1960.

CHALMERS, THOMAS (1780–1847), theologian and writer; professor of moral philosophy at St. Andrew's and of divinity at Edinburgh.

. . . those strange accompaniments of Chalmer's eloquence—the uplifted, half-extracted eye—the large flushed forehead—the pallor of the cheek contrasting with it—the eager lips—the mortal passion struggling within the heaving breast—the short, fin-like, but furious motions of the arms, and the tones of the voice, which seemed sometimes to be grinding their way down into your ear and soul till you were taken by storm . . .

When, years later, we saw Duncan's picture of him he seemed still alive before us. The leonine massiveness of the head, body, and brow—the majestic repose of the attitude—the eye withdrawn upwards into a deep happy dream—the air of simple homely grandeur about the whole person and bearing—were all those of Chalmers, and combined to prove him the Genius of Scotland—the hirsute Forest-God of a rugged but true-hearted land.

SOURCE: George Gilfillan, *Scottish Review*, 1853.

CHAMBERS, ROBERT (1802–1871), publisher and writer.

His manner . . . on first acquaintance, was somewhat solid and unsympathetic. He had a very striking face and figure, as well-known in Edinburgh as St. Giles's Cathedral, but a stranger would have taken him for a divine, possibly even for one of the 'unco' guid'. In London his white tie, and grave demeanour, caused him to be always taken for a clergyman; a very great mistake, which used to tickle him exceedingly. 'When I don't give a beggar the penny he solicits,' he used to say, 'he generally tells me after a few cursory remarks, that the ministers are always the hardest.'

SOURCE: James Payn; quoted in John Lehmann's *Ancestors and Friends*, Eyre and Spottiswoode, 1962.

CHANTREY, SIR FRANCIS LEGATT (1781–1841), sculptor.

I called on Chantrey at Brighton. I had not seen him for eight years, and was astonished and interested. He took snuff in abundance. His nose at the tip was bottled, large and brown, his cheeks full, his person corpulent, his air indolent, his tone a little pompous. Such were the effects of eight years' success. He sat and talked, easily, lazily—gazing at the sun with his legs crossed . . .

To see a man of Chantrey's genius so impose on himself was affecting. Here he was, for that day at least, quite independent; gazing at the sun, sure of his dinner, his fire, his wine, his bed. Why was he not at that moment inventing?

AGED 46.

SOURCE: Benjamin Haydon's *Autobiography*.

CHARLES I (1600–1649), king of England.

He was a person, tho' born sickly yet who came thro' temperance and exercise, to have as firm and strong a body as most persons I ever knew, and throughout all the fatigues of the war, or during his imprisonment, never sick. His appetite was to plain meats, and tho' he took a good quantity thereof, yet it was suitable to an easy digestion. He seldom ate of above three dishes at most, nor drank above thrice; a glass of small beer, another of claret wine, and the last of water . . . His deportment was very majestic; for he would not let fall his dignity, no, not to the greatest foreigners that come to visit him and his Court; for tho' he was far from pride, yet he was careful of majesty, and would be approached with respect and reverence . . . His exercises were manly, for he rose the great horse very well . . . and they were wont to say of him that he failed not to do any of his exercises artificially, but not very gracefully, like some well-proportioned faces which yet want a pleasant air of countenance.

SOURCE: Sir Philip Warwick, *Memoirs of the Reign of Charles I,* 1701.

He went unto the scaffold . . . as a bee unto his hive; with our Saviour, as a lamb unto the slaughter; and cheerfully undrest himself unto his spiritual repose . . .

Observe his great temperance, his exemplary chastity . . . a refined purity from all lasciviousness of either gesture or speech. His abstinence in his feeding gave unto him constancy in health and readiness unto action, and his sobriety in drinking (whom the sun nor all the sons of men ever saw overcome or disguised by ingurgitation of strong liquors) made him unconquerable by wine or woman.

SOURCE: Archbishop William Juxon, March 12, 1648; *Sermon on the Death of Charles I.*

> He nothing common did nor mean
> Upon that memorable scene,
> But with his keener eye
> The axe's edge did try;

Nor call'd the Gods, with vulgar spite,
To vindicate his helpless right;
But bow'd his comely head
Down, as upon a bed.

SOURCE: Andrew Marvell, *An Horatian Ode upon Cromwell's Return from Ireland*, 1650.

Marvell probably witnessed the execution. His tribute is the more remarkable—and gains added veracity—in that he was an ardent republican and, with Milton, was Latin secretary to Cromwell.

An article by J. J. Keevil in the Journal of the History of Medicine and Allied Science, 1954, suggested that the King suffered from rickets as a boy. He is estimated to have been five feet four inches high, though a number of artists made him appear taller; thus, the directions given to Le Sueur for an equestrian statue told him to make the horse 'bigger than a greate Horsse by a foot', and the figure of the King 'proportionable full six foot'.

CHARLES II (1630–1685), king of Great Britain.

. . . at present he is so black that I am ashamed of him.

SOON AFTER BIRTH.

SOURCE: M. A. E. Green, Letters of Henrietta Maria, 1857; quoted in Janet Mackay's *Little Madam*, G. Bell & Sons, 1939. Charles II's mother, Henrietta Maria, was writing to Madame St. George, her old governess and trusted friend.

He is so ugly I am ashamed . . . but his size and fatness supply what he lacks in beauty. I wish you could see the gentleman, for he has no ordinary mien. He is so serious in all he does that I cannot help fancying him far wiser than myself.

AGED 2.

SOURCE: M. A. E. Green, Letters of Henrietta Maria, 1857; quoted in Janet Mackay's *Little Madam*, G. Bell & Sons, 1939. Charles II's mother, Henrietta Maria, was writing to Madame St. George, her old governess and trusted friend.

After the Battle of Worcester, during the future king's flight to the coast, when he had cut his hair, stained his face brown with walnut-tree leaves, and changed garments with a cottager:—

He had on a white steeple-crowned hat, without any other lining besides grease, both sides of the brim so doubled up with handling, that they looked like two waterspouts; a leather doublet, full of holes, and almost black with grease about the sleeves, collar and waist; an old green woodman's coat, threadbare and patched in most places, with a pair of breeches of the same cloth, and in the same condition, the slops hanging down to the middle of the leg; hose and shoes of different parishes; the hose mere grey stirrups, much darned and clouted, especially about the knees, under which he had a pair of flannel stockings of his own, the tops of them cut off; his shoes had been cobbled, being pieced both on the soles and seams, and the upper leathers so cut and slashed to fit them to his feet that they were quite unfit to befriend him either from the water or the dirt.

SOURCE: A contemporary tract, quoted in *Old England, a Pictorial Museum of . . . Antiquities,* 1854.

. . . a tall, black man, six foot two inches high.

AGED 21.

SOURCE: Parliamentary 'wanted' notice.

Those who knew his face, fixed their eyes there; and thought it of more importance to see, than to hear what he said. His face was as little a blab as most men's, yet though it could not be called a prattling face, it would sometimes tell tales to a good observer.

SOURCE: The Marquis of Halifax; from a MS. in the possession of Lady Burlington, Halifax's grand-daughter, published in 1750.

The king is certainly the best bred man in the world; for the queen-mother observed often the great defects of the late king's breeding and the stiff roughness that was in him, by which he disobliged very many and did often prejudice his affairs very much; so she gave strict orders that the young princes should be

bred to a wonderful civility. The king is civil rather to an excess
and has a softness and gentleness with him, both in his air and
expressions, that has a charm in it . . . He is very affable not
only in public but in private, only he talks too much and runs
out too long and too far.

SOURCE: Gilbert Burnet, Bishop of Salisbury, *History of my Own
Time.*

CHARLOTTE AUGUSTA, PRINCESS (1796–1817), only
daughter of George IV.

She was a young lady of more than ordinary personal attractions; her features were regular, and her complexion fair, with
the rich bloom of youthful beauty; her eyes were blue and very
expressive, and her hair was abundant, and of that peculiar
light brown which merges into the golden; in fact, such hair as
the Middle-Age Italian painters associate with their concep-
tions of the Madonna. In figure her Royal Highness was somewhat above the ordinary height of women, but finely proportioned and well developed. Her manners were remarkable for a
simplicity and good-nature which would have won admiration
and invited affection in the most humble walks of life. She
created universal admiration, and I may say a feeling of
national pride, amongst all who attended the ball.

AGED 17.

SOURCE: Captain R. H. Gronow, *Reminiscences.*

She was handsomer than I had expected, with most peculiar
manners, her hands generally folded behind her, her body
always pushed forward, never standing quiet, from time to time
stamping her foot, laughing a great deal, and talking still more.
I was examined from head to foot, without, however, losing my
countenance. My first impression was not favourable. In the
evening she pleased me more. Her dress was simple and in good
taste.

AGED 20.

SOURCE: Dr. Christian von Stockmar, physician and adviser to Leopold of the Belgians, whom Charlotte married in 1816.

CHARLOTTE SOPHIA (1744–1818), queen of George III.

Yes, I do think that the *bloom* of her ugliness is going off.

IN MIDDLE AGE.

SOURCE: Colonel Disbrowe, her chamberlain; quoted by John Timbs in *A Century of Anecdote*, 1760–1860.

We drove to Carlton House; we were shown into a room in old Chinese lacquer, magnificently furnished, but dark and heavy. The Regent arrived half-an-hour late; he excused himself and led us into a large drawing-room, the walls covered in black velvet, blue curtains ornamented with fleur de lis, where we found his mother, the Queen. She is certainly more than seventy years old, small stout; she has nothing distinguished about her looks, but her manner is agreeable. She has a strong German accent, her life is eminently respectable, and most austere and religious.

AGED 71.

SOURCE: The Duchess d'Orleans; quoted by John Timbs in *A Century of Anecdote*, 1760–1860.

Note: Royal birthdays in other centuries were made the occasion for great fashion parades and, one suspects, for immense competition among the female members of the royal household. The following accounts from fashionable magazines for 1807 describe the dresses worn on Queen Charlotte's 63rd birthday:

The Queen was 'extremely neat. Her dress was composed of brown velvet, beautifully embroidered with scarlet and white silk; draperies and bottom trimmed with rich point lace, tied up with silk cords and tassels; the mantle to correspond.' The Princess Augusta wore a 'brown velvet petticoat beautifully embroidered with silver; a large drapery on the right side, with

E

a most brilliant border, with damask and province roses intermised; a small drapery on the left side, tied up with a very rich bouquet, and bordered with Italian chains; train of brown and silver tissue.'

The Princess Elizabeth distinguished herself in a 'magnificent dress of green velvet, superbly embroidered with gold; the right side of the dress composed of a large marking drapery, elegantly striped with gold spangles, and finished at bottom with a massy border of a mosaic pattern, intermixed with pine leaves, richly embroidered in dead and bright gold foil, bullion, etc., the contour of which was strikingly elegant; smaller draperies in shell work, with rich borders, completed this superb dress, which was particularly remarked for taste and effect—the whole finished with a massy border at bottom, of foil and bullion, and looped up with superb cord and tassels.'

Princess Sophia sported 'a puce velvet petticoat, embroidered round the bottom with twist and spangles, over with a most magnificent drapery, superbly embroidered with festoons of variegated geranium leaves of gold, embossed work; under the leaves were suspended an extraordinary rich drapery, with point, terminating in rich gold tassels.'

But perhaps the Duchess of York stole the show on this occasion with a style of dress 'entirely new'. This was of 'white crape petticoat, the ground richly embroidered with gold spangles, in shell patterns, bordered with wreaths of oak and acorns elegantly worked in gold, intermixed with blue velvet; the drapery showered with gold spangles, beautifully interspersed with bunches of acorns, a border of oak to correspond, the pocket holes tastefully ornamented with rich gold cord and tassel; train of blue velvet trimmed with gold fringe, with a profusion of diamonds on the body, sleeves and girdle. Headdress, penache of seven ostrich feathers, with a beautiful heron in the middle bandeau; necklace and earrings of diamonds; a very elegant pair of white silk shoes, richly spangled all over with gold, and ornamented with gold.'

SOURCE: quoted, with many others, in Andrew W. Tuer, *The Follies and Fashions of our Grandfathers*, 1886–1887.

CHATHAM, EARL OF (1708–1778). See Pitt, William, first
Earl of Chatham.

CHATTERTON, THOMAS (1752–1770), poet.

Mention has frequently been made of the wonderful boy's eyes,
of their great brilliancy, and that one was brighter than the
other; but no one has recorded the particular circumstance,
that one was so much brighter than the other as to appear
larger. The fact was well authenticated to me. Their colour was
grey, and it has been observed that Chatterton is the only poet
who gives a beauty grey eyes. The peculiarity of one eye
appearing from its *glittering* (such was the expression of my
informant), larger than the other, is also recorded of Lord
Byron.

SOURCE: C. V. Le Grice, *The Gentleman's Magazine*, August 1838.

CHAUCER, GEOFFREY (1340–1400), poet.

   . . . mine host began to jest
And for the first time looked on me
And spake he thus: 'What man are you?' said he.
'You look as if you hope to find a hare
For always on the ground I see you stare.

'Come nearer now and look up merrily,
Beware you, sirs, and let this man have place.
He is as shapely round the waist as I—
He'd be a poppet, small and fair of face
For any woman in her arm to embrace.
There's something elfish in his countenance,
And with no fellow does he dalliance.'

SOURCE: Geoffrey Chaucer, *The Rime of Sir Thopas, Canterbury
   Tales* (modernised).

These verses, where Chaucer describes the innkeeper's jesting
   insistence on bringing the modest-seeming poet into the circle
   of story-tellers, provide one of the few clues we have to his

appearance. This personal description accords well with the actual portrait of Chaucer included by the poet Thomas Occleve (1370?–1450?) in the manuscript of his *De Regimine Principum* in the British Museum. We do not know the painter, but Occleve tells us it is included 'to remind other men of his personal appearance . . . that those who have least thought and memory of him may recall him by this painting'. It shows the same small, perky face the poet ascribes to himself in Sir Thopas.

CHURCHILL, JOHN, first Duke of Marlborough (1650–1722), soldier.

He is a man of birth: about the middle height, and the best figure in the world: his features without fault, fine sparkling eyes, good teeth, and his complexion such a mixture of white and red that the fairer sex might envy: in brief, except for his legs, which are too thin, one of the handsomest men ever seen . . . He expresses himself well, and even his very bad French is agreeable; his voice is harmonious, and as a speaker in his own language he is reckoned among the best. His address is most courteous, and while his handsome and well-graced countenance engages everyone in his favour at first sight, his perfect manners and his gentleness win over even those who start with a prejudice or grudge against him.

SOURCE: Sicco van Goslinga, *Mémoires;* quoted by Sir Winston Churchill in *Marlborough*, Vol. I, Harrap.

CLARKSON, THOMAS (1760–1846), philanthropist and slave abolitionist.

Clarkson has a head like a patriarch, and in his prime must have been a noble figure. He was very happy to see me, but there is a nervous irritability which is peculiar. He lives too much with adorers, especially women . . . I think Clarkson's intellects are unimpaired, and shine through his infirmities . . . Clarkson has more weaknesses than the Duke. He is not so high bred. He makes a pride of his debilities. He boasts of his swollen legs, and his pills, as if they were so many claims to distinction.

The Duke would not let you see him in his infirmities. He was deaf, but he would not let you see it if possible; he dined like others, ate like others, and did everything like others; and what he did not do like others he did not do before others.

Though Clarkson is a gentleman by birth, and was educated like one, he is too natural for any artifice. He says what he thinks, does what he feels inclined, is impatient, childish, simple.

AGED 81.

SOURCE: Benjamin Haydon's *Autobiography*.

CLOUGH, ARTHUR HUGH (1819–1861), poet.

There were two other guests—Mr. Arthur Hugh Clough, the poet, and his wife . . . He was a very reserved, undemonstrative man, who usually took little share in general conversation. His face had a weary expression which seemed to imply either chronic physical discomfort or chronic mental depression—an apparent depression which suggested the thought that he was oppressed by consciousness of the mystery of things.

AGED 41.

SOURCE: Herbert Spencer, *An Autobiography*, 1904.

COATES, ROBERT (1772–1848), amateur actor; known as 'Romeo Coates'.

About the year 1808, there arrived at the York Hotel, Bath, a person about the age of fifty, somewhat gentlemanlike, but so different from the usual men of the day that considerable attention was directed to him. He was of good figure; but his face was sallow, seamed with wrinkles, and more expressive of cunning than of any other quality. His dress was remarkable: in the daytime he was covered at all seasons with enormous quantities of fur; but the evening costume in which he went to the balls made a great impression from its gaudy appearance; for his buttons, as well as his knee-buckles, were of diamonds.

There was, of course, great curiosity to know who this stranger was; and this curiosity was heightened by an announcement that he proposed to appear at the theatre in the character of Romeo. There was something so unlike the impassioned lover in his appearance—so much that indicated a man with few intellectual gifts—that everybody was prepared for a failure. No one, however, anticipated the reality.

On the night fixed for his appearance, the house was crowded to suffocation. The playbills had given out than 'an amateur of fashion' would, for that night only, perform in the character of Romeo; besides, it was generally whispered that the rehearsals gave indication of comedy rather than tragedy, and that his readings were of a perfectly novel character.

The very first appearance of Romeo convulsed the house with laughter. Benvolio prepared the audience for the stealthy visit of the lover to the object of his admiration; and fully did the amateur give the expression to one sense of the words uttered, for he was indeed the true representative of a thief stealing onwards in the night . . . and disguising his face as if he were thoroughly ashamed of it. The darkness of the scene did not, however, shew his real character so much as the masquerade, when he came forward with a hideous grin and made what he considered his bow—which consisted in thrusting his head forward, and bobbing it up and down several times, his body remaining perfectly upright and stiff, like a toy mandarin with movable head.

His dress was *outré* in the extreme: whether Spanish, Italian, or English, no one could say; it was like nothing ever worn. In a cloak of sky-blue silk, profusely spangled, red pantaloons, a vest of white muslin, surmounted by an enormously thick cravat, and a wig à la Charles the Second, capped by an opera hat, he presented one of the most grotesque spectacles ever witnessed upon the stage. The whole of his garments were evidently too tight for him; and his movements appeared so incongruous, that every time he raised his arm, or moved a limb, it was impossible to refrain from laughter; but what chiefly convulsed the audience was the bursting of a seam in an inexpressible part of his dress, and the sudden extrusion through the red rent of a quantity of white linen sufficient to make a Bourbon flag, which was visible whenever he turned round . . . the total want of flexibility of limb, the awkwardness of his gait, and the idiotic manner in which he stood still, all produced a most ludicrous effect; but when his guttural voice was heard, and his total misapprehension of every passage in the play, especially the vulgarity of his address to Juliet, were perceived, everyone was satisfied that Shakespeare's Romeo was burlesqued on that occasion.

The balcony scene was interruped by shrieks of laughter, for in the midst of one of Juliet's impassioned exclamations Romeo quietly took out his snuff-box and applied a pinch to his nose; on this, a wag in the gallery bawled out: 'I say, Romeo, give us a pinch,' when the impassioned lover, in the most affected manner, walked to the side boxes and offered the contents of his box first to the gentlemen and then, with great gallantry, to the ladies. This new interpretation of Shakespeare was hailed with loud bravos, which the actor acknowledged with his usual grin and nod . . .

The dying scene was irresistibly comic, and I question if Liston, Munden, or Joey Knight, was ever greeted with such merriment; for Romeo dragged the unfortunate Juliet from the tomb, much in the same manner as a washerwoman thrusts into her cart the bag of foul linen. But how shall I describe his death? Out came a dirty silk handkerchief from his pocket, with which he carefully swept the ground; then his opera hat was carefully placed for a pillow, and down he laid himself. After various tossings about, he seemed reconciled to the position; but the house vociferously bawled out, 'Die again, Romeo!' and, obedient to the comment, he rose up and went through the ceremony again. Scarcely had he lain quietly down, when the call was again heard, and the well-pleased amateur was evidently prepared to enact a third death; but Juliet now rose up from her tomb, and gracefully put an end to this ludicrous scene by advancing to the front of the stage and aptly applying a quotation from Shakespeare—

> Dying is such sweet sorrow,
> That he will die again until tomorrow.

Thus ended an extravaganza as has seldom been witnessed; for although Coates repeated the play at the Haymarket, amidst shouts of laughter from the playgoers, there never was so ludicrous a performance as that which took place at Bath on the first night of his appearance.

AGED 26.

SOURCE: Captain R. H. Gronow's *Reminiscences*.

COBBETT, WILLIAM (1762–1835), essayist, politician and farmer.

Those who expected to find Cobbett a rude truculent barbarian were disappointed. They found instead a tall, stout, mild-faced, broad-shouldered, farmer-looking man, with a spice of humour lurking in his eye, but without one vestige of fierceness or malignity either in his look or demeanour. His private manners were simple, unaffected—almost gentlemanly.

SOURCE: George Gilfillan, *Second Gallery of Literary Portraits*, 1850.

COBDEN, RICHARD (1804–1865), statesman and orator.

In his early days, he was slight in frame and build. He afterwards grew nearer to portliness. He had a large and powerful head, and the indescribable charm of a candid eye. His features were not of a commanding type; but they were illuminated and made attractive by the brightness of intelligence, of sympathy and of earnestness. About the mouth there was a curiously winning mobility and play. His voice was clear, varied in its tones, sweet and penetrating; but it had scarcely the compass, or the depth, or the many resources that have usually been found in orators who have drawn great multitudes of men to listen to them. Of nervous fire, indeed, he had abundance, though it was not the fire which flamed up in the radiant colours of a strong imagination. It was rather the glow of a thoroughly convinced reason, of intellectual ingenuity, of argumentative keenness. It came from transparent honesty, thoroughly clear ideas, and a very definite purpose.

SOURCE: John Morley, *Life of Richard Cobden*, Fisher Unwin, 1903.

COCHRANE, THOMAS, tenth Earl of Dundonald (1775–1860), admiral.

By way of initiation into the mysteries of the military profession, I was placed under the tuition of an old sergeant, whose first lessons well accorded with his instructions, not to pay attention to my foibles. My hair, cherished with boyhood pride, was formally cut, and plastered back with a vile composition of candle-grease and flour, to which was added the torture incident to the cultivation of an incipient *queue*. My neck, from childhood open to the lowland breeze, was encased in an inflexible leathern collar or stock, selected according to my preceptor's notions of military propriety; these almost verging on strangulation. A blue semi-military tunic, with red collar and cuffs, in imitation of the Windsor uniform, was provided, and to complete the *tout ensemble*, my father, who was a determined Whig partisan, insisted on my wearing yellow waistcoat and breeches; yellow being the Whig colour, of which I was admonished never to be ashamed. A more certain mode of calling into action the dormant obstinacy of a sensitive, high-spirited lad, could not have been devised than that of converting him into a caricature, hateful to himself, and ridiculous to others.

As may be imagined, my costume was calculated to attract attention, the more so from being accompanied by a stature beyond my years. Passing one day near the Duke of Northumberland's palace at Charing Cross, I was beset by a troop of ragged boys, evidently bent on amusing themselves at the expense of my personal appearance, and, in their particular slang, indulging in comments thereon far more critical than complimentary.

Stung to the quick, I made my escape from them, and rushing home, begged my father to let me go to sea with my uncle, in order to save me from the degradation of floured head, pig-tail, and yellow breeches . . . He at length consented that my commission should be cancelled, and that the renewed offer of my uncle to receive me on board his frigate should be accepted.

AGED 14–18.

SOURCE: The Earl of Dundonald, *The Autobiography of a Seaman.*

COKE, SIR EDWARD (1552–1634), judge and legal writer.

For three things he would give God solemn thanks: that he never gave his body to physic, nor his heart to cruelty, nor his hand to corruption . . .

His parts were admirable: he had a deep judgment, faithful memory, active fancy: and the jewel of his mind was put into a fair case, a beautiful body, with a comely countenance; a case which he did wipe and keep clean, delighting in good clothes well worn, and being wont to say 'that the outward neatness of our bodies might be a monitor of purity to our souls.'

SOURCE: Thomas Fuller, *The English Worthies.*

COLERIDGE, SAMUEL TAYLOR (1772–1834), poet and philosopher.

His appearance was different from what I had anticipated from seeing him before. At a distance, and in the dim light of the chapel there was to me a strange wildness in his aspect, a dusky obscurity, and I thought him pitted with the small-pox. His complexion was at that time clear and bright . . . His forehead was broad and high, light as if built of ivory, with large projecting eyebrows, and his eyes rolling beneath them like a sea with darkened lustre. 'A certain tender bloom his face o'erspread,' a purple tinge as we see it in the pale thoughtful complexions of the Spanish portrait-painters, Murillo and Velasquez. His mouth was gross, voluptuous, open, eloquent; his chin good-humoured and round; but his nose, the rudder of

his face, the index of the will, was small, feeble, nothing—like
what he has done . . .

Coleridge in his person was rather above the common size,
inclining to the corpulent, or like Lord Hamlet, 'somewhat fat
and pursy'. His hair (now, alas! grey) was then black and
glossy as the raven's, and fell in smooth masses over his forehead.
This long, pendulous hair is peculiar to enthusiasts, to those
whose minds tend heavenward . . .

. . . The poet-preacher took leave, and I accompanied him
six miles on the road. It was a fine morning in the middle of
winter, and he talked the whole of the way . . . I observed that
he continually crossed me on the way by shifting from one side
of the foot-path to the other. This struck me as an odd movement; but I did not at that time connect it with any instability
of purpose or involuntary change of principle, as I have done
since.

AGED 25.

SOURCE: William Hazlitt, *My First Acquaintance with Poets*, The
Liberal, 1823.

. . . in spite of my assuring him that time was precious, he drew
me within the door of an unoccupied garden by the road-side,
and there, sheltered from observation by a hedge of evergreen,
he took me by the button of my coat, and, closing his eyes,
commenced an eloquent discourse, waving his right hand
gently, as the musical words flowed in an unbroken stream
from his lips . . . I saw it was of no use to attempt to break away,
so taking advantage of his absorption in his subject, I, with my
penknife, quietly severed the button from my coat, and
decamped. Five hours afterwards, in passing the same garden,
on my way home, I heard Coleridge's voice and, on looking in,
there he was, with closed eyes—the button in his fingers—and
his right hand gracefully waving, just as when I left him.

SOURCE: Charles Lamb. Story told by Lamb to J. R. Dix.

Coleridge sat on the brow of Highgate Hill, in those years,
looking down on London in its smoke-tumult, like a sage
escaped from the inanity of life's battle; attracting towards him

the thoughts of innumerable brave souls still engaged there . . .

The good man, he was now getting old, towards sixty perhaps; and gave you the idea of a life that had been full of sufferings; a life heavy-laden, half-vanquished, still swimming painfully in seas of manifold physical and other bewilderment. Brow and head were round, and of massive weight, but the face was flabby and irresolute. The deep eyes of a light hazel, were as full of sorrow as of inspiration; confused pain looked mildly from them, as in a kind of mild astonishment. The whole figure and air, good and amiable otherwise, might be called flabby and irresolute; expressive of weakness under possibility of strength. He hung loosely on his limbs, with knees bent, and stooping attitude; in walking he rather shuffled than decisively stept; and a lady once remarked, he never could fix which side of the garden-walk would suit him best, but continually shifted, in corkscrew fashion, and kept trying both. A heavy-laden, high-aspiring and surely much-suffering man. His voice, naturally soft and good, had contracted itself into a plaintive snuffle and singsong; he spoke as if preaching—you would have said, preaching earnestly and also hopelessly the weightiest things. I still recollect his 'object' and 'subject' . . . and how he sung and snuffled them into 'om-m-mject' and 'sum-m-mject,' with a kind of solemn shake or quaver, as he rolled along. No talk, in his century or in any other, could be more surprising.

AGED ABOUT 60.

SOURCE: Thomas Carlyle, *Life of John Stirling*, 1851.

Mr. Pollen, a man of fortune and a familiar friend, remarked on Coleridge's shabby dress, and jokingly said, his character would suffer by having a visitor with such a shabby wardrobe. 'Oh,' said Coleridge, 'never mind me; say I am your servant.' 'Servant!' replied Mr. Pollen. 'To keep a servant dressed as you are would totally ruin my character—my servant must always be better dressed than I am.'

SOURCE: D. Stuart, *The Gentleman's Magazine*, August 1838.

Coleridge was fat, and began to lament, in very delightful verses, that he was getting infirm. There was no old age in his verses. I heard him one day, under the Grove at Highgate, repeat one of his melodious lamentations, as he walked up and down, his voice undulating in a stream of music, and his regrets of youth sparkling with visions ever young ... His room looked upon a delicious prospect of wood and meadow, with coloured gardens under the window, like an embroidery to the mantle. I thought, when I first saw it, that he had taken up his dwelling-place like an abbot. Here he cultivated his flowers, and had a set of birds for his pensioners, who came to breakfast with him. He might have been seen taking his daily stroll up and down, with his black coat and white locks, and a book in his hand; and was a great acquaintance of the little children.

SOURCE: Leigh Hunt, *Autobiography*.

COLET, JOHN (1467?–1519), Dean of St. Paul's and founder of St. Paul's School.

In his excursions he would sometimes make me one of his company, and then no man could be more easy and pleasant. He always carried a book with him, and seasoned his conversation with religion. He had an aversion from all impure and improper discourse, and loved to be neat and clean in his apparel, furniture, equipment, books, and whatever belonged to him; but he held all pageantry and magnificence in contempt. Though it was then the custom for the higher clergy to appear in purple, his habit was invariably black. His upper garment, of plain woollen cloth, was in cold weather lined with fur.

SOURCE: Desiderius Erasmus; quoted in Rev. Francis Wrangham's *The British Plutarch*, new edit., 1810.

COLLINGWOOD, CUTHBERT, first Baron Collingwood (1750–1810), admiral.

Being provided with a letter of recommendation to Lord Collingwood, the Commander-in-Chief, I took an early opportunity to wait upon his Lordship ... Lord Collingwood was between fifty and sixty, thin and spare in person, which was then slightly bent, and in height about five feet ten inches. His head was small, with a pale, smooth, round face, the features of which would pass without notice, were it not for the eyes, which were blue, clear, penetrating; and the mouth, the lips of which were thin and compressed, indicating firmness and decision of character. He wore his hair powdered, and tied in a *queue*, in the style of the officers of his age at that time; and his clothes were squared and fashioned after the strictest rules of the good old sea school. To his very ample coat, which had a stiff-stand-up collar, were appended broad and very long skirts—the deep flaps of his single-breasted white waistcoat, descending far below his middle, covered a portion of his thighs; and blue knee-breeches, with white stockings, and buckles to his shoes, completed his attire.

AGED 56.

SOURCE: Midshipman Crawford; quoted by Edward Fraser, in *Champions of the Fleet*, John Lane, 1908.

COLLINS, WILKIE (1824–1889), novelist.

I can see him now as I used to see him in those early unforgotten days: a neat figure of cheerful plumpness, very small feet and hands, a full brown beard, a high and rounded forehead, a small nose not naturally intended to support a pair of large spectacles behind which his eyes shone with humour and friendship; not by any means the sort of man imagination would have pictured as the creator of Count Fosco and the inventor of the terrors of *Armadale* and the absorbing mystery of *The Moonstone*.

SOURCE: Rudolph Lehmann; quoted by John Lehmann in *Ancestors and Friends*, Eyre and Spottiswoode, 1962.

COLLINS, WILLIAM (1721–1759), poet.

About this time [1744] I fell into his company. His appearance was decent and manly; his knowledge considerable, his views extensive, his conversation elegant, and his disposition cheerful ...

The latter part of his life cannot be remembered but with pity and sadness. He languished some years under that depression of mind which enchains the faculties without destroying them, and leaves reason the knowledge of right without the power of pursuing it ... After his return from France, the writer of this character paid him a visit at Islington . . . there was then nothing of disorder discernible in his mind by any but himself; but he had withdrawn from study, and travelled with no other book than an English Testament, such as children carry to school.

SOURCE: Doctor Samuel Johnson, *The Lives of the Most Eminent English Poets*, Vol. IV, 1781.

CONRAD, JOSEPH (1857–1924), novelist.

Very dark he looked in the burning sunlight, tanned, with a peaked brown beard, almost black hair, and dark brown eyes, over which the lids were deeply folded. He was thin, not tall, his arms very long, his shoulders broad, his head set rather forward. He spoke to me with a strong foreign accent ... Fascination was Conrad's great characteristic—the fascination of vivid expressiveness and zest, of his deeply affectionate heart, and his far-ranging, subtle mind.

AGED 35.

SOURCE: John Galsworthy; quoted by Oliver Warner in *Joseph Conrad*, Longmans Green, 1951.

CONSTABLE, JOHN (1776–1837), landscape painter.

He was remarkable among the young men of the village for muscular strength, and being tall and well formed, with good features, a fresh complexion, and fine dark eyes, his white hat and coat were not unbecoming to him, and he was called in the neighbourhood the 'handsome miller'.

AGED ABOUT 18.

SOURCE: C. R. Leslie, *Autobiographical Recollections*, 1860.

I may venture *now* to say, that so finished a model of what is reckoned manly beauty, I never met with as the young painter.

AGED 23.

SOURCE: Mrs. Gilbert, formerly Ann Taylor, *Autobiography*, 1874.

Many of his happiest turns of expression were not to be found in his own notes; they arose at the moment, and were not to be recalled by a reporter unskilled in shorthand; neither can the charm of a most agreeable voice (though pitched somewhat too low), the beautiful manner in which he read the quotations, whether of prose or poetry, or the play of his very expressive countenance, be conveyed to the reader by words.

AGED ABOUT 57.

SOURCE: C. R. Leslie, *Autobiographical Recollections*, 1860.

Constable had another, and very painful, illness, which is thus described by Mr. Evans . . . : 'It was a severe attack of acute rheumatism (or rheumatic fever as it is usually called), which began in February and lasted the greater part of two months . . . I think he was never so well after this severe illness; its effects were felt by him, and showed themselves in his looks ever afterwards . . .'

AGED 58.

SOURCE: C. R. Leslie, *Autobiographical Recollections*, 1860.

COOK, JAMES (1728–1779), explorer and circumnavigator.

. . . a modest man and rather bashful; of an agreeable, lively conversation, sensible and intelligent. In his temper he was somewhat hasty, but of a disposition the most friendly, benevolent and humane. His person was above six feet high, and though a good-looking man, he was plain both in address and appearance. His head was small; his hair, which was dark brown, he wore tied behind. His face was full of expression, his nose exceedingly well-shaped, his eyes were small and of brown cast, quick and piercing; his eyebrows prominent, which gave his countenance altogether a look of austerity.

SOURCE: quoted in *100 Great Lives*, Odhams Press.

CORYATE, THOMAS (1577?–1617), traveller, buffoon and writer; author of *Coryate's Crudities*, etc.

He carried folly (which the charitable call merriment) in his very face. The shape of his head had no promising form, being like a sugar-loaf inverted, with the little end before, as composed of fancy and memory, without any common sense ... so contented with what was present that he accounted those men guilty of superfluity who had more suits and shirts than bodies, seldom putting off either till they were ready to go away from him.

SOURCE: Thomas Fuller, *The Worthies of England*.

CRABBE, GEORGE (1754–1832), poet.

We see the venerable old man, newly returned from a botanical excursion, laden with flowers and weeds (for no one knew better than he that every weed is a flower—it is the secret of his poetry), with his high narrow forehead, his grey locks, his glancing shoe-buckles, his clean neat dress somewhat ruffled in the woods, his mild countenance, his simple abstracted air.

SOURCE: George Gilfillan, *A Second Gallery of Literary Portraits*, 1850.

CROKER, JOHN WILSON (1780–1857), politician and writer; secretary to the Admiralty; introduced the term 'Conservatives'.

Croker was also agreeable, notwithstanding his bitter and sarcastic remarks upon everything and everybody. The sneering, ill-natured expression of his face, struck me as an

F

impressive contrast to the frank and benevolent countenance of Walter Scott.

AGED 35.

SOURCE: Captain R. H. Gronow's *Reminiscences*.

CROMWELL, OLIVER (1599–1658), the Protector.

The first time I ever took notice of him was in the beginning of the Parliament, held in 1640, when I vainly thought myself a courtly young gentleman, for we courtiers valued ourselves much on our good clothes. I came into the House one morning, well clad, and perceived a gentleman speaking (whom I knew not) very ordinarily apparelled, for it was a plain cloth suit that seemed to have been made by an ill country tailor; his linen was plain and not very clean, and I remember a speck or two of blood upon his little band which was not much larger than his collar; his hat was without a hatband; his stature was of a good size; his sword stuck close to his side; his countenance swollen and reddish; his voice sharp and untunable, and his eloquence full of fervour . . . And yet I lived to see this very gentleman, whom out of no ill will to him I thus describe, by multiplied good successes and by real (but usurped) power (having had a better tailor and more converse among good company) . . . appear of a great and majestic deportment and comely presence.

AGED 41.

SOURCE: Sir Philip Warwick, *Memoirs of the Reign of Charles I*.

Mr. Lilly, I desire you would use all your skill to paint my picture truly like me and not flatter me at all but [pointing to his own face] remark all these roughnesses, pimples, warts and everything as you see me; otherwise I will never pay a farthing for it.

SOURCE: Cromwell's own instructions to his painter; George Vertue, *Notebooks*; quoted in David Piper's *The English Face*, Thames and Hudson, 1957.

That sloven, whom you see before you, hath no ornament in his speech; that sloven, I say, if we should ever come to a breach with the king (which God forbid), in such a case, I say, that sloven will be the greatest man in England.

SOURCE: John Hampden; quoted in John Buchan's *Oliver Cromwell.*

Note: A life-mask, taken in about 1656, when Cromwell was 57, shows a thick underlip, with small beard, an upper lip with a pronounced convexity in the centre, and a broad, coarse nose inclining a little towards the left and slightly aquiline. His height was about five feet ten inches.

CUMBERLAND, DUCHESS OF (1747–1808). See Horton, Anne.

CURRAN, JOHN PHILPOTT (1750–1817), Irish judge.

... I saw him in a dress which you would have imagined he had borrowed from his tip-staff; his hands in his sides; his under lip protruded; his face almost parallel with the horizon—and the important step, and the eternal attitude only varied by the pause during which his eye glanced from his guest to his watch, and from his watch reproachfully to his dining room ...

I had often seen Curran—often heard him—often read him; but no man ever knew anything about him who did not see him at his own table, with the few whom he selected. He was a convivial little deity ... At the time I spoke of, he was turned sixty, yet he was as playful as a child. The extremes of youth and age were met in him; he had the experience of the one, and the simplicity of the other.

SOURCE: Charles Phillips, *Life of Curran*; quoted by John Timbs in *A Century of Anecdote, 1760–1860.*

DARWIN, CHARLES ROBERT (1809–1882), naturalist.

He was about six feet in height, but scarcely looked so tall, as he stooped a good deal; in later days he yielded to the stoop;

but I can remember seeing him long ago swinging back his arms to open out his chest, and holding himself upright with a jerk. He gave one the idea that he had been active rather than strong; his shoulders were not broad for his height, though certainly not narrow . . .

He walked with a swinging action, using a stick heavily shod with iron, which he struck loudly against the ground, producing as he went round the 'Sandwalk' at Down a rhythmical click which is with all of us a very distinct remembrance. As he returned from the mid-day walk, often carrying the waterproof or cloak which had proved too hot, one could see that the swinging step was kept up by something of an effort. Indoors his step was often slow and laboured, and as he went upstairs in the afternoon he might be heard mounting the stairs with a heavy footfall, as if each step were an effort. When interested in his work he moved about quickly and easily enough, and often in the midst of dictating he went eagerly into the hall to get a pinch of snuff, leaving the study door open, and calling out the last words of his sentence as he left the room.

In spite of his activity, he had, I think, no natural grace or neatness of movement. He was awkward with his hands, and was unable to draw at all well . . .

His beard was full and almost untrimmed, the hair being grey and white, fine rather than coarse, and wavy or frizzled. His moustache was somewhat disfigured by being cut short and square across. He became very bald, having only a fringe of dark hair behind.

His face was ruddy in colour, and this perhaps made people think him less of an invalid than he was . . . And it must be remembered that at this time he was miserably ill, far worse than in later years. His eyes were bluish grey under deep overhanging brows, with thick, bushy, projecting eyebrows. His high forehead was deeply wrinkled, but otherwise his face was not much marked or lined. His expression showed no sign of the continual discomfort he suffered.

When he was excited with pleasant talk his whole manner was wonderfully bright and animated, and his face shared to the full in the general animation. His laugh was a free and sounding peal ... He often used some sort of gesture with his laugh, lifting up his hands or bringing one down with a slap. I think, generally speaking, he was given to gesture, and often used his hands in explaining anything (e.g. the fertilisation of a flower) in a way that seemed an aid to himself rather than to the listener. He did this on occasions when most people would illustrate their explanations by means of a rough pencil sketch.

He wore dark clothes, of a loose and easy fit. Of late years he gave up the tall hat even in London, and wore a soft black one in winter, and a big straw hat in summer ... Two peculiarities of his indoor dress were that he almost always wore a shawl over his shoulders, and that he had great loose cloth boots lined with fur which he could slip on over his indoor shoes ...

SOURCE: Sir Francis Darwin, *Reminiscences of My Father's Everyday Life*.

DARWIN, ERASMUS (1731–1802), physician, botanist and author.

It was in the course of that autumn that the celebrated Dr. Darwin first came to see my mother at Barr. His arrival was an era in my life; I saw him then with the eyes of a child, and now, in age, I can only describe him from the stores I then locked up in my memory.

It was in the latter part of the morning that a carriage drove up to our door, of that description then called a 'Sulky', because calculated to hold one person only. The carriage was worn, and bespattered with mud. Lashed on the place appropriated to the boot in ordinary carriages was a large pail for the purpose of watering the horses, together with some hay and oats beside it. In the top of the carriage was a skylight, with an awning which could at pleasure be drawn over; this was for the purpose of giving light to the doctor, who wrote most of his works on scraps of paper with a pencil as he travelled.

The front of the carriage within was occupied by a receptacle for writing-paper and pencils, likewise for a knife, fork and spoon; on one side was a pile of books reaching from the floor to nearly the front window of the carriage; on the other, a hamper containing fruit and sweetmeats, cream and sugar, great part of which, however, was demolished during the time the carriage traversed the forty miles which separated Derby from Barr. We all hastened to the parlour window to see Dr. Darwin, of whom we had heard so much, and whom I was prepared to honour and venerate, in no common degree, as the restorer of my mother's health. What then was my astonishment at beholding him as he slowly got out of the carriage! His figure was vast and massive, his head was almost buried on his shoulders, and he wore a scratch wig, as it was then called, tied up in a little bob-tail behind. A habit of stammering made the closest attention necessary, in order to understand what he said.

Meanwhile, amidst all this, the doctor's eye was deeply sagacious, the most so I think of any eye I remember ever to have seen; and I can conceive that no patient consulted Dr. Darwin who . . . was not inspired with confidence in beholding him.

SOURCE: Mary Anne Schimmelpennick; *Life of Mary Anne Schimmelpennick*, 1858.

DAY, THOMAS (1748–1789), author of *Sandford and Merton*, etc.

I have seen him stand between two boards, which reached from the ground higher than his knees; these boards were adjusted with screws, so as barely to permit him to bend his knees, and to rise up and sink down . . . but original formation and inveterate habit resisted all his efforts at personal improvement. I could not help pitying my philosophic friend, pent up in durance vile for hours together, with his feet in the stocks, a book in his hand, and contempt in his heart.

SOURCE: Richard Lovell Edgeworth; quoted in Hesketh Pearson, *Extraordinary People*, Heinemann, 1965. Thomas Day had an ungainly and clumsy figure, and this was one of his more curious efforts to make his joints more flexible and graceful.

DAVY, SIR HUMPHRY (1778–1829), chemist and natural philosopher.

Mr. Davy was announced, and a little, slender youth came in, his hair combed over his forehead, speaking very dandily and drawlingly.

AGED 29.

SOURCE: Benjamin Haydon's *Autobiography*.

DEE, JOHN (1527–1608), mathematician and astrologer.

He had a very fair clear complexion; a long beard as white as milk; a very handsome man; he was tall and slender. He wore a gown like an artist's gown, with hanging sleeves, and a slit. A mighty good man he was.

SOURCE: John Aubrey, *Brief Lives*, edit. Andrew Clark, 1898.

DE LA RAMÉE, MARIE LOUISE (1839–1908), novelist, writing under the pseudonym of **OUIDA**.

... surrounded with dogs—an old lady of sixty or more, with rather a long, impressive face, large forehead, large ears, fine slate-blue eyes, and a bright complexion—a slight body arrayed in light grey satin—very gentle in her manner and wise in her speech which was mostly about European politics. We were ... agreeably surprised to find her thus and not vulgar, masculine or loud.

AGED 61.

SOURCE: Sydney Carlyle Cockerell; quoted in Wilfred Blunt's *Cockerell*, Hamish Hamilton, 1964.

DENHAM, SIR JOHN (1615–1669), poet and surveyor-general.

Sir John Denham was unpolished with the small-pox: otherwise a fine complexion ... He was of the tallest, but a little incurvetting at his shoulders, not very robust. His hair was but thin and flaxen, with moist curl. His gait was slow, and was rather a stalking (he had long legs) ... His eye was a kind of light goose-gray, not big; but it had a strange piercingness, not as to shining and glory, but ... when he conversed with you he looked into your very thoughts.

SOURCE: John Aubrey, *Brief Lives.*

DE QUINCEY, THOMAS (1785–1859), essayist and editor.

A short and fragile, but well-proportioned frame; a shapely and compact head; a face beaming with intellectual light, with rare, almost feminine beauty of face and complexion; a fascinating courtesy of manner; and a fullness, swiftness and elegance of silvery speech—such was the irresistible 'mortal mixture of earth's mould' that men named De Quincey.

SOURCE: *Encyclopaedia Britannica*, 1952 edition, abbreviated from the original account written by J. R. Findlay (1824–1898), a friend of De Quincey's.

He had a morbid value for papers, which accumulated until he was 'snowed up'. When crowded out by such a catastrophe, he promptly locked the door and went elsewhere. . . . Six of these storehouses existed at the time of his death.

SOURCE: Leslie Stephen, in *Dictionary of National Biography*, 1888.

DEVEREUX, ROBERT, second Earl of Essex (1566–1601), favourite of Queen Elizabeth I.

There followed ... a pretty warm dispute, between the Queen and Essex, about the choice of some fit and able persons to superintend the affairs of Ireland ... The Queen looked upon Sir William Knollys, uncle to Essex, as the most proper person for that charge; and Essex contended, on the other side, that Sir George Carew would much better become that post ... : and when the Queen could by no means be persuaded to approve his choice, he quite forgot himself and his duty, and turned his back upon his Sovereign in a kind of contempt. The Queen was not able to bear this insolence, and so bestowed on him a box on the ear, and bade him 'go and be hanged'. He immediately clapped his hand on his sword, and the Lord Admiral, stepping in between, he swore a great oath that he neither could nor would put up with an affront of that nature, nor would he have taken it at the hands of Henry the Eighth himself; and, in a great passion, he immediately withdrew from the Court.

SOURCE: William Camden, *Annals of the Reign of Queen Elizabeth*; quoted in David Jardine's *Criminal Trials*, 1832.

The next day, being Wednesday, the 25th of February 1601, about eight o'clock in the morning, he was brought forth from his chamber by Mr. Lieutenant, attended by the three divines exhorting him, with thirteen of the guard, and divers of the Lieutenant's men also following him. He was apparelled in a gown of wrought velvet, a satin suit, and felt hat, all of black, and with a small ruff about his neck. And at his coming forth of the door, and all the way as he went to the scaffold, he earnestly prayed to God to give him strength, and patience; and again, by the way, he prayed, saying, 'O God, grant me a true and earnest repentance, grant me patience and a true humility!', saying also to the divines, 'I beseech you, brethren, pray for me, and join with me in prayer'; and often entreated those that went with him to pray for him. He requested the clergymen not to leave him, but begged them to observe him closely, and speak to him, if either his eye, his countenance or his speech should betray anything unbecoming his situation.

SOURCE: David Jardine, *Criminal Trials*, 1832; compiled from 'several different relations in the State-Paper Office.'

Such was the fatal, but withal pious and Christian end of Robert Devreux, Earl of Essex, in the 34th year of his age. He was a most accomplished person, and had all those good qualities in perfection that became a nobleman . . . As soon as he got a secure and real interest in the favour of his royal mistress, he made it his business to outstrip all persons, whether of his own or a superior rank; and this was a quarrel which the more politic courtiers had to him, especially when he took it upon him to disparage all whose actions were not of his own square, and to browbeat those who had not the advantage of the royal ear or favour . . .

Nor was he excusable in his deportment to the Queen herself, whom he treated with a sort of insolence, that seemed to proceed rather from a mind that wanted ballast, than any real pride in him; though it looked the more ungrateful, because acted when he had more than once been restored to the Queen's favour, and received fresh instance of her bounty. However, this unhandsome carriage, and a way he had of screwing (as it were) favours from her, joined with a coldness and disrespect towards her person, and backed by the sly management of some that wished him not well, failed not by degrees to lessen, and at the long run to extinguish entirely, the Queen's affection for him. Indeed, he was a person not rightly calculated for a Court, as not being easily brought to any mean compliances. He was of a temper that would readily kindle an injury, but would not so easily forget one; and so far was he of being capable of dissembling a resentment, that he carried his passions in his forehead, and the friend or the enemy were easily read in his face.

SOURCE: William Camden; quoted in David Jardine's *Criminal Trials*, 1832.

DICKENS, CHARLES (1812–1870), novelist.

. . . a dissipated looking mouth with a vulgar draw to it, a muddy olive complexion, shabby fingers and a hand by no means patrician. A hearty off-hand manner, far from well-bred, and a rapid, dashing way of talking.

SOURCE: R. H. Dana, jnr.; quoted in E. F. Payne, *Dickens Days in Boston*, Houghton Mifflin, 1927.

Note: Dana afterwards modified his opinion of some of Dickens' characteristics, e.g. 'The gentlemen all talking their best, but Dickens natural and unpretending. He couldn't have behaved better. He did not say a single word for display'; and, 'He is full of life . . . I never saw a face fuller of life.'

He has the finest of eyes; and his whole countenance speaks life and action—the face seems to flicker with the *heart's* and the *mind's* activity. You cannot tell how dead the faces around him seemed.

SOURCE: R. H. Dana, Snr., quoted in E. F. Payne, *Dickens Days in Boston*, Houghton Mifflin, 1927.

Dickens himself is frank and hearty, and with a considerable trace of rowdyism in his manner. But his eyes are fine and the whole muscular action of the mouth and lower part of the face beautifully free and vibratory.

SOURCE: Henry James, *William Whetmore Story and His Friends*, Houghton Mifflin, 1904.

Gay, free and easy, fine bright face; blue eyes, long black hair, and with a slight touch of the Dick Swiveller about him.

SOURCE: *Longfellow and Dickens, the Story of a Trans-Atlantic Friendship*, Cambridge Historical Society, vol. 28, 1942.

Note: These descriptions were all given during Dickens' first American tour, at the age of 30 and are quoted in *Charles Dickens, His Tragedy and Triumph*, Victor Gollancz, 1953.

My father had one very vivid memory of Dickens. 'I cannot have been more than six or seven years old when my father and mother took me to one of his readings at, I think, St. James's Hall. First he read the death of Paul Dombey, which left me in floods of tears, and next came the trial scene from *Pickwick*. I shall never forget my amazement when he assumed the character of Mr. Justice Stareleigh. The face and figure that I knew, that I had seen on the stage a moment before, seemed to vanish as if by magic, and there appeared instead a fat, pompous, pursy little man, with a plump imbecile face, from which every vestige of good temper and cheerfulness—everything in fact except an expression or self-sufficient stupidity—had been removed. The upper lip had become long, the corners of the mouth dropped, the nose was short and podgy, all the angles of the chin had gone, the chin itself had receded into the throat, and the eyes, lately so humorous and human, had become as malicious and obstinate as those of a pig. It was a marvellous effort in transformation.'

SOURCE: John Lehmann, *Ancestors and Friends*, Eyre and Spottiswode, 1963.

... The features were very good. He had a capital forehead, a firm nose with full wide nostrils, eyes wonderfully beaming with intellect and running over with humour and cheerfulness, and a rather prominent mouth strongly marked with sensibility. The head was altogether well formed and symmetrical, and the air and carriage of it were extremely spirited. The hair, so scant and grizzled in later days, was then of a rich brown and most luxuriant abundance, and the bearded face of his last two decades had hardly a vestige of hair or whisker. . . .

SOURCE: John Forster, *Life of Dickens*, Book 2.

DIGBY, SIR KENELM (1603–1665), royalist, naval commander, writer.

Sir Kenelm Digby was held to be the most accomplished cavalier of his time ... He was such a goodly handsome person, gigantic and great voice, and had so graceful elocution and noble address, etc., that had he been dropped out of the clouds in any part of the world, he would have made himself respected ... He was a person of very extraordinary strength. I remember one at Sherbourne ... protested to us that as he, being a middling man, being set in [a] chair, Sir Kenelm took him up, chair and all, with one arm.

SOURCE: John Aubrey, *Brief Lives*.

DISRAELI, BENJAMIN, first Earl of Beaconsfield (1804–1881), statesman and man of letters.

Never in my life had I been so struck by a face as I was by that of Disraeli. It was lividly pale, and from beneath two finely-arched eyebrows blazed out a pair of intensely black eyes. I never have seen such orbs in mortal sockets, either before or since. His physiognomy was strictly Jewish. Over a broad, high forehead were ringlets of coal-black glossy hair, which, combed away from his right temple, fell in luxuriant clusters or bunches over his left cheek and ear, which it entirely concealed from view. There was a sort of half-smile, half-sneer, playing about his beautifully formed mouth, the upper lip of which was curved as we see it in the portraits of Byron . . . He was very showily attired in a dark bottle-green frock-coat, a waistcoat of the most extravagant fashion, the front of which was almost covered with glittering chains, and in fancy-pattern pantaloons. He wore a plain black stock, but no collar was visible. Altogether he was the most intellectual-looking exquisite I had ever seen.

He minced his phrases in apparently the most affected manner, and whilst he was speaking, placed his hands in all imaginable positions: not because he felt awkward . . . but apparently for the purpose of exhibiting to the best advantage the glittering rings which decked his white and taper fingers. Now he would place his thumbs in the armholes of his waistcoat, and spread out his fingers on its flashing surface; then one set of digits would be released and he would lean affectedly on the table, supporting himself with his right hand; anon he would push aside the curls from his forehead . . . But as he proceeded all traces of this dandyism and affectation were lost . . . His voice, at first so finical, gradually became full, musical, and sonorous, and with every varying sentiment was beautifully modulated.

AGED 31.

SOURCE: *Pen and Ink Sketches of Poets, Preachers and Politicians*, 1846; quoted in Monypenny and Buckle's '*Life*', 1910–1918.

When he rose to speak he rested his hands for a moment on the Box . . . The attitude he found most conducive to happy delivery was to stand balancing himself on heel and toe with hands in his coat-tail pockets. In this pose, with head hung down as if he were mentally debating how best to express a thought just born to him, he slowly uttered the polished and poisoned sentences, over which he had spent laborious hours in the study. The merest tyro knew a moment beforehand when Disraeli was approaching what he regarded as the most effective opening for dropping the gem of phrase he made believe to have just dug up from an unvisited corner of his mind. He saw him lead up to it; he noted the disappearance of a hand in the direction of the coat-tail pocket, sometimes a pocket-handkerchief brought out and shaken with careless air, most often to extend the coat-tails, whilst, with body gently rocked to and fro and an affected hesitancy of speech, the *bon mot* was flashed forth.

SOURCE: Henry Lucy, *Sixty Years in the Wilderness*, John Murray, 1909.

DODGSON, CHARLES LUTWIDGE (1832–1898), mathematician, and writer of children's books under pseudonym of **LEWIS CARROLL.**

Another silk hat which I well remember—but this always a sleek and respectable one, was that of 'Lewis Carroll'—to give him his proper name, the Reverend Charles Dodgson, student of Christ Church. I was just of the generation to appreciate as a boy Alice in Wonderland and Through the Looking Glass, which I read at school with glee, and ere I came to Oxford I knew most of Dodgson's verse by heart. What a surprise then to find this purveyor of joys for young and old, when he was identified, to be an austere cleric, always dressed in the correct garb of a clergyman of low-church tendencies—sober black, with a waistcoat cut rather low, a large, well-arranged white tie, and an impeccable tall hat. He looked severe to the passer-by, and no-one outside the limited sphere in Christ Church in which he moved would have suspected him of being the author of such cascades of riotous fun . . .

SOURCE: Sir Charles Oman, *Memories of Victorian Oxford*, Methuen, 1941.

The quiet humour of his voice, a very pleasant voice, the occasional laugh—he was not a man that often laughed, though there was often a smile playing about his sensitive mouth—and the slight hesitation that whetted some of his wittiest sayings—all those that knew him must remember ... Dodgson was a good teller of anecdote ... a fantastic weaver of paradox and propounder of puzzles, a person who never let the talk flag, but never monopolised it, who had rather set others talking than talk himself, and was as pleased to hear a twice-told tale as to retail his own store of reminiscences.

SOURCE: Oliver Elton, *Frederick York Powell, A Life and a Selection of His Letters and Occasional Writings*, 1906; quoted in Derek Hudson, *Lewis Carroll*, Constable, 1954.

His intense shyness and morbid dislike of publicity made him a figure apart. Only in Common Room, when the port had gone round, and only then on a lucky night, would a tiny drop of fantasy fall from Mr. Dodgson's lips, after which the venerable humorist would resume his tantalizing taciturnity. A dull and steady routine governed the days of this fantastic friend of all the children. Every afternoon he could be seen in his tall silk hat and flowing clerical black striding out to take the air with his inseparable companion the genial and benevolent Vere Bayne, yet another silver-haired Christ Church cleric ...

SOURCE: H. A. L. Fisher, *An Unfinished Autobiography*, O.U.P., 1940.

DONNE, JOHN (1573–1631), poet and divine.

He was of a stature moderately tall, of a straight and equally proportioned body, to which all his words and actions gave an unexpressible addition of comeliness. The melancholy and pleasant humour were in him so contempered that each gave advantage to the other, and made his company one of the delights of mankind ...

His aspect was cheerful and, as such, gave a silent testimony of a clear, knowing soul, and of a conscience at peace with itself. His melting eye shewed that he had a soft heart, full of noble compassion; of too brave a soul to offer injuries, and too much a Christian not to pardon them in others.

SOURCE: Izaak Walton, *Life of Dr. Donne*, 1640.

DOUGLAS, SIR JAMES, called 'The Good' (1286?–1330), soldier; knighted at Bannockburn.

> In visage he was some deal gray,
> And had black hair, as I heard say,
> But then of limbs, he was well made,
> With bones great, and shoulders braid.
> His body well made and lenzie,
> As they that saw him said to me.
> When he was blyth, he was lovely
> And meek, and sweet in company;
> But who in battle might him see,
> Another countenance had he;
> And in his speech he lispt some deal,
> But that set him right wonder well.

SOURCE: John Barbour, *The Bruce*, c. 1376.

DRAKE, SIR FRANCIS (1540?–1596), admiral and circumnavigator.

Round headed, brown hair, full bearded, his eyes round, large and clear, well favoured, fair and of a cheerful countenance.

SOURCE: John Stow, *Annales*.

Francis Drake knows no language but English and I talked with him through interpreters in Latin or French or Italian. He had with him an Englishman who understood Spanish a little and sometimes acted as interpreter. Drake is a man of medium stature, blond, rather heavy than slender, merry, careful. He commands and governs imperiously. He is feared and obeyed by his men. He punishes resolutely. Sharp, restless, well-spoken inclined to liberality and to ambition, vainglorious, boastful, not very cruel. These are qualities I noted in him during my negotiations with him.

AGED 47.

SOURCE: Garcia Fernandez de Torrequemada, factor and inspector to the royal treasury, reporting to Philip II. Irene R.

Wright (trans. and edit.), *Further English Voyages to Spanish America*, 1583–1594, Hakluyt Society, 1951.

Thirty sails were assembled, belonging to the queen, to Drake and to other private persons, aboard which were sent 3,000 young men, the eldest being Francis Drake himself who admits that he is 46 years old. He is red complexioned, under medium in stature.

SOURCE: Diego Hidalgo, to King Philip II. Irene R. Wright (trans. and edit.), *Further English Voyages to Spanish America*, 1583–1594, Hakluyt Society, 1951.

He is called Francisco Drac, and is a man of about 35 years of age, low of stature, with a fair beard, and is one of the greatest mariners that sail the seas, both as a navigator and as a commander . . . He is served on silver dishes with gold borders and gilded garlands, in which are his arms. He said that many of these had been given to him by the Queen.

SOURCE: Don Francisco da Zarate, in Richard Hakluyt's *The Principall Navigations, Voiages and Discoveries of the English Nation.*

> As he was walking up Totnes' long street:
> He asked me whose I was? I answered him.
> He asked me if his good friend were within?
> A fair red orange in his hand he had;
> He gave it me, whereof I was right glad,
> Takes and kissed me, and prays 'God bless my boy.'

SOURCE: Robert Hayman, *Quodlibets.* Hayman was a Devonshire lad who went up to Oxford and later became Governor of Newfoundland. He published, among other books, a volume called *Quodlibets*, which included this boyhood recollection of Drake, just back from a voyage and enquiring in the steep main street of Totnes for Hayman's father.

DRYDEN, JOHN (1631–1700), poet.

The two cavaliers had now approached within the throw of a lance, when the stranger desired a parley, and, lifting up the vizor of his helmet, a face hardly appeared from within, which,

G

after a pause, was known for that of the renowned Dryden. The brave Ancient [i.e. the poet Virgil] suddenly started, as one possessed with surprise and disappointment together; for the helmet was nine times too large for the head, which appeared situate in the hinder part, even like the lady in a lobster, or like a mouse under a canopy of state, or like a shrivelled beau, from within the pent-house of a modern periwig; and the voice was suited to the visage, sounding weak and remote.

SOURCE: Dean Swift, *The Battle of the Books*, 1704.

Note: Swift calls Dryden 'my dear relation', though the Dean seems to have been only the son of Dryden's second cousin. References to Dryden's appearance are fragmentary. A contemporary epigram refers to 'old Nassau's hook-nosed head'; Luke Milbourne (1649–1720) hints at the poet's good looks in his youth, describing him as:

> Still smooth, as when, adorn'd with youthful pride,
> For thy dear sake the blushing virgins died.

In later years, Rochester (1647–1680) nicknamed him, in *An Allusion to the Tenth Satire*, 'The Poet Squab', probably a reference to Dryden's increasing corpulency. His voice, at least when reading his own productions, was flat and dull. Cibber's *Apology* records: 'When Dryden, our first master of verse and harmony, brought his play of Amphityron to the stage, I heard him give it his first reading to the actors; in which, though it is true he delivered the plain sense of every period, yet the whole was in so cold, so flat, and unaffecting manner, that I am afraid of not being believed, when I affirm it.'

DUDLEY, ROBERT, Earl of Leicester (1532?–1588), Queen Elizabeth's favourite.

He was a very goodly person, tall and singularly well featured, and all his youth well favoured, of a sweet aspect, but high foreheaded which (as I should take it) was of no discommendation.

SOURCE: Sir Robert Naunton, *Fragmenta Regalia*, compiled c. 1630: quoted in J. S. Millward, *Sixteenth Century*, Hutchinson.

DUNDAS, HENRY, first Viscount Melville (1742–1811).

His figure tall, manly, and advantageous; his countenance open, cheerful and expressive, prejudiced in his favour. Neither the Scotticisms with which his speeches abounded, nor an accent peculiarly northern, as well as uncouth, could prevent his assuming and maintaining that place in the Ministerial ranks to which his pre-eminent parts entitled him. These very defects of elocution or of diction, by the ludicrous effect they produced, became often converted into advantages; as they unavoidably operated to force a smile from his bitterest opponents, and chequered with momentary good humour the personalities of debate . . . Never did any man conceal deeper views of every kind under the appearance of careless inattention to self-interest . . . His voice, strong and sonorous, enabled him to surmount the noise of a popular assembly, and almost to command attention at moments of the greatest clamour or impatience. Far from shunning the post of danger, he always seemed to court it; and was never deterred from stepping forward to the assistance of Ministers by the violence of the Opposition, by the unpopularity of the measure to be defended or by the difficulty of the attempt. His speeches, able, animated and argumentative, were delivered without hesitation, and unembarrassed by any timidity. If they displayed no ornaments of style and no beauties of composition, it was impossible to accuse them of any deficiency in sterling sense, or in solid ability.

SOURCE: Sir N. William Wraxall, *Historical Memoirs of My Own Life*, 1815.

DUNCAN, ADAM, Viscount Duncan (1731–1804), admiral; victor of Camperdown.

Imagine a man upwards of six feet four inches in height, with limbs of proportionate frame and strength. His features are nobly beautiful, his forehead high and fair, and his hair as white as snow. His movements are all stately and unaffected, and his manner easy though dignified.

AGED 66.

SOURCE: quoted by Christopher Lloyd in *St. Vincent and Camperdown*, Batsford, 1963. In his younger days, Duncan had the reputation of being the handsomest lieutenant in the Royal Navy.

EDWARD, called **THE CONFESSOR** (d. 1066), king of the English.

He used to stand with lamb-like meekness and tranquil mind at the holy offices of the divine mysteries and masses, a worshipper of Christ manifest to all the faithful; and at these times, unless he was addressed, he seldom spoke to anyone.

Moreover, it was quietly, and only for the occasion—in any case, it should be distinctly said, with no mental pleasure—that he displayed the pomp of royal finery in which the queen obligingly arrayed him. And he would not have cared at all if it had been provided at far less cost. He was, however, grateful for the queen's solicitude in these matters, and with a certain kindness of feeling used to remark on her zeal most appreciatively to his intimates.

SOURCE: F. Barlow (edit.), *The Life of Edward the Confessor*, Nelson's Mediaeval Texts, 1962; quoted by Christopher Brooke in *The Saxon and Norman Kings*, Batsford, 1963.

EDWARD I (1239–1307), king of England, nicknamed 'Longshanks'.

He was of fine figure and tall stature, head and shoulders above the ordinary people; his hair in boyhood verging from a colour almost silver to flaxen, in manhood changing to black, and turning to a swanlike whiteness which gave charm to his old age; the forehead broad and the rest of his face regular, except that the drooping lid of the left eye showed a resemblance to his father; a stammer which did not detract from a persuasive eloquence in long speeches. None were more suited, by reason of their sinewy vigour, than his supple arms, proportionate in length to the rest of his body, to the wielding of the sword. His chest stuck out beyond his belly, and his great length of leg gave him a sure seat on noble horses, running or jumping.

SOURCE: Nicholas Trivet or Trevet, *Annales Sex Regum Anglie*. Edward's tomb was opened in 1774 by the Society of Antiquaries and he was found to measure 6 feet 2 inches in height, a stature much above the average for his time. His nickname of 'Longshanks' is therefore readily understandable.

EDWARD III (1312–1377), king of England.
(Before the Battle of Crecy)

The king then mounted a small palfrey, having a white wand in his hand, and attended by his two marshals on each side of him: he rode [at] a foot's pace through all the ranks, encouraging and intreating the army, that they would guard his honour and defend his right. He spoke so sweetly, and with such a cheerful countenance, that all who had been dispirited were directly comforted by seeing and hearing him.

When he had thus visited all the battalions, it was near ten o'clock: he retired to his own division, and ordered them all to eat heartily, and drink a glass after. They ate and drank at their ease; and having packed up pots, barrels, etc. in the carts, they returned to their battalions, according to the marshals' orders, and seated themselves on the ground, placing their helmets and bows before them, that they might be the fresher when their enemies should arrive.

SOURCE: Sir John Froissart, *Chronicles*, Thomas Johnes's translation, 1806.

EDWARD IV (1442–1483), king of England.

The handsomest prince my eyes ever beheld.

SOURCE: Philip de Commines, *The Memoirs of Philip de Commines, Lord of Argenton*, edit. Scoble, 1856.

He was a goodly personage and very princely to behold, of

heart courageous . . . He was of visage lovely, of body mighty, strong and clean-made; howbeit, in his latter days, with over-liberal diet, somewhat corpulent and burly, and, nevertheless, not uncomely.

SOURCE: *The History of King Richard the Thirde writen by Master Thomas More.*

This Edward was a goodly man of personage, of stature high, of countenance and beauty comely, of sight quick, broad breasted, and well set, in every other part conformable to his body; of a pregnant wit, of stomach stout, and high of courage.

SOURCE: John Hardyng, *Chronicle* (Continuation).

ELIOT, GEORGE (pseudonym of **CROSS, MARY ANN**) (1819–1880), novelist.

Nature had disguised George Eliot's apparently stoical, yet really vehement and sensitive spirit, and her soaring genius, in a homely and insignificant form. Her countenance was equine—she was rather like a horse; and her head had been intended for a much longer body—she was not a tall woman. She wore her hair in not pleasing, out-of-fashion loops, coming down on either side of her face, so hiding her ears; and her garments concealed her outline—they gave her a waist like a milestone . . .

She had a measured way of conversing; restrained, but impressive. When I happened to call she was nearly always seated in the chimney corner on a low chair, and she bent forward when she spoke. As she often discussed abstract subjects, she might have been thought pedantic, especially as her language was sprinkled with scientific terminology; but I do not think she was a bit of a pedant. Then, though she had a very gentle voice and manner, there was, every now and again, just a suspicion of meek satire in her talk . . . I have been told that she was most agreeable *en tête-a-tête*; that when surrounded by admirers she was apt to become oratorical—a different woman. She did not strike me as witty or markedly humorous; she was too much in earnest; she spoke as if with a sense of responsibility, and one cannot be exactly captivating when one is doing that.

SOURCE: Frederick Locker-Lampson, *My Confidences*, 1896.

She had a large head and most striking and somewhat Dante-esque features. She was distinctly plain, but her voice was soft and melodious and always exercised a spell on me.

SOURCE: Frederick Lehmann; quoted by John Lehmann in *Ancestors and Friends*, Eyre and Spottiswoode, 1962.

ELIZABETH I (1533–1603), queen of England.

She was a lady upon whom nature had bestowed and well placed many of her fairest favours: of stature mean*, slender, straight and aimiably composed; of such state in her carriage as every motion of her seemed to bear majesty. Her hair was inclined to pale yellow, her forehead large and fair, a seeming seat for princely grace; her eyes lively and sweet, but short-sighted; her nose somewhat rising in the midst; the whole compass of her countenance somewhat long, but yet of admirable beauty; not so much in that which is termed the flower of youth, as in a most delightful composition of majesty and modesty in equal mixture.

SOURCE: Sir John Hayward, *The Beginning of the Reigne of Queen Elizabeth;* printed in *Annals of Queen Elizabeth*, by Sir John Hayward, Kt., edit. John Bruce (Camden Society, 1840).

. . . when she smiled it was pure sunshine, that everyone did choose to bask in, if they could: but anon came a storm from a sudden gathering of clouds, and the thunder fell in wondrous manner on all alike.

SOURCE: Sir John Harington, *Nugae Antiquae*.

As for her face, it is and appears to be, very aged, and her teeth are very yellow and unequal compared with what they were formerly, and on the left side less than the right. Many

* i.e., of average height.

of them are missing, so that one cannot understand her when she speaks quickly. Her figure is fair and tall and graceful in whatever she does; so far as may be she keeps her dignity, yet humbly and graciously withal.

AGED 64.

SOURCE: André Horault, Sieur de Maisse, Ambassador Extraordinary from Henry IV of France. *Journal of Sieur de Maisse*, trans. by Harrison and Jones, Nonesuch Press, 1931.

Next came the Queen, in the 65th year of her age (as we were told), very majestic; her face oblong, fair but wrinkled; her eyes small, yet black and pleasant; her nose a little hooked, her lips narrow, and her teeth black (a defect the English seem subject to, from their too great use of sugar); she had in her ears two pearls with very rich drops; her hair was of an auburn colour, but false; ... her hands were slender, her fingers rather long, and her stature neither tall nor low; her air was stately, her manner of speaking mild and obliging.

SOURCE: Paul Hentzer, *A Journey into England in the year MDXCVIII.*

She was most lavishly attired in a gown of pure white satin, gold-embroidered, with a whole bird of Paradise for panache, set forward on her head studded with costly jewels; she wore a string of huge pearls about her neck and elegant gloves over which were drawn costly rings. In short, she was most gorgeously apparelled, and although she was already seventy-four, she was very youthful still in appearance, seeming no more than twenty years of age. She had a dignified and regal bearing.

AGED 66.

SOURCE: Thomas Platter; quoted in Ian Dunlop's *Palaces and Progresses of Elizabeth I*, Jonathan Cape, 1962. Platter, a visitor from Germany, must have made the mistake of asking another lady the Queen's age, since he was eight years out.

ESGROVE, LORD (1724?–1804). See Rae, Sir David.

ESSEX, EARL OF (1566–1601). See Devereux, Robert, second Earl.

EVANS, WILLIAM (fl. 1630), porter to King Charles I; noted for his great stature.

William Evans was born in this county [Monmouthshire] and may justly be accounted the giant of our age for his stature, being full two yards and a half in height. He was porter to King Charles the First, succeeding Walter Perrons in his place and exceeding him two inches in height, but far beneath him in equal proportion of body; for he was not only what the Latins call *compernis*, knocking his knees together, and going out squalling with his feet, but also halted a little; yet he made a shift to dance in an antimasque at Court, where he drew Jeffery the dwarf out of his pocket, first to the wonder, then to the laughter of the beholders.

SOURCE: Thomas Fuller, *The English Worthies*.
Note: See Hudson, Jeffery, for an account of 'Jeffrey the dwarf'.

FALCONER, WILLIAM (1732–1769), poet.

In person, Falconer was about five feet seven inches in height, of a thin, light make, with hard features, and a weather-beaten complexion. His hair was brown, and he was marked with the smallpox. In his common address, it is said, he was blunt and forbidding: but quick and fluent in conversation. His observation was keen, and his judgments acute and severe. By natural temper he was cheerful, and used to amuse his companions, the seamen, with acrostics, which he made on their favourite nymphs. He was a good and skilful seaman.

SOURCE: John Mitford, *Life of Falconer*, prefaced to Aldine edition of Falconer's Poetical Works.

FANSHAWE, SIR RICHARD (1608–1666), writer and diplomatist.

He was of the highest size of men, strong, and of the best proportion, his complexion sanguine, his skin exceeding fair, his hair dark brown and very curling, but not very long, his eyes grey and penetrating, his nose high, his countenance gracious and wise, his motion good, his speech clear and distinct. He never used exercise but walking, and that generally with some book in his hand, which often-time was poetry, in which he spent his idle hours. Sometimes he would ride out to take the air; but his most delight was to go only with me in a coach some miles, and there discourse of those things which then most pleased him of what nature soever. He was very obliging to all, and forward to serve his master, his country and friends, cheerful in conversation, his discourse ever pleasant, mixed with the sayings of wise men and their histories, repeated as occasion offered; yet so reserved that he never shewed the thought of his heart in its greatest sense but to myself only.

SOURCE: *Memoirs of Lady Fanshawe*, printed 1829–1830.

FAWKES, GUY (1570–1606), Gunpowder Plot conspirator.

. . . a man of great piety, of exemplary temperance, of mild and cheerful demeanour, an enemy of broils and disputes, a faithful friend, and remarkable for his punctual attendance upon religious observances.

SOURCE: Father Oswald Greenway; quoted in David Jardine's *Criminal Trials*, 1832.

Last of all [at the execution] came the great devil of all, Fawkes, *alias* Johnson, who should have put fire to the powder. His body being weak with torture and sickness, he was scarce able to go up the ladder, but yet, with much ado, by the help of the hangman, went high enough to break his neck with the fall; who made no long speech, but, after a sort, seeming to be sorry for his offence, asked a kind of forgiveness of the King and the state for his bloody intent; and with his crosses and idle ceremonies, made his end upon the gallows and the block . . .

SOURCE: *Harleian Miscellany;* quoted in David Jardine's *Criminal Trials*, 1832.

FISHER, JOHN (1459–1535), bishop of Rochester; beheaded for refusing to acknowledge Henry VIII as supreme head of the Church.

In stature of body he was tall and comely, exceeding the common and middle sort of men; for he was to the quantity of 6 foot in height, and being therewith very slender and lean, was nevertheless upright and well framed, straight backed, big jointed and strongly sinewed. His hair by nature black, though in his later time, through age and imprisonment, turned to hoarness or rather whiteness, his eyes long and round, neither full black nor full grey, but of a mixed colour between both; his forehead smooth and large, his nose of a good and even proportion, somewhat wide mouthed and big jawed, as one ordained to utter speech much, wherein was notwithstanding a certain comeliness; his skin somewhat tawny mixed with many blue veins; his face, hands, and all his body so bare of flesh as is almost incredible, which came the rather (as may be thought) by the great abstinence and penance he used upon himself many years together, even from his youth. In his countenance he bore such a reverent gravity, and therewith in his doings exercised such discreet severity, that not only of his equals, but even of his superiors he was both honoured and feared . . . And generally in all things belonging to the care and charge of a true bishop, he was to all the bishops of England living in his days the very mirror and lantern of light.

SOURCE: *A Treatise contayninge the lyfe and manner of death of that most holy prelat and constant martyr of Christ, John Fisher, Bishop of Rochester* . . . Harleian MS. 6382, printed by the Early English Text Society, 1921.

Furthermore, I beseech you to be good master unto me in my necessity; for I have neither shirt, nor suit, nor yet other clothes that are necessary for me to wear, but that be ragged and rent shamefully. Notwithstanding, I might easily suffer that if they would keep my body warm. But my diet also, God knoweth how slender it is at many times; and in mine age my stomach may not away but with a few kinds of meats, which if I want,

I decay forthwith, and fall into coughs and diseases of my body, and cannot keep myself in health.

SOURCE: Bishop Fisher, in a letter to Thomas Cromwell during his imprisonment in the Tower.

FLAXMAN, JOHN (1755–1826), sculptor and draughtsman.

Here he touched my knee familiarly, and leaned forward, and his old, deformed, humped shoulder protruded as he leant, and his sparkling old eye and his apish old mouth grinned on one side, and he rattled out of his throat, husky with coughing, a jarry, inward, hesitating hemming sound . . .

AGED 71.

SOURCE: Benjamin Haydon's *Autobiography*.

FORBES, EDWARD (1815–1854), naturalist; professor of botany at King's College, London, president of the Geological Society and professor of natural history at Edinburgh.

About seventeen years ago, there was a very remarkable cluster of youths attending the University of Edinburgh, and well known on its streets and public walks. Three of them were especially prominent, and were often seen together. One was a tall, fair-complexioned young man, with a somewhat stooping gait, long yellow hair hanging over his shoulders, in the style of ancient pictures, and dull and downcast, but thoughtful eyes. Arm-in-arm with him there often walked a thinner youth, with hair as dark as the raven's wing, floating down in masses, and forming a piquant contrast to the bright locks of his companion, a pale, long face, nose slightly hooked, high, well-arched forehead, and searching, rather than brilliant eyes. The opinions were divided about this singular pair. Many set them down as intolerable and empty coxcombs. Others stamped them as irredeemable and impudent young scamps . . . Often, but not habitually, there appeared in their company another, less ostentatiously singular in his appearance, about the middle size in height; his hair not quite so Absolomic in its longitude, his aspect simply that of an ordinary clever student, save for a certain rapt expression which glimmered in his grey eye, and over his thin pale visage; his gait elastic, and his air joyous. Such was the trinity of Edinburgh scientific genius in the years 1838-9-40. The name of the first was Cunningham, who promised to become one of the first geologists of the day, but who died early, without having done anything to justify the estimation of his friends. The second was Edward Forbes . . . ; and the third was Samuel Brown . . . Let us treasure up a few reminiscences of the only time we met the first of these . . .

He was about twenty-five years of age . . . His manner was easy and agreeable, but wanted that buoyant frankness, and beaming cordiality which, in his happier moods, distinguished Brown above all men we ever knew. In select social society, however, and when perfectly at home, Forbes, we have heard, became a most genial and even joyous being. Sitting with a chairman of considerable bulk between us, we could not pursue any consecutive stream of talk, or do more than telegraph across the human continent, a few scattered observations . . .

SOURCE: George Gilfillan, *Scottish Review*, October 1857. Samuel Brown, the third member of the trio described above, became a distinguished chemist and wrote on the atomic theory.

FOX, CHARLES JAMES (1749–1806), statesman.

. . . a prodigious dandy, wearing a little odd French hat, shoes with red heels, etc.

AGED ABOUT 20.

SOURCE: Alexander Dyce, *Recollections of the Table-talk of Samuel Rogers*, 1856.

It was impossible to contemplate the lineaments of his countenance, without instantly perceiving the indelible marks of genius. His features, in themselves dark, harsh, and saturnine, like those of Charles the Second, from whom he descended in the maternal line, derived nevertheless a sort of majesty, from the addition of two black and shaggy eye-brows, which sometimes concealed, but oftener developed, the workings of his mind. Even these features, however seemingly repulsive, yet did not readily assume the expression of anger, or of enmity; whereas they frequently, and as it were naturally, relaxed into a smile, the effect of which became irresistible, because it appeared to be the index of a benevolent and complacent disposition. His figure, broad, heavy and inclined to corpulency, appeared destitute of all elegance and grace, except what was conferred on it by the emanations of intellect, which at all times diffused over his whole person when speaking, the most impassioned animation. In his dress, which had constituted an object of his attention earlier in life, he had then become negligent, even to a degree not altogether excusable in a man whose very errors or defects produced admirers and imitators. He constantly, or at least usually, wore in the House of Commons a blue frock coat and a buff waistcoat, neither of which seemed in general new, and sometimes appeared to be threadbare . . .

In this dress he always took his seat, not upon the front Opposition bench, but on the third row behind, close to that pillar supporting the gallery, which is nearest to the Speaker's chair. It was not till 1783, or rather till the beginning of 1783, that, with Lord North by his side, he first began to sit on the Opposition bench.

AGED 32.

SOURCE: Sir N. William Wraxall, *Historical Memoirs of My Own Time*, 1815.

This same celebrated Charles Fox is a short, fat and gross man, with a swarthy complexion and dark; and in general he is badly dressed. There is certainly something Jewish in his looks. But upon the whole, he is not an ill made or an ill looking man: and there are many marks of sagacity and fire in his eyes.

AGED 33.

SOURCE: *Travels of Carl Philipp Moritz in 1782*, Clarendon Press.

. . . I saw Mr. Fox, fat and jovial, though he was then declining.

He, who had been a 'beau' in his youth, then looked something quaker-like as to dress, with plain coloured clothes, a broad round hat, white waistcoat, and, if I am not mistaken, white stockings. He was standing in Parliament Street, just where the street commences as you leave Whitehall; and was making two young gentlemen laugh heartily at something which he seemed to be relating.

SOURCE: Leigh Hunt, *Autobiography*.

FRANKLIN, SIR JOHN (1786–1847), arctic explorer; lost on the search for the North-West passage.

... an old man, with broad shoulders, thick and heavier-set than Captain Hall, with grey hair, full face and bald head. He wore spectacles, was quite lame, and appeared sick when they last saw him ... But despite his ill health he was always laughing ...

SOURCE: A description given by two Esquimaux who had camped alongside Franklin's ships; given to Captain Charles F. Hall, an American who spent several years with the Esquimaux, mainly in the Repulse Bay region, searching for news of the expedition; from *Narrative of the Second Arctic Expedition made by C. F. Hall*, 1829.

FREDERICK AUGUSTUS, DUKE OF YORK (1763–1827), second son of George III and guardian of the king's person during his illness; commander-in-chief of English army.

He was simply dressed in a plain riding costume, and was, without exception, one of the finest men England could boast of. He stood above six feet; was rather stout, but well proportioned; his chest broad, and his frame muscular; his face bore the stamp of authority, and every feature was handsome; his brow was full and prominent, the eye grayish, beaming with benevolence; and a noble forehead, with premature gray hairs ...

SOURCE: Captain R. H. Gronow's *Reminiscences*.

Saw the Duke of York. The change in H.R.H. is most wonderful. From a big, burly, stout man, with a thick and sometimes an inarticulate mode of speaking, he has sunk into a thin-faced, slender-looking old man, who seems diminished in his very size ... He speaks much more distinctly than formerly; his complexion is clearer.

AGED 63.

SOURCE: Sir Walter Scott's *Journal*.

FROWD, DOCTOR JOHN (fl. 1816), naval chaplain and Fellow of Corpus Christi; present in the *Queen Charlotte* at the bombardment of Algiers, 1816.

He was a very little man, an irrepressible, unwearied chatterbox, with a droll interrogative face, a bald shining head, and a fleshy under-lip which he could push nearly up to his nose ...

As the action [at Algiers] thickened, he was seized with a comical religious frenzy, dashing round the decks and diffusing spiritual exhortation amongst the half-stripped busy sailors, till the First Lieutenant ordered a hen-coop to be clapped over him, whence his little head, emerging, continued its devout cackle, quite regardless of the balls which flew past him.

SOURCE: Rev. W. Tuckwell, *Reminiscences of Oxford*, 1901; quoted by Michael Lewis in *A Social History of the Navy*, George Allen and Unwin, 1960.

FULLER, THOMAS (1608–1661), divine and author.

... of stature somewhat tall, exceeding the mean, with a proportional bigness to become it, but no way inclining to corpulency; of an exact straightness of the whole body, and an exact symmetry in every part thereof. He was of a sanguine constitution, which beautified his face with a pleasant ruddiness, but of so grave and serious an aspect that it awed and discountenanced ... that complexion. His head adorned with a comely light-coloured hair, which was so by nature exactly curled (an ornament enough of itself in this age to denominate a handsome person and wherefore all skill and art is used) but not suffered to overgrow to any length unseeming his modesty and profession.

His gait and walking was very upright and graceful, becoming his well-shaped bulk: approaching near to that we term majestical; but that the doctor was so well known to be void of any affectation or pride. Nay, so regardless was he of himself in his garb and raiment, in which no doubt his vanity would have appeared, as well as in his stately pace, that it was with some trouble to himself to be either neat or decent; it mattered not for the outside ...

That which was most strange, and very rare in him, was his way of writing, which something like the Chinese, was from the top of the page to the bottom, the manner thus:—he would write near the margin the first words of every line down to the foot of the paper, then would be beginning at the head again, fill up every one of these lines, which without any interlineations or spaces, but with full and equal length, would so adjust the sense and matter, and aptly connect and conjoin the ends and beginnings of the said lines, that he could not do it better, as he hath said, if he had writ all out in a continuation.

SOURCE: *The Life of that Reverend Divine and Learned Historian Dr. Thomas Fuller*, 1661.

FUSELI, HENRY (Johann Heinrich Fuessli) (1741–1825), painter and author, keeper of the Royal Academy.

I expected the floor to give way—I fancied Fuseli himself to be a giant. I heard his footsteps and saw a little bony hand slide round the edge of the door, followed by a little white-headed lion-faced man in an old flannel dressing-gown, tied round his waist with a piece of rope, and upon his head the bottom of Mrs. Fuseli's work-basket.

AGED 64.

In his temper he was irritable and violent, but appeased in an instant. In his person small, with a face of independent,

H

unregulated fire. I have heard he was handsome when young, and with women (when gratified by their attentions) no man could be more gentle.

SOURCE: Benjamin Haydon's *Autobiography*.

GALTON, SIR FRANCIS (1822–1911), scientist; founder of the science of eugenics; invented the method of crime detection by finger-prints.

Even today I can conjure up, from memory's misty deep, that tall figure with its attitude of perfect physical and mental poise; the clean-shaven face, the thin compressed mouth with its enigmatical smile; the long upper lip and firm chin; and, as if presiding over the whole personality of the man, the prominent dark eyebrows from beneath which gleamed, with penetrating humour, contemplative grey eyes.

SOURCE: Mrs. Sidney Webb; quoted in Hesketh Pearson's *Extraordinary People*, Heinemann, 1965.

Although, when I knew him, the eyebrows were white and his body was bent, I doubt if he could ever have been more than five feet eight inches high; so I assume his statistical mind made him appear tall to Mrs. Webb. That he was of medium height is proved by the fact that whenever as a young man he went to see a public procession or similar show he carried a wooden brick under his arm, done up as a brown paper parcel. If the people in front of him obstructed his vision, he would quietly lower the brick, which was attached to a piece of cord, stand on it, view the proceedings, draw it up again, and resume his normal stature.

SOURCE: Hesketh Pearson, *Extraordinary People*, Heinemann, 1965.

GARNETT, HENRY (1555–1606), Jesuit; executed for alleged complicity in Gunpowder Plot.

... of middling stature, full-faced, fat of body, of complexion fair, his forehead high on each side, with a little thin hair coming down upon the middest of the forepart of his head: the hair of his head and beard grizzled. Of age between fifty and three score. His beard on his cheeks cut close, and his gait upright and comely for a feeble man.

SOURCE: Proclamation for his arrest, 1606; quoted by Philip Caraman in *Henry Garnet and the Gunpowder Plot*, Longmans, 1964.

GARNETT, RICHARD (1835–1906), scholar and Keeper of Printed Books at the British Museum.

Mr. Garnett, as all who know him must admit, is one of the most amiable and benign of men; he is also very tall. One day I saw him stretching himself to the utmost to reach one of the top shelves of the Reading Room Reference Library, so I said, 'Why, Mr. Garnett, you are the very embodiment of Milton's line *of linked sweetness long drawn out*.' He was much pleased.

(Samuel Butler).

... the smiling, learned, tall, stooping, myopic figure that seemed to come up out of the very dim depths of thought to lend a patient, and in no degree condescending, attention to my vicarious question ...

(Ford Madox Ford).

SOURCE: quoted in Carolyn G. Heilbrun's *The Garnett Family*, George Allen and Unwin, 1961.

GEORGE I (1660–1727), king of Great Britain.

The person of the King is as perfect in my memory as if I saw him but yesterday. It was that of an elderly man, rather pale, and exactly like his pictures and coins; not tall; of an aspect rather good than august; with a dark tie-wig, a plain coat, waistcoat, and breeches of snuff-coloured cloth, with stockings of the same colour, and a blue riband over all.

SOURCE: Horace Walpole, *Reminiscences written in 1788*.

GEORGE II (1683–1760), king of Great Britain and Ireland.

He had no better parts than his father, but much stronger animal spirits, which made him produce and communicate himself more. Everything in his composition was little; and he had all the weaknesses of a little mind, without any of the virtues, or even the vices, of a great one. He loved to act the king, but mistook the part; and the royal dignity shrunk into the electoral pride . . . In his dress and in his conversation he affected the hero . . . He was very well-bred; but it was in a stiff and formal manner, and produced in others that restraint which they saw he was under himself. He bestowed his favours so coldly and ungraciously, that they excited no warm returns in those who received them.

SOURCE: Lord Chesterfield, *Miscellaneous Works*, 1777.

Note: George II's favourite artist was the German, Frederick Zincke, who drew many pictures of the Royal family. As evidence of the reliability of royal portraits, it is worth noting that the Queen advised Zincke to make the King's portrait look young—not above twenty-five. The King was pleased with his work and instructed him not to make the Queen look more than twenty-eight. They were both about forty-five at the time.

GEORGE III (1738–1820), king of Great Britain and Ireland.

I once saw George III walking with his favourite son, the Duke of York, with whom he talked incessantly, repeating his 'Yes, yes, yes, Frederick,' in his usual loud voice. His beard was of unusual length, and he stooped very much. He wore the Windsor uniform, with a large cocked hat, something like that with which Frederick the Great is usually represented. The doctors walked behind the King, which seemed greatly to annoy him, as he was constantly looking round. It was said, and I believe with truth, that the poor King could not hear Dr. Willis's name spoken without shuddering.

AGED 81.

SOURCE: Captain R. H. Gronow's *Reminiscences*.

In the King's countenance, a physiognomist would have distinguished two principal characteristics: firmness, or as his enemies denominated it, obstinacy; tempered with benignity. The former expression was, however, indisputably more marked and prominent than the latter sentiment. He seemed to have a tendency to become corpulent, if he had not repressed it by systematic and unremitting temperance.

SOURCE: Sir N. William Wraxall, *Historical Memoirs of My Own Life,* 1815.

GEORGE IV (1762–1830), king of Great Britain.

Anybody who could have seen his disgusting figure, with a wig, the curls of which hung down his back, and quite bending beneath the weight of his robes and his sixty years, would have been quite sick . . .

SOURCE: Harriet Arbuthnot; Duke of Wellington (edit.) *The Journal of Mrs. Arbuthnot, 1820–1832,* Macmillan, 1950.

He made himself a strange figure by drawing in his great body with a broad belt, and by the close buttoning of a kind of uniform jacket . . . hiding the lower part of his face with a long black neckcloth, and then swelling out his shoulders and the upper part of his person with tags and embroidery and covering it with orders.

SOURCE: Mr. Wollaston; quoted by Mary Hopkins in *Queen Adelaide,* John Murray, 1946.

George IV always carried a snuff-box; but it appeared to me as if his Majesty took snuff for fashion's sake. He would take the box in his left hand, and, opening it with his right thumb and forefinger, introduce them into this costly reservoir of snuff, and with a consequential air convey the same to the nose; but never suffered any to enter: indeed, those who were well acquainted with his Majesty frequently told me that he took snuff for effect, but never liked it, and allowed all of it to escape from his finger and thumb before it reached the nose.

SOURCE: Captain R. H. Gronow's *Reminiscences.*

GEORGE WILLIAM FREDERICK CHARLES, second Duke of Cambridge (1819–1904), field marshal, and commander-in-chief of the British army.

The frank and joyous eye of the Duke was much admired, but not much else of the Duke's face was visible; he was bearded 'like the pard'—lip, cheek and chin alike being innocent of the razor. In a camp shaving is pursued under considerable disadvantages; and the Duke is no doubt right; but our young men at home, who can ring for their shaving water as usual on getting up in the morning, are beginning to make his royal highness the 'glass of fashion and the mould of form', and are cultivating a beard in addition to a luxuriant moustache and whisker. Let Sheffield look to it, therefore, and pray for an early termination of the war.

AGED 36.

SOURCE: *The Manchester Guardian,* reporting on a meeting in honour of Florence Nightingale; quoted in David Piper's *The English Face,* Thames and Hudson, 1957.

GERARD, JOHN (1564–1637), Jesuit.

John Gerrard, the Jesuit, is about 30 years old. Of good stature, somewhat staring in his look or eyes, curled hair by nature and blackish and apt not to have much hair of his beard. I think his nose somewhat wide and turning up, blubbered lips turning outward, expecially the over-lip most upwards towards the nose; curious in speech . . . and smiles much and a faltering or lisping, or doubling of his tongue in his speech.

SOURCE: Richard Topcliffe (c. 1598).

. . . of stature tall, high shouldered, especially when his cope is on his back, blackhaired, and of complexion swarth, hawk-nosed, high templed, and for the most part attired costly and defencibly in buff leather garnished with gold or silver lace, satin doublet, and velvet hose of all colours . . . and rapiers and daggers gilt or silvered.

SOURCE: Report of William Byrd to Cecil, 1601, preserved in the Hatfield House papers; quoted by Philip Caraman in *John Gerard, the Autobiography of an Elizabethan*, Longmans Green, 1951.

Of stature tall, and according thereunto well set; his complexion swart or blackish; his face large; his cheeks sticking out, and somewhat hollow underneath the cheeks; the hair of his head long, if it be not cut off, his beard close, saving little mustachoes, and a little tuft under his lower lip; about forty years old.

SOURCE: A description circulated at the time of the Gunpowder Plot (1605). *P.R.O. Proclamation Book;* quoted in Philip Caraman's *John Gerard, the Autobiography of an Elizabethan*, Longmans Green, 1951.

GERMAIN, GEORGE SACKVILLE, first Viscount Sackville (1716–1785), soldier and statesman.

He had a frame of body naturally robust, and a vigorous constitution secured him almost uninterrupted health. In his person, which rose to near six feet, he was muscular and capable of enduring much bodily as well as mental fatigue. Though his features were strongly pronounced and saturnine, yet considered together as a whole their effect by no means displeased. An air of high birth and dignity, illuminated by strong sense, pervaded every lineament of his face.

SOURCE: Sir N. William Wraxall, *Historical Memoirs of My Own Life*, 1815.

GLADSTONE, CATHERINE (1812–1900), wife of William Ewart Gladstone.

She was tall and splendidly shaped, with a bearing which was queen-like in its stateliness and girl-like in its ease and elasticity ... Her beauty was on the grand scale—a noble brow, shaded by magnificent dark and wavy hair, eyes full of light and expression, and a wide though well-formed mouth. She was, not only by blood and training, but by temperament and instinct, emphatically a great lady (I eschew the French equivalent, and 'aristocratic' sounds pompous). Her walk and curtsey as she passed the Royal presence at the Drawing Room was long the admiration of those whose official duty obliged them to stand by the Throne or in the 'general circle'. All her habits, manners, and ways of speech belonged to that old school, which in these matters was certainly the best school. The effectiveness of her appearance owed nothing to art or study. She was by nature careless and untidy; and it was only the unremitting attentions of zealous maids that made her even presentable.

SOURCE: G. W. E. Russell, *Portraits of the Seventies*, 1916.

GLADSTONE, WILLIAM EWART (1809–1898), statesman.

His manner in speech making was more strongly marked by action than was that of his only rival, John Bright. He emphasised points by smiting the open palm of his left hand with sledge-hammer fist. Sometimes he, with gleaming eyes—'like a vulture's' Mr. Lecky genially described them—pointed his forefinger straight at his adversary. In the hottest moments he beat the brass-bound Box with clamorous hand that occasionally drowned the point he had to make. Sometimes with both hands raised above his head; often with left elbow leaning on the Box, right hand with closed fist shaken at the head of an unoffending country gentleman on the back bench opposite; anon, standing half a step back from the Table, left hand hanging at his side, right uplifted, so that he might with thumb-nail lightly touch the shining crown of his head, he trampled his way through the argument . . .

SOURCE: Henry Lucy, *Sixty Years in the Wilderness*, John Murray, 1909.

I sat near to the organ in the west gallery, and immediately in front of me sat Mr. Gladstone. A strong Tory supporter of Church and State in those days, he had been more than an occasional worshipper in the little Chapel, for he belonged to the old High Church party, which was far from being a Romanizing body. Always a keen observer, and knowing it was a great man who sat there, I critically examined him. At that time he had black hair and a good deal of it; but it was not that which struck me, but the great thickness of his neck, and the position of his ears, which was very low. The skull was not really wide at the base, the ears were almost on a level with the mouth. The neck and skull, as seen from the back, appeared to be almost in one line, broken only by prominent, but not too prominent, ears.

SOURCE: William Richmond, in *The Richmond Papers*, Heinemann, 1926.

Mr. Gladstone was a great walker. However bad the weather, it never stopped him from his daily exercise. I never saw him use an umbrella at Hawarden. A very old slouch hat, with brim turned down, drained off the rain on to a thick Scotch tweed cloak, which fell to his knees, an old pair of trousers, sometimes frayed at the bottom, a thick pair of boots on his abnormally large and flat feet, a stout walking-stick of rude make, completed his outdoor equipment, and off he started at four miles an hour, never relaxing his speed, never loitering, always talking with immense vivacity and spirit . . .

Mr. Gladstone was then fifty-eight, his hair was still black, his skin was dark, almost southern in its darkness, that pallor which spread over his complexion in later years had not begun. He looked full of health, was abnormally strong and very thin; his bones were enormous.

AGED 58.

SOURCE: William Richmond, in *The Richmond Papers*, Heinemann, 1926.

That white-hot face, stern as a Covenanter's yet mobile as a comedian's; those restless, flashing eyes; that wondrous voice whose richness its northern burr enriched as the tang of the wood brings out the mellowness of a rare old wine; the masterly cadence of his elocution; the vivid energy of his attitudes; the fine animation of gestures—sir, when I am assailed through

eye and ear by a compacted phalanx of assailants, what wonder
the stormed outposts of the senses should spread the contagion
of their own surrender through the main encampment of the
mind . . .

SOURCE: Henry Duff Traill, *The New Lucian*, 1884.

GLOUCESTER, DUKE OF (1776–1834). See William Frederick,
second Duke of Gloucester.

GODOLPHIN, SYDNEY, first Earl of Godolphin (1645–1712),
statesman; lord high treasurer under Queen Anne.

As to his person, the Lord Godolphin was of a middle stature,
well set, and of a strong constitution; his face of a brown
complexion, somewhat disfigured with the small-pox, but
enlivened with a quick, piercing eye; and the usual severity of
his countenance was now and then sweetened with a smile.

SOURCE: Abel Boyer, *History of the Life and Reign of Queen Anne.*

GODRIC (1065?–1170), merchant, hermit and pilgrim.

For he was vigorous and strenuous in mind, whole of limb and
strong in body. He was of middle stature, broad-shouldered
and deep-chested, with a long face, grey eyes most clear and
piercing, bushy brows, a broad forehead, long and open
nostrils, a nose of comely curve, and a pointed chin. His beard
was thick, and longer than the ordinary, his mouth well
shaped, with lips of moderate thickness; in youth his hair was
black, in age as white as snow; his neck was short and thick,
knotted with veins and sinews; his legs were somewhat
slender, his instep high, his knees hardened and horny with
frequent kneeling; his whole skin rough beyond the ordinary,
until all this roughness was softened by old age . . . In labour
he was strenuous and assiduous above all men; and, when by
chance his bodily strength proved insufficient, he compassed

his ends with great ease by the skill which his daily labours had given and by a prudence born of long experience.

SOURCE: *Life of St. Godfric*, Surtees Society, 1847; quoted in G. C. Coulton, *Medieval Panorama*, C.U.P., 1938. Godfric was a Norfolk boy who began life as a chapman and pedlar, travelling widely in this country and abroad, and eventually becoming a substantial merchant and shipowner. He visited many shrines and then, after sixteen years as a merchant, turned his mind to solitude and the religious life. For sixty years he lived as a hermit at Finchdale on the Wear, where he was often visited by one of the Durham monks who tells us that he wrote down the hermit's saying and reminiscences on the very day that he heard them.

GOLDSMITH, OLIVER (1728–1774), author.

His person was short, his countenance coarse and vulgar, his deportment that of a scholar awkwardly affecting the easy gentleman.

SOURCE: James Boswell, *The Life of Samuel Johnson*.

I hear that Goldsmith, who is a very great sloven, justified his disregard of cleanliness and decency by quoting my practice; and I am desirous this night to show him a better example.

AGED 31.

SOURCE: Doctor Johnson, when asked why he was taking unusual trouble with his dressing; James Boswell, *The Life of Samuel Johnson*.

Dr. Goldsmith was in stature rather under the middle size, his body strongly built, his limbs more sturdy than elegant, his complexion pale, his forehead low, his face almost round and pitted with the small-pox; but marked with the strong lines of thinking. His first appearance was not captivating; but, when he grew easy and cheerful in company, he relaxed into such a display of good humour, as speedily removed every unfavourable impression.

SOURCE: Rev. Francis Wrangham, *The British Plutarch*, new edit., 1816.

The most delightful man was Goldsmith. She saw him and Garrick keep an immense party laughing till they shrieked. Garrick sat on Goldsmith's knee; a tablecloth was pinned under Garrick's chin and brought behind Goldsmith, hiding both their figures. Garrick then spoke, in his finest style, Hamlet's speech to his father's ghost. Goldsmith put his hands on each side of the cloth and made burlesque action, tapping his heart and putting his hand to Garrick's head and nose, all at the wrong time.

SOURCE: Benjamin Haydon, recording a conversation with Sir Joshua Reynold's niece; *Autobiography*.

Note: The London Museum contains a suit which belonged to Goldsmith. It is of plum-coloured velvet, collarless, slightly cut away in front and buttoned to the waist. There are fan-shaped pleats and deep pocket flaps. The waistcoat, of similar material, reaches half-way down the thighs and has a V-opening. Boswell, for October 16th, 1769, describes a dinner party at his lodgings when Goldsmith 'strutted about, bragging of his dress', which was 'bloom-coloured'. Perhaps the Museum suit is the one. Johnson did not, apparently, share Goldsmith's enthusiasm. He said it would serve as an advertisement for John Filby, the tailor, only because it showed 'how well he could make a coat even of so absurd a colour'.

GOSCHEN, GEORGE JOACHIM, first Viscount Goschen (1831–1907), statesman.

He obtained a high reputation as a debater and speaker, yet he had great physical difficulties to overcome: his voice was raucous, his gestures ungainly, and he was so blind that not only could he not see his audience, but found difficulty in reading his notes.

SOURCE: Lord George Hamilton, *Parliamentary Reminiscences and Reflections, 1868–1885*, John Murray, 1917.

GRACE, WILLIAM GILBERT (1848–1915), cricketer; known as 'W.G.'.

Finally, it may be said of W. G. that he did more to popularise cricket than any man who ever lived; his genial personality, his Jovian form, his inexhaustible vitality and stamina and enthusiasm, all combined with his prodigious prowess to make him the focus for an empire's devotion to the game. He was imcomparably the greatest 'draw' of all the sportsmen of history; he was the nearest approach to a living embodiment of John Bull that England has seen.

SOURCE: H. S. Altham, *A History of Cricket*, George Allen and Unwin, 1962.

His fielding, when he was a tall and athletic youth, was admirable in any position, but especially to his own bowling. In later life his massive figure is recalled at point, when little escaped his large and capable hands.

Grace's style of batting was solid and efficient. The bat looked curiously light in his hands, an impression perhaps created by the ease with which he wielded it. His defence was always first-rate; he watched the ball closely, and though at his best he was more comfortable with fast than with slow bowling, he was quick on his feet for so heavy a man. Like other famous executants, he was more occupied with practice than theory, and, according to a contemporary anecdote, his contribution to a technical discussion on forward and back play was confined to an explanation that his own plan was to put the bat against the ball.

While he was master of all the usual scoring strokes, his play on the leg side was specially noted for its accuracy and power ... His burly figure and thick black beard were familiar beyond the cricket field; his fame was celebrated constantly in prose and verse; he was the hero of anecdote and legend.

SOURCE: Alfred Cochrane, *Dictionary of National Biography*, 1927.

GRAHAM, JAMES, first Marquis of Montrose (1612–1650).

He was of a middle stature, and most exquisitely proportioned limbs; his hair of a light chestnut, his complexion betwixt pale and ruddy, his eye most penetrating, though inclining to grey; his nose rather aquiline than otherwise. As he was strong of body and limbs, so was he most agile, which made him excel most others in those exercises where these two are required . . . He was pleasant and witty in conversation, with an affability in private becoming a comrade; scandalous and obscene wit durst not appear before him.

SOURCE: anonymous pamphlet, published 1661.

GRAHAM, JOHN, of Claverhouse, first Viscount Dundee (1649?– 1689), soldier and Jacobite.

Dundee had inflamed his mind from his earliest youth, by the perusal of ancient poets, historians, and orators, with the love of the great actions they praise and describe. He is reported to have inflamed it still more, by listening to the ancient songs of the highland bards . . . He was obliged continually to shift his quarters by prodigious marches, in order to avoid, or harass his enemy's army, to obtain provisions, and sometimes to take advantages . . . In some of those marches, his men wanted bread, salt, and all liquors, except water, during several weeks; yet were ashamed to complain, when they observed that their commander lived not more delicately than themselves. If any good thing was brought him to eat, he sent it to a sick soldier. If a soldier was weary, he offered to carry his arms. He kept those who were with him from sinking under their fatigues, not so much by exhortation, as by preventing them from attending to their sufferings. For this reason he walked on foot with the men; now by the side of one clan, but anon by that of another. He amused them with jokes. He flattered them with his knowledge of their genealogies. He animated them by a recital of the deeds of their ancestors, and of the verses of their bards.

SOURCE: Sir John Dalrymple, *Memoirs of Great Britain and Ireland, from the Dissolution of the last Parliament of Charles II until the Sea-battle off La Hogue,* 1771.

GRANBY, MARQUIS OF (1721–1770). See Manners, John, Marquis of Granby.

GRANVILLE, EARL (1690–1763). See Carteret, John, Earl Granville.

GRAY, THOMAS (1716–1771), poet.

His constitution was weak ... His character I am willing to adopt, as Mr. Mason has done, from a nameless writer; and am as willing as his warmest friend to believe it true. 'Perhaps he was the most learned man in Europe. He was equally acquainted with the elegant and profound parts of science ... He knew every branch of history, both natural and civil ... and was a great antiquarian. Criticism, metaphysics, morals, politics, made a principal part of his study; voyages and travels of all sorts were his favourite amusement; and he had a fine taste in paintings, prints, architecture and gardening ... There is no character without some speck, some imperfection; and I think the greatest defect in his was an affectation in delicacy, or rather effeminacy, and a visible fastidiousness, or contempt and disdain of his inferiors in science ...'

To this character Mr. Mason has added a more particular account of Gray's skill in zoology. He has remarked, that Gray's effeminacy was affected most before *those whom he did not wish to please;* and that he is unjustly charged with making knowledge his sole reason of preference, as he paid his esteem to none whom he did not likewise believe to be good.

SOURCE: Dr. Samuel Johnson, *The Lives of the Most Eminent English Poets*, 1781.

GREENWAY, OSWALD (1563–1635). See Tesimond, Oswald.

GRENVILLE, SIR RICHARD (1541?–1591), naval commander.

Richard Grenville seemed to be a man of quality, for he was served elaborately on silver and gold plate, by servants. Many musical instruments were played when he dined, and his appearance was that of an important person.

SOURCE: Enrique Lopez; Irene R. Wright (trans. and edit.), *Further English Voyages to Spanish America, 1583–1594*, Hakluyt Society, 1951. Lopez was a passenger on the *Santa Maria de San Vincente*, which was captured by Grenville and stripped of some 120,000 ducats-worth of gold, silver, pearls and general merchandise.

GRONOW, CAPTAIN REES HOWELL (1794–1865), soldier, member of Parliament and writer of reminiscences; fought at Waterloo.

Mr. Gronow, when I knew him, was small, spare and about fifty years of age; his hair was thinning, and he wore a small moustache, of which the edge was daily shaved, which did not disguise the circumstance that the Captain's latent vanity had recourse to a brown dye. He always wore a blue tight-fitting coat closely buttoned, just allowing a white line of waistcoat to be visible.

With the head of his well-known stick pressed to his lips, the Captain spent his days seated at the window ... He was very 'good form', had a great respect for everything that was proper and convenient, and a strong propensity to become eccentric. He committed the greatest follies, without in the slightest disturbing the points of his shirt collar. He had married a lady of the *corps de ballet*, and would rather have blown out his brains than gone to the opera in morning costume.

This little man, with his hair well arranged, scented, cold and phlegmatic ... was evidently intimate with everybody of note in Europe.

AGED 50.

SOURCE: H. de Villemessant, French journalist.

GROTE, GEORGE (1794–1871), historian, and **MRS. GROTE.**

What I saw of Mr. and Mrs. Grote on this and other such occasions, reminded me of the saying ascribed to Rogers—'Ah!

I like the Grotes very much; she is so gentlemanly and he is so ladylike.' The saying was unfair to Mr. Grote, however; for his extreme suavity did not prevent his manliness from being manifest. I liked him very much, but I did not care about her; and I suppose this fact was displayed in my manner, for I have no power of disguising my feelings. She was a masculine woman, alike in size, aspect, character, and behaviour; and I greatly dislike masculine women. Moreover, she had been accustomed to a great deal of incense, and I, little given to administering it in any case, was in her case deterred by the tacit claim; for when there is an assumption without adequate achievement to justify it, I always feel prompted to resent it.

SOURCE: Herbert Spencer, *An Autobiography*, Watts and Company, 1904.

HAMILTON, EMMA, Lady (1765–1815), wife of Sir William Hamilton, ambassador.

This morning she was to show her attitudes. She came, and her appearance was more striking than I can describe, or could have imagined. She was draped exactly like a Grecian statue, her chemise of white muslin was exactly in that form, her sash in the antique manner, her fine black hair flowing over her shoulders. It was a Helena, Cassandra or Andromache, no Grecian or Trojan Princess could have had a more perfect or commanding form. Her attitudes, which she performed with the help alone of two shawls, were varied—every one was perfect—everything she did was just and beautiful. She then sung and acted the mad scene in *Nina*—this was good, but I think chiefly owing to her beautiful action and attitudes . . .

In the evening she came again but we ought to have closed with the morning. She looked handsome certainly . . . but her conversation, though good-natured and unaffected, was uninteresting, and her pronunciation very vulgar.

AGED 26.

SOURCE: Lady Elizabeth Foster; quoted by Hugh Tours in *The Life and Letters of Emma Hamilton*, Victor Gollancz, 1963.

I

In conformity with her husband's taste, she was generally dressed in a white tunic, with a belt round her waist, her hair down her back or turned up by a comb, but dressed in no special way. When she consented to give a performance, she would provide herself with two or three cashmere shawls, an urn, a scent-box, a lyre, and a tambourine. With these few properties, and her classical costume, she took up her position in the middle of the room. She threw a shawl over her head which reached the ground and covered her entirely, and thus hidden, draped herself with the other shawls. Then she suddenly raised the covering, either throwing it off entirely or half raising it, and making it form part of the drapery of the model which she represented. But she always appeared as a statue of most admirable design . . .

She took her inspiration from the antique statues, and without making any servile copy of them, recalled them to the poetical imagination of the Italians by improvised gesture. Others have tried to imitate Lady Hamilton's talent, but I doubt if anyone has succeeded. It is a business in which there is but a step from the sublime to the ridiculous. Moreover, to equal her success, the actor must first be of faultless beauty from head to foot, and such perfection is rare . . .

Apart from this artistic instinct, Lady Hamilton was entirely vulgar and common. When she exchanged her classical tunic for ordinary dress she lost all distinction. Her conversation showed no interest and little intelligence.

SOURCE: The Comtesse de Boigne, *Memoirs, 1781–1814*; quoted by Hugh Tours in *The Life and Letters of Emma Hamilton*, Victor Gollancz, 1963.

Dined at Mr. Elliot's with the Nelson party. It is plain that Lord Nelson thinks of nothing but Lady Hamilton, who is totally occupied by the same object. She is bold, forward, coarse, assuming and vain. Her figure is colossal, but, excepting her feet, which are hideous, well shaped. Her bones are large, and she is exceedingly *embonpoint*. She resembles the bust of

Ariadne; the shape of all her features is fine, as is the form of her head, and particularly her ears; her teeth are a little irregular, but tolerably white; her eyes light blue, with a brown spot in one, which, though a defect, takes nothing away from her beauty or expression. Her eyebrows and hair are dark, and her complexion coarse. Her expression is strongly marked, variable, and interesting; her movements in common life ungraceful; her voice loud, yet not disagreeable.

The chief of her imitations are from the antique. Each representation lasts about ten minutes. It is remarkable that, though coarse and ungraceful in common life, she becomes highly graceful, and even beautiful, during this performance. It is also singular that, in spite of the accuracy of her imitation of the finest ancient draperies, her usual dress is tasteless, vulgar, loaded, and unbecoming. She has borrowed several of my gowns, and much admires my dress, which cannot flatter, as her own is so frightful. Her waist is absolutely between her shoulders.

AGED 35.

SOURCE: Melesina St. George; quoted by Hugh Tours in *The Life and Letters of Emma Hamilton*, Victor Gollancz, 1963.

HAMMOND, DOCTOR HENRY (1605–1660), chaplain to Charles I.

The frame of his body was such as suited with the noble use to which it was design'd, the entertaining a most pure and active soul, built equally to the advantages of strength and comeliness. His *stature* was of just height and all proportionate dimensions, avoiding the extremes of gross and meagre, advantag'd by a graceful carriage, at once most grave, and yet most obliging. His *face* carried dignity and attractiveness in it, scarce ever clouded with a frown, or so much as darkened by reservedness. His *eye* was quick and sprightful, his *complexion* clear and florid, so that (especially in his youth) he had the esteem of a very beauteous person; which was lessened only by the colour of his hair ...

To this outward structure was joined that strength of *constitution*, patient of severest toil and hardship; insomuch that for the most part of his life, in the fiercest extremity of cold he took no other advantage of a fire, than at the greatest distance that he could to look upon it. As to diseases (till immoderate study had wrought a change) he was in a manner only liable to fevers, which too constant temperance did in great measure prevent, and still assisted to relieve and cure ...

His *sight* was quick to an unusual degree; insomuch that if by chance he saw a knot of men, a flock of sheep or herd of cattle, being engaged in discourse, and not at all thinking of it, he would involuntarily cast up their number, which others after long delays could hardly reckon. His *ear* was accurate and tun'd to his harmonious soul, so that having never learn'd to sing by book or study, he would exactly perform his part of many things to a *harpsicon* or *theorbo;* and frequently did so in his more vigorous years after the toil and labour of the day, and before the remaining studies of the night. His *elocution* was free and graceful, prepared at once to charm and command his audience ...

In the time of his full and more vigorous health he seldom did eat or drink more than once in twenty-four hours, and some fruit towards night; and two days in every week, and in Lent and Ember week three days, he ate but once in thirty-six ... His temperance in sleep resembled that of his meats, midnight being the usual time of his going to rest, and four or five and very rarely six, the hour of his rising.

SOURCE: John Fell, *Life of Dr. H. Hammond*, 1661.

HAMPDEN, JOHN (1594–1643), parliamentarian; opposed ship-money levy; one of the five members whose arrest was attempted by Charles I; mortally wounded at Chalgrove Field.

He was a gentleman of a good extraction, and a fair fortune, who, from a life of great pleasure and licence, had on a sudden

retired to extraordinary sobriety and strictness, and yet
retained his usual cheerfulness and affability ... He was not a
man of many words, and rarely began the discourse, or made
the first entrance upon any business that was assumed; but a
very weighty speaker, and after he had heard a full debate, and
observed how the House was like to be inclined, took up the
argument, and shortly, and clearly, and craftily, so stated it
that he commonly conducted it to the conclusion he desired ...
He made so great a show of civility, and modesty, and humility,
and always of mistrusting his own judgment, and esteeming his
with whom he conferred for the present, that he seemed to have
no opinions or resolutions, but such as he contracted from the
information and instruction he received upon the discourses of
others; whom he had a wonderful art of governing, and leading
to his principles and inclinations, whilst they believed that he
wholly depended upon their counsel and advice. No man had
ever a greater power over himself, or was less the man than he
seemed to be; which shortly after appeared to everybody, when
he cared less to keep on the mask.

SOURCE: Edward, Earl of Clarendon, *The History of the Rebellion
and Civil Wars in England, Begun in the Year 1641.*

HARLEY, ROBERT, first Earl of Oxford (1661–1724), statesman;
  chancellor of the exchequer and leader of Tory ministry under
  Queen Anne.

He was a cunning and dark man, of too small ability to do
much good, but of all the qualities requisite to do mischief and
to bring on the ruin and destruction of a nation. The mischiev-
ous darkness of his soul was written in his countenance, and
plainly legible in a very odd look, disagreeable to everybody at
first sight, which, being joined with a constant awkward
motion or rather agitation of his head and body, betrayed
dishonesty within, even in the midst of all those familiar and
jocular bowing and smiling, which he always affected to cover
what would not be covered.

SOURCE: Sarah, Duchess of Marlborough, *An Account of the Conduct of the Duchess of Marlborough;* quoted in *English Historical Documents, 1660–1714,* edit. Andrew Browning, Eyre and Spottiswoode, 1953.

HARRIS, DAVID (fl. 1800), Hambledon cricketer.

Having finished with the best batter of his own age—or, perhaps, of any age—Beldham, we proceed to the very best bowler; a bowler who, between any one and himself, comparison must fail . . . He was a muscular, bony man, standing about five feet nine and a half inches. His features were not regularly handsome, but a remarkably kind and gentle expression amply compensated the defect of mere linear beauty. The fair qualities of his heart shone through his honest face, and I can call to mind no worthier, or, in the active sense of the word, not a more '*good*' man than David Harris . . .

It would be difficult, perhaps impossible, to convey in writing an accurate idea of the grand effect of Harris's bowling; they only who have played against him can fully appreciate it. His attitude when preparing to deliver the ball would have made a beautiful study for the sculptor. Phidias would certainly have taken him for a model. First of all, he stood erect like a soldier at drill; then, with a graceful curve of the arm, he raised the ball to his forehead, and drawing back his right foot, started off with his left. The calm look and general air of the man were uncommonly striking, and from this series of preparations he never deviated . . . His mode of delivering the ball was very singular. He would bring it from under the arm by a twist, and nearly as high as his armpit, and with this action *push* it, as it were, from him. How it was that the balls acquired the velocity they did by this mode of delivery I never could comprehend . . . In bowling, he never stooped in the least in his delivery, but kept himself upright all the time.

SOURCE: John Nyren, *The Young Cricketer's Tutor,* edit. Charles Cowden Clarke, 1833.

HARVEY, WILLIAM (1578–1657), physician and discoverer of the circulation of the blood.

He was much and often troubled with the gout, and his way of cure was thus: he would then sit with his legs bare, if it were a frost, on the leads of Cockaine House, put them into a pail of water, till he was almost dead with cold, and betake himself to his stove, and so 'twas gone . . .

He was not tall; but of the lowest stature, round faced, olivaster complexion; little eye, round, very black, full of spirit; his hair was black as a raven, but quite white 20 years before he died.

SOURCE: John Aubrey, *Brief Lives*, edit. Andrew Clark, 1898.

HASTINGS, HENRY (1551–1650), sportsman.

Mr. Hastings, by his quality, being the son, brother and uncle to the Earls of Huntingdon, and his way of living, had the first place among us. He was peradventure an original in our age, or rather the copy of our nobility in ancient days in hunting and not warlike times; he was low, very strong and very active, of a reddish flaxen hair, his clothes always green cloth, and never all worth when new five pounds. His house was perfectly of the old fashion, in the midst of a large park well stocked with deer.

. . . He kept all manner of sport-hounds that ran buck, fox, hare, otter and badger, and hawks long and short-winged; he had all sorts of nets for fishing; he had a walk in the New Forest and the manor of Christ Church. This last supplied him with red deer, sea and river fish; and indeed all his neighbours' grounds and royalties were free to him, who bestowed all his time in such sports.

He lived to a hundred, never lost his eyesight, but always writ and read without spectacles, and got to horse without help.

SOURCE: Ashley Cooper, 1st Earl of Shaftesbury; *Fragment of Autobiography*, first printed 1753. 'Some features of his character may have been worked up by Addison into his portraits of Sir Roger de Coverley and Will Wimble.' (Dict. of National Biography).

HAYDON, BENJAMIN ROBERT (1786–1846), historical painter.

He wore concave glasses, so concave as greatly to diminish objects. Through these glasses he used to contemplate his model and picture from a distance. He would then run up to his picture, raise his glasses, and paint, using the naked eye. He would then run to a mirror and examine the reflection of his picture, often through two pairs of such concave spectacles, and then would return again as before, raising the spectacles to work on his picture. His 'dashing' at his pictures—usually interpreted as an expression characteristic of his enthusiastic energy—was thus literally descriptive of his approach to a canvas.

SOURCE: Tom Taylor's account in his edition of Haydon's *Autobiography*, 1853.

HAZLITT, WILLIAM (1778–1830), essayist.

For depth, force, and variety of intellectual expression, a finer head and face than Hazlitt's were never seen. I speak of them when his countenance was not dimmed and obscured by illness, or clouded and deformed by those fearful indications of internal passion which he never even attempted to conceal. The expression of Hazlitt's face, when anything was said in his presence that seriously offended him or when any peculiarly painful recollection passed across his mind, was truly awful—more so than can be conceived as within the capacity of the human countenance ... But when he was in good health, and in a tolerable humour with himself and the world, his face was more truly answerable to the intellect that spoke through it, than any other I ever saw, either in life or on canvas; and its crowning portion, the brow and forehead, was, to my thinking, quite unequalled, for mingled capacity and beauty.

For those who desire a more particular description, I will add that Hazlitt's features, though not cast in any received classical mould, were regular in their formation, perfectly consonant with each other, and so finely 'chiselled' (as the phrase is), that they produced a much more prominent and striking effect than their scale of size might have led one to expect. The forehead, as I have hinted, was magnificent; the nose precisely that (combining strength with lightness and elegance) which physiognomists have assigned as evidence of a fine and highly cultivated taste; though there was a peculiar character about the nostrils, like that observable in those of a fiery unruly horse. The mouth, from its ever-changing form and character, could scarcely be described, except as to its astonishingly varied power of expression, which was equal to, and greatly resembled, that of Edmund Kean. His eyes, I should say, were not good. They were never brilliant, and there was a furtive and at times a sinister look about them, as they glanced suspiciously from under their overhanging brows, that conveyed a very unpleasant impression to those who did not know him. And they were seldom directed frankly and fairly towards you; as if he were afraid that you might read in them what was passing in his mind concerning you. His head was nobly formed and placed; with (until the last few years of his life) a profusion of coal-black hair, richly curled; and his person was of the middle height, rather slight, but well formed and put together.

SOURCE: P. G. Patmore, *My Friends and Acquaintance*, 1854.

HENLEY, WILLIAM, ERNEST (1849–1903), poet and dramatist.

His portrait, a lithograph by Rothenstein, hangs over my mantelpiece among portraits of other friends. He is drawn standing, but because doubtless of his crippled legs he leans forward, resting his elbows upon some slightly suggested object —a table, or a window-sill. His heavy figure and powerful head the disordered hair standing upright, his short irregular beard and moustache, his lined and wrinkled face, his eyes steadily fixed upon some object in complete confidence and self-possession, and yet as in half-broken reverie, all are there exactly as I remember him.

AGED ABOUT 40.

SOURCE: W. B. Yeats, *Autobiographies*, Macmillan, 1955.

HENRIETTA MARIA (1609–1669), queen of Charles I.

Her garments were exceeding rich and sumptuous, her gown being of cloth of gold cut upon cloth of silver and richly embroidered all over with fleur-de-lys of gold, chased and interlaced with diamonds, rubies, pearls and other rich jewellery of inestimable value.

AGED 16.

SOURCE: '*A True Relation of the Royal Passages, Triumphs and Ceremonies observed at the Marriage of the High and Mighty Charles, King of Britain, and the Most Excellent of Ladies, the Lady Henrietta Maria of Bourbon.*'

... nimble and quick, black-eyed, brown-haired and a brave lady.

SOURCE: *Sloane MSS.*

On Thursday I went to Whitehall purposely to see the Queen, which I did fully all the time she sat at dinner and perceived her to be a most absolute delicate lady after I had exactly surveyed all the features of her face much enlivened by her radiant and sparkling black eye. Besides, her deportment amongst her women was so sweet and humble and her speech and looks to her other servants so mild and gracious as I could not abstain from divers deep-pitched sighs to consider that she wanted the knowledge of the true religion.

SOURCE: Sir Simonds D'Ewes. *Autobiography of Sir Simonds d'Ewes*, ed. J. O. Halliwell, 1845.

The Queen, a very little, plain old woman, and nothing more

in her presence in any respect nor garb than any ordinary woman.

AGED 50.

SOURCE: Samuel Pepys, *Diary*.

HENRY I (1068–1135), king of England.

He was of middle stature, exceeding 'the diminutive but exceeded by the very tall: his hair was black, but scanty near the forehead; his eyes mildly bright, his chesty brawny; his body fleshy . . . He was heavy to sleep, which was interrupted by frequent snoring. His eloquence was rather unpremeditated than laboured, not rapid but deliberate.

SOURCE: William of Malmesbury's *Chronicle of the Kings of England*, edit. J. A. Giles, 1847.

HENRY II (1133–1189), king of England.

He was taller than the tallest men of middle height, and was blessed with soundness of limb and comeliness of face, in fact, whom men flocked to gaze upon, though they had scrutinised him a thousand times already. In agility of limb he was second to none, failing in no feat which anyone else could perform; with no polite accomplishment was he unacquainted; he had skill of letters as far as was fitting or practicably useful . . . There does not seem to be anyone beside him possessed of such temper and affability . . . He does nothing in a proud or overbearing manner.

SOURCE: Walter Map; M. R. James (edit.), *De Nugis Curialium*, Hon. Cymmrodorion Society.

You ask me to send you an accurate description of the appearance and character of the King of England. That surpasses my powers, for the genius of a Vergil would hardly be equal to it. That which I know, however, I will ungrudgingly share with you. Concerning David, we read that it was said of him, as evidence for his beauty, that he was ruddy. You may know then that our king is still ruddy, except as old age and whitening hair have changed his colour a little. He is of medium stature so that among small men he does not seem large, nor yet among large men does he seem small. His head is spherical, as if the abode of great wisdom and the special sanctuary of lofty intelligence. The size of his head is in proportion to the neck and the whole body. His eyes are full, guileless and dove-like when he is at peace, gleaming like fire when his temper is aroused, and in bursts of passion they flash like lightning. As to his hair, he is in no danger of baldness, but his head has been closely shaved. He has a broad, square, lion-like face. His feet are arched and he has the legs of a horseman. His broad chest and muscular arms show him to be a strong, bold, active man. His hands show by their coarseness that he is careless and pays little attention to his person, for he never wears gloves except when he goes hawking . . . Although his legs are bruised and livid from hard riding, he never sits down except when on horseback or at meals . . . He always has his weapons in his hands when not engaged in consultation or at his books. When his cares and anxieties allow him to breathe, he occupies himself with reading, or in a circle of clerks tries to solve some knotty question . . .

SOURCE: Peter of Blois, *Epistolae*, edit. John Allen Giles, 1848.

Henry II, king of England, was a man of reddish, freckled complexion with a large round head, grey eyes which glowed fiercely and grew bloodshot in anger, a fiery countenance and a harsh cracked voice. His neck was somewhat thrust forward from his shoulders, his chest was broad and square, his arms strong and powerful. His frame was stocky with a pronounced tendency to corpulence, due rather to nature than to indulgence, which he tempered by exercise. For in eating and drinking he was moderate and sparing, and in all things frugal in the degree permissible to a prince . . . In stature he was of middle height, and in this he was matched by none of his sons, for the two eldest were a little above the average, while the two younger stopped short of it. Except when troubled in mind or moved to anger, he was a prince of great eloquence and, what is remarkable in these days, polished in letters.

SOURCE: Giraldus Cambrensis, *Liber de Principis Instructione:* included in Douglas and Greenaway, *English Historical Documents, Volume II, 1042–1189*, Eyre and Spottiswoode, 1953.

HENRY III (1207–1272), king of England.

He was, however, of moderate stature, of compact body, with the lid of one eye rather drooping, so that it concealed part of the blackness of the pupil; robust in strength, but impulsive in action . . .

SOURCE: Nicholas Trivet or Trevet, *Annales Sex Regum Anglie.*

HENRY IV (1367–1413), king of England.

The coronation of the king:

The Duke of Lancaster left the Tower this Sunday after dinner, on his return to Westminster: he was bare-headed, and had round his neck the order of the king of France. The Prince of Wales, six dukes, six earls, eighteen barons, accompanied him; and there were, of knights and other nobility, from eight to nine hundred horse in the procession. The duke was dressed in a jacket, after the German fashion, of cloth of gold, mounted on a white courser, with a blue garter on his left leg. He passed through the streets of London, which were all handsomely decorated with tapestries and other rich hangings: there were nine fountains in Cheapside, and other streets he passed through which perpetually ran with white and red wines. He was escorted by prodigious numbers of gentlemen with their servants in liveries and badges; and the different companies of London were led by their wardens clothed in their proper livery, and with ensigns of their trade. The whole cavalcade amounted to six thousand horse, which escorted the duke from the Tower to Westminster.

The same night the duke bathed, and on the morrow confessed himself, as he had good need to do, and according to his custom heard three masses. The prelates and clergy who had been assembled then came in a large body in procession from Westminster Abbey, to conduct the king thither, and returned in the same manner, the king and his lords following them.

The dukes, earls, and barons, wore long scarlet robes, with mantles trimmed with ermine, and large hoods of the same. The dukes and earls had three bars of ermine on the left arm, a quarter of a yard long, or thereabout: the barons had but two. All the knights and squires had uniform cloaks of scarlet lined with miniver.

In the procession to the church, the duke had borne over his head a rich canopy of blue silk, supported on silver staves, with four golden bells that rang at the corners, by four burgesses of Dover, who claimed it as their right. On each side of him were the Sword of Mercy and the Sword of Justice: the first was borne by the Prince of Wales, and the other by the Earl of Northumberland, constable of England . . . The Earl of Westmorland, marshal of England, carried the sceptre.

The procession entered the church about nine o'clock; in the middle of which was erected a scaffold covered with crimson cloth, and in the centre a royal throne of cloth of gold. When the duke entered the church, he seated himself on the throne, and was thus in regal state, except having the crown on his head. The archbishop of Canterbury proclaimed from the four corners of the scaffold how God had given them a man for their lord and sovereign, and then asked the people if they were consenting to his being consecrated and crowned king. They unanimously shouted out, 'Aye!', and held up their hands, promising fealty and homage.

After this, the duke descended from his throne and advanced to the altar to be consecrated. This ceremony was performed by two archbishops and ten bishops: He was stripped of all his royal state before the altar, naked to his shirt, and was then anointed and consecrated at six places; that is to say, on the head, the breast, the two shoulders, before and behind, on the back and hands; they then placed a bonnet on his head; and, while this was doing, the clergy chanted the litany . . .

The king was now dressed in a churchman's clothes like a deacon; and they put on him shoes of crimson velvet, after the manner of a prelate. Then they added spurs with a point, but no rowel, and the Sword of Justice was drawn, blessed and delivered to the king, who put it into the scabbard, when the archbishop of Canterbury girded it about him. The crown of St. Edward, which is arched over like a cross, was next brought and blessed, and placed by the Archbishop on the king's head.

SOURCE: Sir John Froissart, *Chronicles*.

HENRY V (1387–1422), king of England.

His head is round, a sign of great prudence and wisdom. This is his cardinal virtue, the most praiseworthy quality in a ruler, and his smooth brow signifies a sound and healthy mind. His thick brown hair is evenly cut, he has a straight nose and wide, handsome features. His aspect is florid . . . his eyes sparkle brightly, having a reddish tinge when wide open. In peace they resemble those of a dove, but in rage are like a lion's. His teeth are snowy, strong and even . . . He has a cleft chin and his neck is everywhere evenly thick . . . His skin is completely white . . . but his lips are scarlet. His limbs are well-formed and strong with bone and sinews, without any signs denoting violence . . .

SOURCE: Rolls series, *Memorials of Henry V*, edit. Charles Augustus Cole, 1858.

The most serene prince of whose appearance this attempts to treat was neither of unseemly Titan size nor stunted in poor, pigmy-like shortness. He was very well-favoured, his neck was wide, his body graceful, his limbs not over-muscled . . . He outstripped all his equals in age at running and jumping . . . in so much that, with two chosen companions, he frequently, by sheer speed of running and without any help of whatever kind, killed the swiftest fallow deer driven out in to the plain from the woodland shades.

SOURCE: Thomas de Elmham, *Vita et Gesta Henrici Quinti Anglorum Regis*, edit. Thomas Hearne, 1727.

HENRY VI (1421–1471), king of England.

In church or oratory he never indulged himself by sitting on a seat, or by walking to and fro, as is the manner of worldly men during divine service, but always with his head bare, and his royal limbs seldom erect, but continually making genuflexions before the Book, with eyes and hands raised he sought inwardly to repeat the prayers, epistles and gospels of the Mass with the celebrant . . .

Concerning his humility in his gait, raiment and demeanour, he was wont from a youth to wear square shoes and boots like a farmer. Also his cloak was long, with a round hood such as a burgess wears, and his tunic reached below his knees, all dove-coloured, and he avoided anything fanciful.

SOURCE: John Blakman, *De Virtutibus et Miraculis Henrici VI*, pub. 1732 by Thomas Hearne; quoted (trans. and abridged) in M. W. Keatinge and N. L. Fraser, *A History of England for Schools*, 1911.

HENRY VIII (1491–1547), king of England.

. . . nine years old, and having already something of royalty in his demeanour in which there was a certain dignity combined with singular courtesy.

AGED 9.

SOURCE: Desiderius Erasmus (1499). F. M. Nichols (Trans.), *Epistles of Erasmus*, Longmans, Green and Co.

His Majesty is the handsomest potentate I ever set eyes on: above the usual height, with an extremely fine calf to his leg; his complexion fair and bright, with auburn hair combed straight and short in the French fashion, and a round face so very beautiful that it would become a pretty woman, his throat being rather long and thick.

AGED ABOUT 18.

SOURCE: Pasqualigo, the Venetian. *Giustinian's Despatches;* quoted by J. S. Brewer in *The Reign of Henry VIII,* John Murray, 1884.

Extremely handsome. Nature could not have done more for him. He is much handsomer than any other sovereign in Christendom; a great deal handsomer than the King of France; very fair and his whole frame admirably proportioned ... It is the prettiest thing in the world to see him play, his fair skin glowing through his shirt of the finest texture.

AGED 29.

SOURCE: Sebastian Giustinian, Venetian Ambassador. *Giustinian's Despatches;* quoted by J. S. Brewer in *The Reign of Henry VIII,* John Murray, 1884.

In this Eighth Henry God has combined such corporeal and intellectual beauty as not merely to surprise, but to astound all men ... His face is angelic rather than handsome; his head imperial and bold; and he wears a beard, contrary to the English custom.

AGED 38.

SOURCE: Ludovico Falier, Venetian Ambassador; *Venetian Calendar,* P.R.O.

He wore a cap of crimson velvet, in the French fashion, and the brim was looped up all round with lacets and gold enamelled tags. His doublet was in the Swiss fashion, striped alternately with white and crimson satin, and his hose were scarlet, and all slashed from the knee upwards. Very close round his neck he had a gold collar, from which there hung a rough cut diamond, the size of the largest walnut I ever saw, and to this was suspended a most beautiful and very large round pearl. His mantle was of purple velvet lined with white satin, the

K

sleeves open, with a train more than four Venetian yards long. This mantle was girt in front like a gown, with a thick gold cord from which there hung large golden acorns like those suspended from a cardinal's hat; over this mantle was a very handsome gold collar, with a pendant St. George entirely of diamonds. Beneath the mantle he wore a pouch of cloth of gold, which covered a dagger; and his fingers were one mass of jewelled rings.

SOURCE: *Giustinian's Despatches;* quoted by J. S. Brewer in *The Reign of Henry VIII*, John Murray, 1884.

HERBERT, GEORGE (1593–1633), poet and divine.

He was for his person of a stature inclining towards tallness; his body was very straight, and, so far from being cumbered with too much flesh, that he was lean to an extremity. His aspect was cheerful, and his speech and motion did both declare him a gentleman; for they were all so meek and obliging that they purchased love and respect from all that knew him.

SOURCE: Izaak Walton, *Life of George Herbert*, 1670.

HICKMAN, TOM (1785–?), prize-fighter; known as 'the Gaslight Man', 'Gas-man' or 'the Gas'.

The Gas-man came forward with a conscious air of anticipated triumph, too much like the cock-of-the-walk. He strutted about more than became a hero, sucked oranges with a supercilious air, and threw away the skin with a toss of his head . . . If Neate was like Ajax, 'with Atlantean shoulders fit to bear' the pugilistic reputation of all Bristol, Hickman might be compared to Diomed, light, vigorous, elastic, and his back glistened in the sun, as he moved about, like a panther's hide.

AGED 36.

SOURCE: William Hazlitt, *New Monthly Magazine*, February 1822.

Note: See entry for his opponent, Bill Neate, who defeated him in eighteen rounds on December 11, 1821.

HIGHLANDERS, THE (in 1689, under Graham of Claverhouse).

Their dress, which was the last remains of a Roman habit in Europe, was well suited to the nature of their country, and still better to the necessities of war. It consisted of a roll of light woollen, called a plaid, six yards in length, and two in breadth, wrapped loosely round the body, the upper lappet of which rested on the left shoulder, leaving the right arm at full liberty; a jacket of thick cloth, fitted tightly to the body; and a loose short garment of light woollen, which went round the waist and covered the thigh. In rain, they formed the plaid into folds, and, laying it on the shoulders, were covered as with a roof. When they were obliged to lie abroad in the hills, in their hunting parties, or tending their cattle, or in war, the plaid served them both for bed and for covering; for, when three men slept together, they could spread three folds of cloth below, and six above them. The garters of their stockings were tied under the knee, with a view to giving more freedom to the limb; and they wore no breeches, that they might climb mountains with the greater ease. The lightness and looseness of their dress, the custom they had of going always on foot, never on horseback, their love of long journeys, but above all, their patience of hunger, and every kind of hardship, which carried their bodies forward even after their spirits were exhausted, made them exceed all other European nations in speed and perseverance of march . . .

Their arms were a broad sword, a dagger, called a dirk, a target, a musket, and two pistols: so that they carried the long sword of the Celts, the pugio of the Romans, the shield of the ancients, and both kinds of modern fire arms, all together. In battle, they threw away the plaid and under garment, and fought in their jackets, making thus their movements quicker and their strokes more forcible. Their advance to battle was rapid, like the charge of dragoons. When near the enemy, they stopped a little to draw breath and discharge their muskets, which they then dropped on the ground. Advancing, they fired their pistols, which they threw almost at the same instant against the heads of their opponents; and then rushed into their ranks with the broad sword, threatening, and shaking the sword as they ran on, so as to conquer the enemy's eye, while his body was yet unhurt. They fought, not in long and regular lines, but in separate bands, like wedges condensed and firm; the army being ranged according to the clans which composed it, and each clan according to its families; so that there arose a competition in valour of clan with clan, of family with family, of brother with brother.

SOURCE: Sir John Dalrymple, *Memoirs of Great Britain and Ireland,* 1771.

HILL, OCTAVIA (1838–1912), philanthropist and social reformer.

. . . an unobtrusive, plainly dressed little lady, everlastingly knitting an extraordinarily fine piece of work, whose face attracts you at first, and charms you as you become acquainted with the power of the mind, and sweetness of character to which it gives expression, a lady of great force and energy, with a wide, open, and wellstored brain, but withal as gentle and womanly as she can be, and possessed of a wonderful tact, which makes her the most instructive, and the pleasantest companion in the establishment.

SOURCE: Sydney John Cockerell, writing to his sister in 1871; quoted by Wilfrid Blunt in *Cockerell,* Hamish Hamilton, 1964.

. . . Queen Elizabeth among her admirals and pirate explorers. For the solid, little figure with powerful head, masses of loose grey hair, large, benign, but watchful brown eyes, and mouth closing tight like a trap when she was displeased, displayed all the great Queen's indomitable resolution, power of personal affection or dislike, and scrupulous regard for every halfpenny spent or received.

SOURCE: H. W. Nevinson; quoted by Wilfrid Blunt in *Cockerell,* Hamish Hamilton, 1964.

HOBBES, THOMAS (1588–1629), philosopher.

In his youth unhealthy; of an ill yellowish complexion . . . from forty, or better, he grew healthier, and then he had a fresh, ruddy complexion ... In his old age he was very bald ... yet within door, he used to study, and sit, bareheaded, and said he never took cold in his head, but that the greatest trouble was to keep off the flies from pitching on the baldness ... His skin was soft of that kind which my Lord Chancellor Bacon ... calls a goose-skin, i.e. of a wide texture. *Face* not very great; ample forehead; whiskers, yellowish-reddish, which naturally turned up—which is a sign of a brisk wit ... Below, he was shaved close, except a little tip under his lip ... He had two kind of looks; when he laugh't, was witty, and in a merry humour, one could scarce see his eyes; by and by, when he was serious and positive, he open'd his eyes round ... He was six foot high, and something better, and went indifferently erect, or rather, considering his great age, very erect.

In cold weather he commonly wore a black velvet coat, lined with fur; if not some other coat so lined. But all the year he wore a kind of boots of Spanish leather, laced or tied along the sides with black ribbons.

He had the shaking palsy in his hands; which began in France before the year 1650, and has grown upon him by degrees, ever since, so that he has not been able to write very legibly since 1665 or 1666, as I find by some letters he hath honoured me withal.

SOURCE: John Aubrey, *Brief Lives*, edit. Andrew Clark, 1898.

HOGG, THOMAS (1755–1820), wanderer.

In my native village of Heanor, in Derbyshire, some sixteen or seventeen years ago, there appeared a singular character whose arrival created a sensation, and became an epoch in its history. Some boys who had been strolling to a distance brought an account that a little man, with a barrow as large as a house, was coming along the lane, at 'a snail's gallop'. Forth sallied a troop of gazers, who found a small, thick-set, round-faced man, in an old, red, soldier's jacket, and cocked hat, sitting on the handle of his barrow, which was built and roofed after the manner of a caravan; and was a storehouse of some kind of merchandise, what they yet knew not. He sat very quietly as they came round him, and returned their greetings in a way short and dry, and which became markedly testy and impatient, as they crowded more closely, and began to ask questions . . .

At length he rose, and, by the aid of a strong strap passed over his shoulders, heaved up the handles of his barrow, and placing his head against it, like a tortoise under a stone, proceeded at a toilsome rate of some few hundred yards per hour. This specimen of patient endurance amazed the villagers. A brawny labourer would have thought it a severe toil to wheel it a mile; and yet this singular being, outdoing the phlegmatic perseverance of an ass, casting Job himself in the background for patience, from league to league, from county to county, and from year to year, urged on his ponderous vehicle with almost imperceptible progression.

It was soon found that he was not more singular in appearance, than eccentric in mind. A villager, thinking to do him a kindness, offered to wheel his barrow, but what was the surprise of the gazers to see him present the man payment when he had moved it a considerable way, and on its being refused, to behold him quietly raise the barrow, turn it round, and wheel it back to the identical spot whence the villager set out.

On reaching the hamlet, he took up his quarters in a stable and opened his one-wheeled caravan, displaying a good assortment of cutlery ware. It was there that I first saw him, and was struck with his grave and uncomplying air, more like that of a beadle stationed to keep off intruders, than of a solicitous vendor of wares. He was standing with a pair of pliers, twisting wire into scissor-chains*; keeping, at the same time, a shrewd eye upon the goods. The prices were so wonderfully low that it was whispered the articles could not be good, or they were stolen . . . In fact, his goods were *goods*. So much so, that many of them are in use in the village to this day; he desired only so much a profit as would supply the necessities of one who never slept in a bed, never approached a fire for

---

* Scissors were often carried suspended from the house-wife's belt, along with a medley of other things.

the sake of its warmth, nor ever indulged in any luxury . . .

I well remember my boyish astonishment when he quoted to me maxims of Plato and Seneca, and when I heard him pouring out abundance of anecdote from the best sources. He had a real spirit of kindliness in him, though the most immediately striking features of his mind were shrewdness and rigid notions of truth . . . He had a tame hedgehog which partook his fare, slept in a better nest than himself, and was evidently a source of affectionate enjoyment. He was fond of children; but he had a stern spirit of independence which made him refuse gifts and favours, unless permitted to make some return . . . He always slept with his barrow chained to his leg; and on Sundays kept himself totally shut up, except during service time, standing the day through, reading his Bible.

When his character was known, he grew to be a general favourite. His stable became a sort of school, where he taught, to a constant audience, more useful knowledge than has emanated from many a philosopher, modern or antique. The good-will he excited evidently pleased the old man; he came again and again, till at length years rolled away without his reappearance, and he was considered as dead. But not so. For ten or eleven years he was still going on his pilgrimage, a wanderer and an outcast.

SOURCE: *The Everyday Book and Table Book, or Everlasting Calendar of Popular Amusements*, 1830.

Note : William Hogg wrote some verse of merit, and there is a strong likelihood that he came from Jedburgh and was a relative of the better-known James Hogg (1770–1835), the 'Ettrick Shepherd'. In 1820, William, sometimes known as *Cheap Tommy*, turned up in Midsomer Norton, near Bristol, without his eccentric barrow, which he had become too old to push. He died there at the end of January, having walked back from Bristol through the deep snow with half a hundredweight of wire on his back, bought to carry on his old trade. The vicar, Mr. Read, later wrote a rare little account of him, called *The Scottish Wanderer*.

HOOK, THEODORE EDWARD (1788–1841), novelist and wit.

I remember, one day at Sydenham, Mr. Theodore Hook coming

in unexpectedly to dinner, and amusing us very much with his talent at extempore verse. He was then a youth, tall, dark, and of a good person, with small eyes, and features more round than weak; a face that had character and humour, but no refinement.

SOURCE: Leigh Hunt, *Autobiography*.

Croker came to breakfast, and we were soon after joined by Theodore Hook, *alias* 'John Bull'; he has got as fat as the actual monarch of the herd.

SOURCE: Sir Walter Scott, *Journal*.

Note: Hook was the editor of a satirical Sunday newspaper, started in 1820, called 'John Bull'.

HOOKER, RICHARD (1554?–1600), divine and author.

His complexion (if we may guess by him at the age of forty) was sanguine, with a mixture of choler; and yet his motion was slow even in his youth, and so was his speech, never expressing an earnestness in either of them, but an humble gravity suitable to the occasion.

AGED 40.

SOURCE: Izaak Walton, *Life of Richard Hooker*, 1665.

HORTON, ANNE (1747–1808), married clandestinely to Henry Frederick, Duke of Cumberland and Strathearn.

The new Princess of the Blood is a young widow of twenty-four, extremely pretty, very well made, with the most amorous eyes in the world and eye-lashes a yard long; coquette beyond measure, artful as Cleopatra and completely mistress of her passions and projects. Indeed, eyelashes three-quarters of a yard shorter would have served to conquer such a head as she has turned.

AGED 24.

SOURCE: Horace Walpole, to Sir Horace Mann, 1771; *Letters of Horace Walpole, Earl of Orford*, edit. Peter Cunningham, 1861.

HOWARD THOMAS, second Earl of Arundel and Surrey (1586–1646), soldier, royalist and art collector.

He was tall of stature, and of shape and proportion rather goodly than neat; his countenance was majestical and grave, his visage long, his eyes large, black and piercing; he had a hooked nose, and some warts or moles on his cheeks; his countenance was brown, his hair thin both on his head and beard; he was of stately presence and gait, so that any man that saw him, though in never so ordinary habit, could not but conclude him to be a great person, his garb and fashion drawing more observation than did the rich apparel of others; so that it was a common saying of the late Earl of Carlisle, 'Here comes the Earl of Arundel in his plain stuff and trunk hose, and his beard in his teeth, that looks more like a noble man than any of us.'

SOURCE: Sir Edward Walker, *Historical Discourses Upon Several Occasions*, 1705.

HOWE, RICHARD, Earl Howe (1726–1799), admiral of the fleet; first lord of the admiralty; won victory of the Glorious First of June, 1794.

Among the sailors he was known, from his dark complexion, by the epithet of 'Black Dick'. If no genius could be discovered in the lines of his face, there was in them an expression of serene and passive fortitude, which could not be mistaken. His profile bore, indeed, a very strong resemblance to the portraits of George the First, from whom, by his mother, he descended . . .

In Parliament, Lord Howe made, if possible, a worse figure than Keppel; who, when he addressed the House, was at least intelligible, though he might not greatly illuminate the subject. Lord Howe's ideas were commonly either so ill conceived by himself, or so darkly and ambiguously expressed, that it was by no means easy to comprehend his precise meaning.

This oracular and confused mode of delivery, rendered still more obscure by the part of the House where he usually sat, which was on a back row at a distance from the Speaker's chair, increased, however, the effect of his oratory; and seemed to exemplify Burke's assertion that 'obscurity is a source of the sublime.'

SOURCE: Sir N. William Wraxall, *Historical Memoirs of My Own Life*, 1815.

HUDSON, JEFFERY (1619–1682), dwarf; captain of horse in Civil War; captured by pirates off the coast of France; imprisoned for suspected complicity in 'Popish Plot'.

His father ... presented him at Burley-on-the-Hill to the Duchess of Buckingham, being then nine years of age and scarce a foot and a half in height, as I am informed by credible persons then and there present, and still alive. Instantly Jeffery was heightened, not in stature but in condition, from one degree above rags into silk and satin, and two tall men to attend him.

He was without any deformity, wholly proportionable ... It was not long before he was presented in a cold baked pie to King Charles and Queen Mary at an entertainment; and ever after lived (whilst the court lived) in great plenty therein.

SOURCE: Thomas Fuller, *The Worthies of England*, 1662.

Note: Hudson was eighteen inches high till he was 30, but afterwards reached three feet six or a few inches more.

HUME, DAVID (1711–1776), historian and philosopher.

Nature I believe never formed any man more unlike his real character than David Hume. The powers of physiognomy were baffled by his countenance; neither could the most skilful in that science pretend to discover the smallest trace of the faculties of his mind in the unmeaning features of his visage. His face was broad and fat, his mouth wide, and without any other expression than that of imbecility. His eyes vacant and spiritless; and the corpulence of his whole person was far better fitted to communicate the idea of a turtle-eating alderman than that of a refined philosopher. His speech in English was rendered ridiculous by the broadest Scottish accent, and his French was, if possible, still more laughable; so that wisdom most certainly never disguised herself before in so uncouth a garb ... he was healthy and strong; but his health and strength, far from being advantageous to his figure, instead of manly comeliness had only the appearance of rusticity.

AGED 38.

SOURCE: Francis Hardy, *Memoirs of ... Earl of Charlemont*, 1810; quoted by Robert Chambers in *A Biographical Dictionary of Eminent Scotsmen*, 1837.

HUNT, JAMES HENRY LEIGH (1784–1859), essayist and poet.

... we began to talk, and he to hold forth, and I thought him, with his black bushy hair, black eyes, pale face and 'nose of taste', as fine a specimen of a London editor as could be imagined; assuming yet moderate, sarcastic yet genial, with a smattering of everything and mastery of nothing; affecting the dictator, the poet, the politician, the critic and the sceptic, whichever would at the moment give him the air to inferior minds of being a very superior man. I listened ... though hating his effeminacy and cockney peculiarities.

AGED 27.

SOURCE: Benjamin Haydon's *Autobiography*.

HUTCHINSON, COLONEL JOHN (1615–1664), parliamentarian and regicide.

He was of a middle stature, of a slender and exactly well-proportion'd shape in all parts, his complexion fair, his hair of light brown, very thick set in his youth, softer than the finest silk, curling into loose great rings at the ends, his eyes of a lively grey, well-shaped and full of life and vigour, graced with many becoming motions, his visage thin, his mouth well made, and

his lips very ruddy and graceful, although the nether chap*
shut over the upper, yet it was in such a manner as was not
unbecoming, his teeth were even and white as the purest
ivory, his chin was something long, and the mould of his face,
his forehead was not very high, his nose was raised and sharp,
but withal he had a most amiable countenance, which carried
in it something of magnanimity and majesty mixed with
gentleness, that at the same time bespoke love and awe in all
that saw him; his skin was smooth and white, his legs and feet
excellently well made, he was quick in his pace and turns,
nimble and active and graceful in all his motions, he was apt
for any bodily exercise, and any that he did became him, he
could dance admirably well, but neither in youth nor riper
years made any practise of it, he had skill in fencing such as
became a gentleman, he had a great love of music, and often
diverted himself with a viol, on which he played masterly . . .
he was wonderful neat, cleanly and genteel in his habit, and
had a very good fancy in it, but he left off very early the wearing
of anything that was costly, yet in his plainest negligent habit
appear'd very much a gentleman . . . there was a life of spirit
and power in him that is not to be found in any copy drawn
from him.

SOURCE: Lucy Hutchinson, *Memoirs of the Life of Colonel Hutchinson,
Governor of Nottingham Castle and Town* . . ., first published 1806.

HYDE, ANNE, Duchess of York (1637–1671), wife of James, Duke
of York, afterwards James II.

She had a heartier appetite than any other woman in the
kingdom . . . It was an edifying spectacle to watch Her
Highness eat and, while the Duke on his side frittered away
his substance in the continual pursuit of fresh passions and
grew progressively more meagre, his poor consort . . . waxed
so fat that it was a marvel to see.

SOURCE: Anthony Hamilton, *Mémoires de la Vie du Comte de
Gramont.*

* i.e., his lower jaw.

JAMES I (1566–1625), king of England.

He was of a middle stature, more corpulent through his clothes than in his body, yet fat enough, his clothes ever being made large and easy, the doublets quilted for stiletto proof, his breeches in great pleats and full stuffed. He was naturally of a timorous disposition, which was the reason for his quilted doublets; his eyes large, ever rolling after any stranger came in his presence, insomuch as many for shame left the room, as being out of countenance. His beard was very thin, his tongue too large for his mouth, which ever made him speak full in the mouth, and made him drink very uncomely, as if eating his drink, which came out into the cup of each side of his mouth. His skin was as soft as taffeta sarsnet, which felt so because he never washed his hands, only rubbed his finger ends slightly with the wet end of a napkin. His legs were very weak, having had (as was thought) some foul play in his youth, or rather before he was born, that he was not able to stand at seven years of age; that weakness made him ever leaning on other men's shoulders.

SOURCE: Sir Anthony Weldon, *Court and Character of King James I*, 1650.

JAMES II (1633–1701), king of England.

I had desired him to take a ribbon with him [Colonel Bampfield] and bring me the bigness of the Duke's waist and his length, to have clothes made to fit for him ... When I gave the measure to my tailor to enquire how much mohair would serve to make a petticoat and waistcoat to a young gentlewoman of that bigness and stature, he considered it a long time, and said he had made many gowns and suits, but he had never made any to such a person in his life. I thought he was right; but his meaning was, he had never seen any woman of so low a stature have so big a waist; however, he made it as exactly fit as if he had taken the measure himself. It was a mixed mohair of a light hair colour and black, and the under petticoat was scarlet ...

His Highness called, 'Quickly, quickly, dress me,' and putting off his clothes, I dressed him in the woman's habit that was prepared, which fitted His Highness very well, and he was very pretty in it.

AGED 15.

SOURCE: *Autobiography of Anne, Lady Halkett*, Camden Society, 1875. After the Battle of Edgehill, the future king, James II, was handed over to the Parliamentarians and kept in custody at St. James's Palace. He was rescued, after several vain attempts, in April 1648, by Anne Murry, later Lady Halkett, and Colonel Joseph Bampfield, by dressing him in woman's clothes and having him conveyed to the Continent.

The reverse process was carried out for the little Princess Henrietta, aged two. The plucky Lady Dalkeith disguised herself as a disreputable hunchback and made for Dover with the princess, scruffily dressed as a boy, named Pierre. Henrietta, with typical Stuart awkwardness, nearly ruined the whole attempt by announcing to all and sundry that she was not a small boy, but the Princess Henrietta. Fortunately Lady Dalkeith managed to persuade the hearers that her charge was indulging in childish flights of fancy.

He was something above the middle stature, well-shaped, very nervous and strong; his face was rather long, his complexion fair, his countenance engaging; his outward carriage was a little stiff and constrained ... In his conversation and arguing, he endeavoured rather to convince with good reason than fine expressions, and having something of a hesitation in his speech, his discourse was not so graceful as it was judicious and solid.

SOURCE: *Life of James II*, edit. J. S. Clarke; quoted by David Ogg in *England in the Reigns of James II and William III*, Oxford 1955.

JEFFREYS, GEORGE, first **BARON JEFFREYS** (1648–1689), judge; lord chief justice; conducted the 'Bloody Assize', 1685, after Monmouth's rebellion.

His friendship and conversation lay much among the good fellows and humourists; and his delights were, accordingly, drinking, laughing, singing, kissing, and all the extravagances of the bottle. He had a set of banterers, for the most part, near him; as, in old time, great men kept fools to make them merry . . . When he was in temper, and matters indifferent came before him, he became his seat of justice better than any other I ever saw in his place . . . He had extraordinary natural abilities, but little acquired, beyond what practice in affairs had supplied. He talked fluently, and with spirit; and his weakness was that he could not reprehend without scolding; and in such Billingsgate language as should come out of the mouth of any man . . .

Many times, on days of causes at his house, the company have waited five hours in a morning, and, after eleven, he hath come out inflamed, and staring like one distracted. And that visage he put on when he animadverted on such as he took offence at, which made him a terror to real offenders; whom he also terrified, with his face and voice, as if the thunder of the day of judgment broke over their heads: and nothing ever made men tremble like his vocal inflictions.

SOURCE: Roger North, *Life of . . . Francis North Baron Guilford*, 1742.

JENKINSON, CHARLES, first Earl of Liverpool (1727–1808), statesman.

At this time [in 1781] he was about fifty-four years of age, and in his person he rose above the common height. The expression of his countenance, I find it difficult to describe, as without having in his face any lines strongly marked, it was not destitute of deep intelligence. Reflection and caution seemed to be stamped on every feature; while his eyes were usually, even in conversation, directed downwards to the earth. Something imperious and inscrutable seemed to accompany and to characterise his demeanour . . . His enemies asserted that he resembled a Dark Lanthorn; and, as much as the human figure or physiognomy can ever be supposed to offer such a strange similarity, unquestionably it existed in him. Even the twinkling motion of his eyelids, which he half-closed from time to time in speaking, made the illusion, however fanciful, more close and striking.

His manners were polite, calm and unassuming; grave if not cold; but not distant, without any mixture of pride or affectation in society; though reserved, he was not silent; and though guarded in certain topics, communicative on ordinary subjects. He always appeared as if desirous to disclaim and to reject the consideration which he involuntarily attracted.

AGED 54.

SOURCE: Sir N. William Wraxall, *Historical Memoirs of My Own Life*, 1815.

JENYNS, SOAME (1704–1787), wit and author; cousin of Sarah Jennings, Duchess of Marlborough.

He dressed himself to do your party honour, in all the colours of the jay; his lace, indeed, had long since lost its lustre, but his coat had faithfully retained its cut since the days when gentlemen wore embroidered figured velvets, with short sleeves, boot cuffs, and buckram skirts. As nature cast him in the exact mould of an ill-made pair of stiff stays, he followed her so close in the fashion of his coat, that it was doubted if he did not wear them; because he had a protuberant wen just under his poll, he wore a wig that did not cover above half his head. His eyes were protruded, like the eyes of the lobster, who wears them at the end of his feelers, and yet there was room between one of them and his nose for another wen, that added nothing to his beauty; yet this good man was heard very innocently to remark, when Gibbon published his history, 'that he wondered anybody so ugly could write a book!'

SOURCE: quoted in Sir Bernard Burke's *The Rise of Great Families*, 1873.

JERSEY, FRANCES, Countess of (1753?–1821).

Shall I tell you what Lady Jersey is like? She is like one of her numerous gold and silver musical dickey birds, that are in all the show rooms of this house. She begins to sing at eleven o'clock, and, with the interval of the hour she retires to her cage to rest, she sings till 12 at night without a moment's interruption. She changes her feathers for dinner, and her plumage both morning and evening is the happiest and most beautiful I ever saw. Of the *merits* of her songs I say nothing till we meet.

AGED 67.

SOURCE: *Creevey Papers*, edit. Sir H. Maxwell, 1903; a useful recent re-publication is *The Creevey Papers* (1793–1838), edit. John Gore, Batsford.

JERVIS, JOHN, Earl of St. Vincent (1735–1823), admiral of the fleet.

From the moment he entered the room, no listless countenance, no wandering eye, betrayed unoccupied thoughts. His natural demeanour was grave; but he had all the carriage and ease of polished society, and of the accomplished statesman. He was one of the few eminent public men who were very agreeable in their domestic life: and they who were honoured with most frequent and intimate participation of Lord St. Vincent's remarkable hospitality, can now best testify, the constancy of friendship, the ever-varying kindness, the fund of entertainment with which he charmed them . . . Well can they recollect how, to suit the occasion of the moment's drama, collecting into his face fun and drollery, or with an assumption of an admirably pretended importance, he would, by his playful sallies, or his excellent fabrications, raise laughter the most irresistible, and then in an instant resume his natural guise, the serious, over-awing presence of a great man. His stature indicated rather the strength of his robust constitution than elegance; his countenance was one of thoughtfulness, dignity, and a firmness which no man would even attempt to shake. The resolute determination of the blue large eye beneath his bold prominent brow, was overpowering; and such the ubiquity of his attention, that, however numerous the circle, however

L

diversified the characters, not an unusual look, gesture, or tone, beyond the individual's ordinary habit, escaped his penetrating notice. His voice, when exerted, was exceedingly strong; at other times, though it was never quite free from the gruffness habitual to the weather-beaten sailor, yet had it such impressively varying intonation, that even to those not listening, it was continually dropping upon the ear. He always wore the Star of the Order of the Bath; and to a child who one day asked what it was, and where he had found it, he replied, 'I found it upon the sea; and if you become a sailor, and search diligently, perhaps you may find just such another.'

SOURCE: Jedediah Stephens Tucker, *Memoirs of Admiral the Right Hon. the Earl of St. Vincent*, 1844.

JOHN (1167?–1216), king of England.

Then the king heaved deep sighs, began to feel the utmost irritation, started to turn in upon himself and languish . . . He started to gnash his teeth and roll his staring eyes in fury. Then he would pick up sticks and straws and gnaw them like a lunatic and sometimes he would cast them away half-chewed. His uncontrolled gestures gave indications of the melancholy, or rather of the madness, that was upon him.

SOURCE: Matthew Paris, *Chronica Majora* (Rolls Series, 1874).

Note: No reliable contemporary description of King John seems to have survived. Even the account given above is highly suspect. But we have an eye-witness account of the opening of his tomb in Worcester Cathedral on July 24th, 1797:—

'The venerable shrine of this monarch was opened on Monday last in consequence of a general reparation of the Cathedral Church at Worcester. The remains of the illustrious personage appear entire, his robes, in which he was interred, they are undecayed, but the colour through length of time is indiscernible. On one side of him lay a sword, the bones of his left arm lying on his breast . . .; his remains measured five feet five inches, being his stature when living.'

SOURCE: Gough MSS; quoted by A. L. Poole *in Domesday Book to Magna Carta*, Oxford.

JOHNSON, ESTHER (1681–1728), Dean Swift's 'Stella'.

I knew her from six years old, and had some share in her educa-
tion, by directing what books she should read, and perpetually
instructing her in the principles of honour and virtue; from
which she never swerved in any one action or moment of her
life. She was sickly from her childhood until about the age of
fifteen; but then grew into perfect health, was looked upon as
one of the most beautiful, graceful, and agreeable young
women in London, only a little fat. Her hair was blacker than
a raven, and every feature of her face in perfection.

SOURCE: Jonathan Swift, *Character of Mrs. Johnson;* see Vol. XI
of *Swift's Prose Works*, edit. Temple Scott, 1907.

JOHNSON, DOCTOR SAMUEL (1709–1784), lexicographer.

... while talking or even musing as he sat in his chair, he
commonly held his head to one side towards his right shoulder,
and shook it in a tremulous manner, moving his body backwards
and forwards, and rubbing his left knee in the same direction
with the palm of his hand. In the intervals of articulating he
made various sounds with his mouth; sometimes as if ruminat-
ing, or what is called chewing the cud, sometimes giving a
half-whistle, sometimes making his tongue play backwards
from the roof of his mouth, as if clucking like a hen, and sometimes protruding it against his upper gums in front, as if
pronouncing quickly under his breath, *too, too, too:* all this
accompanied sometimes with a thoughtful look, but more
frequently with a smile. Generally when he had concluded a
period, in the course of a dispute ... he used to blow out his
breath like a whale ...

SOURCE: James Boswell, *Life of Doctor Samuel Johnson, LL.D.*

His figure was large and well-formed, and his countenance of
the cast of an ancient statue; yet his appearance was rendered
strange and somewhat uncouth, by convulsive cramps, by the
scars of that distemper which it was once imagined the royal
touch could cure, and by a slovenly mode of dress. He had the

use of only one eye . . . he never knew the natural joy of a free and vigorous use of his limbs; when he walked, it was like the struggling gait of one in fetters; when he rode, he had no command or direction of his horse, but was carried as if in a balloon.

SOURCE: James Boswell, *Life of Doctor Samuel Johnson, LL.D.*

His stature was remarkably high, and his limbs exceedingly large; his strength was more than common, I believe, and his activity was greater than his size gave one cause to expect. His features were strongly marked, though his complexion was fair, a circumstance somewhat unusual; his sight was near, and otherwise imperfect, yet his eyes though of a light blue colour were so wild, so piercing, and at times so fierce, that fear was I believe the first emotion in the hearts of all his beholders.

SOURCE: *Thraliana, the Diary of Mrs. Hester Lynch Thrale, 1776–1809*, edit. Katherine C. Balderston, 1942.

In the midst of this performance, Dr. Johnson was announced. He is indeed very ill favoured; is tall and stout, but stoops terribly; he is almost bent double. His mouth is almost constantly opening and shutting as if he was chewing. He has a strange method of frequently twirling his fingers and twisting his hands. His body is in a continual agitation *see-sawing* up and down; his feet are never a moment quiet; and in short his whole person is in *perpetual motion*. His dress too, considering the times and that he had meant to put on his *best becomes*, being engaged to dine in a large company, was so much out of the common road as his figure; he had a large wig, snuff colour coat and gold buttons but no ruffles to his shirt . . . and black worsted stockings. He is shockingly near-sighted, and did not, till she held out her hand to him, even know Mrs. Thrale.

AGED 68.

SOURCE: *The Early Diary of F. Burney*, edit. A. R. Ellis, 1889. Standard edit. of *The Diary and Letters* is that by Austin Dobson, 1905; for useful smaller edition, see *The Diary of Fanny Burney*, edit. Christopher Lloyd, Roger Ingram, 1948.

JONSON, BEN (1573?–1637), dramatist.

He was (or rather had been) of a clear and fair skin; his habit was very plain. I have heard Mr. Lacy, the player, say that he was wont to wear a coat like a coachman's coat with slits under the armpits.

Ben Jonson had one eye lower than t'other, and bigger.

SOURCE: John Aubrey, *Brief Lives*, edit. Andrew Clark, 1898.

. . . punched full of eylet-holes like the cover of a warming pan . . . the most ungodly face . . . it looks for all the world like a rotten russet-apple, when 'tis bruised. It's better than a spoonful of cinnamon-water next my heart, for me to hear him speak; he sounds it so i' the nose, and talks and rants . . . it's cake and pudding to me to see his face make faces when he reads his songs and sonnets.

SOURCE: Thomas Dekker, *Satiro-mastix*. Dekker deliberately drew a recognisable picture of Jonson in the character of Horace in his play *Satiro-mastix*, which was a reply to Jonson's own *Poetaster*, another satire on some of his contemporaries. The first words are a reference to the ravages of smallpox.

JORDAN, DOROTHEA or **DOROTHY** (1762–1816), actress.

We congratulate the public on the re-engagement for three years of that deservedly famous favourite actress, Mrs. Jordan: and . . . we were in hopes . . . that she intended to play chiefly those hoydenish characters, in the delineation of which she shines so conspicuously, and to leave to Miss Duncan, who is certainly much better calculated, both in figure and manners, the representation of the lively woman of fashion. But we were woefully mistaken. Mrs. Jordan, coarse in figure, drawling in sentiment, inelegant in manner, boisterous when she should be gay . . . chooses to play the lively woman of the world.

SOURCE: A magazine report (1807).

JOWETT, BENJAMIN (1817–1893), classical scholar and master of Balliol.

He was like Jenkyns [a former Master of Balliol], short in stature, but without his pompous voice and strut. The head and countenance of Jenkyns arrested attention, the face of Jowett was to the last youthful, as simple as was that of a child. He was shy and retiring in manner, but won respect from all brought under his influence ... Jowett was all brain; the ordinary feelings which made life amiable and interesting had little attraction for him: work, work, seemed his delight.

SOURCE: Richard W. Hiley, *Memories of Half a Century*, Longmans, Green & Co. 1899.

... though he had passed his prime as a teacher of philosophy, this quaint white-haired, rosy-cheeked little clergyman, who tripped about Oxford in an old-fashioned swallow-tailed coat, was still a figure among young men and old. His will was firm, his tongue sharp, his discipline strict ... In weight of character and in his tonic influence on the lives of younger men he was probably in his own day unequalled. In his mellow old age he was untiring in quiet benevolence.

SOURCE: H. A. L. Fisher, *An Unfinished Autobiography*, O.U.P., 1940.

KATHERINE OF ARRAGON (1485–1536), first queen of Henry VIII.

She is not handsome, but has a very beautiful complexion.

SOURCE: Sebastian Giustinian, Venetian ambassador; *Despatches*.

She is rather ugly than otherwise.

SOURCE: Nicolo Sagudino, secretary to the ambassador Giustinian; *Despatches*.

KEAN, EDMUND (1787–1833), actor.

Well, I went to see Mr. Keane, and was thoroughly disgusted. This monarch of the stage is a little insignificant man, slightly deformed, strongly ungraceful, seldom pleasing the eye, still seldomer pleasing the ear—with a voice between grunting and croaking, a perpetual hoarseness which suffocates his words, and a vulgarity of manner which his admirers are pleased to call nature . . . I am quite sure that in any character where he can possibly raise his voice above conversation pitch—where there is anything like strong writing that he can contrive to rant, or anything resembling strong passion for him to tear to rags—his acting will always be, if not actually insupportable, yet unequal, disappointing, and destructive of all illusion.

SOURCE: Mary Russell Mitford, *Letters*.

KEATS, JOHN (1795–1821), poet.

He was below the middle size, with a low forehead, and an eye that had an inward look, perfectly divine, like a Delphian priestess who saw visions . . .

Keats was the only man I ever met who seemed and looked conscious of a high calling, except Wordsworth . . .

In fireside conversation, he was weak and inconsistent, but he was in his glory in the fields. The humming of a bee, the sight of a flower, the glitter of the sun, seemed to make his nature tremble; then his eyes flashed, his cheek glowed, his mouth quivered.

SOURCE: Benjamin Haydon's *Autobiography*.

He was under the middle height; and his lower limbs were small in comparison with the upper, but neat and well turned. His shoulders were very broad for his size: he had a face in which energy and sensibility were remarkably mixed up; an eager power, checked and made patient by ill-health. Every feature was at once strongly cut, and delicately alive. If there was any faulty expression, it was in the mouth, which was not without something of a character of pugnacity. His face was

rather long than otherwise; the upper lip projected a little
over the under; the chin was bold, the cheeks sunken; the eyes
mellow and glowing; large, dark, and sensitive. At the recital
of a noble action, or a beautiful thought, they would suffuse
with tears and his mouth trembled . . . His hair, of a brown
colour, was fine, and hung in natural ringlets. The head was a
puzzle for the phrenologists, being remarkably small in the
skull; a singularity which he had in common with Byron and
Shelley, whose hats I could not get on. Keats was sensible of
the disproportion above noticed, between his upper and lower
extremities; and he would look at his hand, which was faded
and swollen in the veins, and say it was the hand of a man of
fifty.

SOURCE: Leigh Hunt, *Autobiography . . . with Reminiscences of Friends
and Contemporaries*, 1850.

KEMBLE, JOHN PHILIP (1757–1823), actor.

The Kembles, indeed, as Garrick had been, were received
everywhere among the truly best circles; that is to say, where
intelligence was combined with high breeding; and they
deserved it: for whatever difference of opinion may be entertained as to the amount of genius in the family, nobody who
recollects them will dispute that they were a remarkable race,
dignified and elegant in manners, with intellectual tendencies,
and in point of aspect very like what has been called 'God
Almighty's nobility'.

I remember once standing behind John Kemble and a noble
lord at a sale . . . What a difference! and what a voice! Kemble's
voice was none of the best; but, like his profile, it was nobleness
itself compared with that of the noble lord.

SOURCE: Leigh Hunt, *Autobiography . . . with Reminiscences of Friends
and Contemporaries*, 1850.

Too much praise cannot be given to Mr. Kemble's performance
of Macbeth. He was 'himself again', and more than himself. His
action was decided, his voice audible. His tones had occasionally

indeed a learned quaintness, like the colouring of Poussin . . . In that prodigious prosing paper, the *Times*, which seems to be written as well as printed by a steam-engine, Mr. Kemble is compared to the ruin of a magnificent temple, in which the divinity still resides. This is not the case. The temple is unimpaired; but the divinity is sometimes from home.

SOURCE: William Hazlitt, *The Examiner*, June 15th, 1816.

KENYON, LLOYD, first Baron Kenyon (1732–1802), lord chief justice.

Chief-Justice Kenyon was curiously economical about the adornment of his head. It was observed for a number of years before he died that he had two hats and two wigs. Of the hats and the wigs, one was dreadfully old and shabby, the other comparatively spruce. He always carried into court with him the very old hat and the comparatively spruce wig, or the very old wig and the comparatively spruce hat. On the days of the very old hat and the comparatively spruce wig, he shoved his hat under the bench and displayed his wig; but on the days of the very old wig and the comparatively spruce hat, he always continued covered.

SOURCE: John Timbs, *A Century of Anecdote, 1760–1860.*

KEPPEL, AUGUSTUS, first Viscount Keppel (1725–1786), Admiral of the White; first lord of the Admiralty.

There appeared neither dignity in his person, nor intelligence in his countenance, the features of which were of the most ordinary cast; and his nose, which, in consequence of an accident that befell him in the course of his professional life, had been laid almost flat, gave him an equally vulgar and unpleasant air.

SOURCE: Sir N. William Wraxall, *Historical Memoirs of My Own Life*, 1815.

KINGSLEY, CHARLES (1819–1875), author; wrote *Westward Ho!*, etc.; professor of modern history at Cambridge.

I met Kingsley the other day—the author of 'Alton Locke,' 'Yeast,' the 'Saint's Tragedy,' etc. He is a capital fellow: I might with propriety say a *jolly* fellow. We met at a picnic. No one would suspect him of being a clergyman. We had a great deal of talk together . . . He is evidently a man of immense energy. He seems to have so much steam that he can scarcely sit still. He said that if he could do something whilst asleep it would be a great gratification. He stammers in conversation, but not, they say, in preaching.

AGED 33.

SOURCE: Herbert Spencer, *An Autobiography*, 1904.

KNIGHT, A (15th Century). The arming and appearance of a man being prepared to fight on foot.

He shall have no shirt upon him, but a doublet of fustian lined with satin, cut full of holes. The doublet must be strongly laced where the points are set about the great [part] of the arm, and the best before and behind, and the gussets of mail must be sewed to the doublet at the bend of the arm and under the arm. The arming points must be made of fine twine such as men used to make strings for crossbows, and they must be tied small and pointed as points. They must be waxed with shoe-maker's wax, and then they will neither stretch nor break. He shall have a pair of hose of worsted cloth, and a pair of short pads of thin blanket to put about his knees to prevent chafing of his leg harness; also a pair of shoes of thick leather, and they must be fastened with small whipcord, three knots upon a cord, and three cords must be fast sewed to the heel of the shoe, and fine cords in the middle of the sole of the same shoe, and there must be between the cords of the heel and those of the middle of the shoe the space of three fingers.

SOURCE: Viscount Dillon, *On a MS Collection of Ordinances of Chivalry of the Fifteenth Century;* quoted in *Chaucer's World*, Columbia University Press.

LAMB, CHARLES (1775–1834), essayist.

Lamb was an amiable, gentle boy, very sensible and keenly observing, indulged by his schoolfellows and by his master on account of his infirmity of speech. His countenance was mild; his complexion clear brown, with an expression which might lead you to think he was of Jewish descent. His eyes were not each of the same colour; one was hazel, the other had specks of grey in the iris, mingled as we see red spots in the bloodstone. His step was plantigrade, which made his walk slow and peculiar, adding to the staid appearance of his figure . . . His delicate frame and his difficulty of utterance, which was increased by agitation, unfitted him for joining in any boisterous sports.

SOURCE: Charles Valentine le Grice, *Reminiscences* contributed to *Lamb's Letters*, edit. by Sir Thomas Noon Talfourd.

Lamb I recollect coming to see the boys, with a pensive, brown, handsome, and kindly face, and a gait advancing with a motion from side to side, between involuntary consciousness and attempted ease. His brown complexion may have been owing to a visit to the country; his air of uneasiness to a great burden of sorrow. He dressed with Quaker-like plainness.

SOURCE: Leigh Hunt, *School-Days;* included in *Christ's Hospital, Recollections of Lamb, Coleridge, and Leigh Hunt*, edit. R. Brimley Johnson, 1896.

Charles Lamb had a head worthy of Aristotle . . . and limbs very fragile to sustain it . . . There never was a true portrait of Lamb. His features were strong yet delicately cut: he had a fine eye as well as forehead; and no face carried in it greater marks of thought and feeling.

SOURCE: Leigh Hunt, *Autobiography*.

There is something due to manners and customs, and I should apologise to you and Mrs. Asbury for being absolutely carried home upon a man's shoulders thro' Silver Street, up Parson's Lane, by the Chapels (which might have taught me better) and then to be deposited like a dead log at Gaffer Westwood's . . .

Not that the mode of conveyance is objectionable ... I protest I thought myself in a palanquin, and never felt myself so grandly carried. It was a slave under me. There was I, all but my reason. And what is reason?

SOURCE: Letter from Charles Lamb to his physician, Doctor J. V. Asbury.

For God's sake (I never was more serious) don't make me ridiculous any more by terming me gentle-hearted in print, or do it in better verses ... In the next edition ... please to blot out *gentle-hearted* and substitute drunken dog, ragged head, seldom-shaven, odd-eyed, stuttering, or any other epithet which truly and properly belongs to that gentleman in question.

SOURCE: Letter from Charles Lamb, to Samuel Taylor Coleridge.

LANDOR, WALTER SAVAGE (1775–1864), author.

Made the acquaintance of Walter Savage Landor, ten days ago, and have seen him nearly every day since ... There is a natural dignity which appertains to him that suits perfectly with the style of his conversation and his general appearance. His head is one of the most intellectual ones imaginable, and would serve as a good illustration in support of the theories of phrenology. The forehead broad and prominent; the mental organs largely developed; the eyes quick and intelligent; and the mouth full of benevolence.

AGED 52.

SOURCE: Marguerite, Countess of Blessington, *The Idler in Italy;* quoted by Malcolm Elvin in *Landor*, Macdonald, 1958.

He was a man of florid complexion, with large full eyes and altogether a *leonine* man, and with a fierceness of tone well suited to his name; his decisions, being confident, and on all subjects whether of taste or of life, unqualified ... But why should I trouble myself to describe him? He is painted by a master hand in Dickens' novel, Bleak House ...

AGED 55.

SOURCE: *Diary, Reminiscences and Correspondence of Henry Crabb Robinson*, 1869; quoted in Malcolm Elvin, *Landor*, Macdonald, 1958.

Note : The *Bleak House* reference is to the character of Mr. Boythorne, which Dickens based on Landor. He describes him 'with his head thrown back like an old soldier, his stalwart chest squared, his hands like a clean blacksmith's, and his lungs!—there's no simile for his lungs. Talking, laughing or snoring, they made the beams of the house shake . . . there was a sterling quality in this laugh, and in his vigorous healthy voice, and in the roundness and fulness with which he uttered every word he spoke, and in the very fury of his superlatives, which seemed to go off like blank cannons and hurt nothing . . . He was not only a very handsome old gentleman . . . with a massive grey head, a fine composure of face when silent, a figure that might have become corpulent but for his being so continually in earnest that he gave it no rest, and a chin that might have subsided into a double chin but for the vehement emphasis in which it was constantly required to assist; but he was such a true gentleman in his manner, so chivalrously polite, his face was lighted by a smile of so much sweetness and tenderness, and it seemed so plain that he had nothing to hide, but showed himself exactly as he was . . . that really I could not help looking at him with equal pleasure as he sat at dinner, whether he smilingly conversed . . . or threw up his head like a bloodhound, and gave out that tremendous Ha, ha, ha!'

LATIMER, HUGH (1485?–1555), bishop and martyr.

After him [Ridley] came Master Latimer in a poor Bristow frieze frock, all worn, with his buttoned cap, and a kerchief on his head all ready to the fire, a new long shroud hanging over his hose down to the feet; which at the first sight stirred men's hearts . . . Master Latimer . . . very quickly suffered his keeper to pull off his hose, and his other array, which to look unto was very simple; and being stripped unto his shroud, he seemed as comely a person to them that were present as one should lightly see; and whereas in his clothes he appeared a withered and crooked, silly old man, he now stood bolt upright, as comely a father as one might lightly behold.

AGED 70.

SOURCE: John Foxe, *Book of Martyrs*, 1563.

LAUD, WILLIAM (1573–1645), archbishop of Canterbury; impeached of high treason by the Long Parliament and beheaded, 1645.

One of low stature, but high parts; piercing eyes, cheerful countenance, wherein gravity and pleasantness were well compounded.

SOURCE: Thomas Fuller, *The Worthies of England*.

LAUDERDALE, EARL OF (1612–1682). See Maitland, John, second Earl and first Duke of Lauderdale.

LAWRENCE, SIR THOMAS (1769–1830), portrait painter, president of the Royal Academy.

As a man, Sir Thomas Lawrence was amiable, kind, generous and forgiving. His manner was elegant, but not high-bred. He had too much the air of always submitting. He had smiled so often and so long, that at last his smile had the appearance of being set in enamel.

SOURCE: Benjamin Haydon's *Autobiography*.

Note: See also entry for Siddons, Sarah.

LEAKE, SIR JOHN (1656–1720), admiral of the fleet.

Sir John Leake was of a middle stature, well set and strong, a little inclining to corpulency, but not so as to incommode in the least. His complexion was florid, his countenance open, his eye sharp and piercing, and his address both graceful and manly, denoting both the military man and the gentleman. As he had a good person he had also a good constitution, hardly ever knowing what it was to be sick. And though he took his bottle freely, as was the custom in his time in the fleet, yet he was never disguised, or impaired his health by it. His disposition was naturally cheerful and good-humoured . . . In his dress he was neat and plain, never very fine, being as free from ostentation and from vanity in all things, as from pride, which knew him not. In short, as to his person and natural qualities, he was what physicians define a perfect man; namely, he had a sound mind in a sound body.

SOURCE: Stephen Martin-Leake, *The Life of Sir John Leake*, Navy Records Society, 1920.

LEAR, EDWARD (1812–1888), artist and writer; author of 'Book of Nonsense'; gave drawing lessons to Queen Victoria.

He had an ingrained conviction that he was too ugly for any woman to accept him. No doubt he *was* ugly . . . and his plainness of face was made the more emphatic by his nearness of sight, awkward slouch, and a style of dress which can only be called careless by courtesy. He may have thought that dress was of no concern for one for whom it could do nothing.

SOURCE: R. E. Francillon, *Victorian Memories*.

LEWIS, MATTHEW GREGORY (1775–1818), writer; known as 'Monk' from his authorship of 'The Monk', 1795; friend of Scott.

. . . Matt, though a clever fellow, was a bore of the first description. Moreover, he looked always like a schoolboy . . . Matt had queerish eyes—they projected like those of some insects, and were flattish on the orbit.

SOURCE: Sir Walter Scott, *Journal*, pub. 1890.

LIDDELL, HENRY GEORGE (1811–1898), dean of Christ Church, Oxford; father of Lewis Carroll's 'Alice'.

In most people the Dean inspired awe . . . He disliked shyness in others, although he was the shyest of men himself. A certain aloofness of manner was the result, which could easily be broken down by meeting him with perfect straightforwardness . . . His relationship with his family was beautiful. They feared him not one whit, although he would at times reprimand them with asperity if they were inaccurate or made what he considered silly statements. It was a household of quite exceptional physical beauty. The Dean was as handsome a specimen of aristocratic manhood as could be seen in a lifetime.

Enoch Arden came out while I was staying with the Dean. He read it aloud in the evenings, and the other poems in the same volume, while I drew and the girls sewed. He read very splendidly with restrained dramatic force, and great feeling. He especially admired the sermon in Aylmer's Fields; and when Enoch comes back, looks in at the window, and sees the new husband and the wife of his youth among their children, he fairly broke down; the stern, strong man was moved beyond his power of restraint—for so it was with him—a very sensitive, tender, emotional nature was hidden under what many people thought a hard, critical exterior.

AGED ABOUT 52.

SOURCE: William Richmond, *The Richmond Papers*, Heinemann, 1926.

LIVINGSTONE, DAVID (1813–1873), missionary and explorer.

There is a group of respectable Arabs, and as I come nearer I see the white face of an old man among them. He has a cap with a gold band round it; his dress is a short jacket of red blanket cloth; and his pants—well, I didn't observe. I am shaking hands with him. We raise our hats, and I say, 'Doctor Livingstone, I presume?' and he says, 'Yes'.

AGED 58.

SOURCE: H. M. Stanley, *How I Found Livingstone*, 1872.

LLANDAFF, VISCOUNT (1826–1913). See Matthews, Henry, Viscount Llandaff.

LOVELACE, RICHARD (1618–1658), cavalier and poet.

Having by that time [i.e. after the execution of Charles I, and his release from imprisonment] consumed all his estate, he grew very melancholy . . . became very poor in body and purse, was the object of charity, went in ragged clothes (whereas when he was in his glory he wore cloth of gold and silver) and mostly lodged in obscure and dirty places, more befitting the worst of beggars and poorest of servants.

SOURCE: Anthony à Wood, *Athenæ Oxoniensis*.

LOWE, SIR HUDSON (1769–1844), lieutenant-general and governor of St. Helena during Napoleon's captivity there.

Saw Sir Hudson Lowe today in the streets. Micheli and an Italian had stopped me. Micheli's friend had sailed with and knew him. We all walked by, and then turned, and had a d——d good stare. He turned and looked fiercely at us, and gave us a good opportunity by crossing. A meaner face no assassin ever had. He answered Napoleon's description to a T.

AGED 63.

SOURCE: Benjamin Haydon's *Autobiography*.

His eye is that of a hyæna caught in a trap.

SOURCE: Napoleon.

LYTTON, BULWER (1803–1873). See Lytton, Edward George Earle Lytton Bulwer, first Baron Lytton.

LYTTON, EDWARD GEORGE EARLE LYTTON BULWER, first Baron Lytton (1803–1873), novelist.

In a dirty shirt and frayed trousers and stooping much, he looked 70 at least . . . Before dinner he apparently took a

M

pick-me-up, which infused new life into him. He came down in evening dress, as spruce as possible and seemingly twenty years younger than when he left us to dress . . . About 11, the power of the elixir, or whatever it was, seemed to wane. Lytton became again a bent old man, his talk flagged, and he faded away from us to work, for he was the most industrious of mortals and was said often to work half the night . . .

For a large part, his deafness prevented him from joining freely in the conversation, but with a few friends round him willing and eager to listen, I remember no talk like his. He was essentially a monologist, but Dickens—the only man who could perhaps have disputed the palm with him—used to call him the greatest conversationalist of the age.

AGED 58.

SOURCE: Frederick Lehmann; John Lehmann, *Ancestors and Friends*, Eyre and Spottiswoode, 1963.

MACAULAY, THOMAS BABINGTON, first Baron Macaulay (1800–1859), historian.

The moment he stood up to speak, Whigs and Tories crowded the benches of the House; without the external qualities of the orator, he produced great oratorial effect. On a massive bust (if it is thus he is represented) rose a strong and expressive head. His feet remained as if fixed to the ground. His left arm flung behind him while with his right, and by some abrupt movements, he seemed to push, as it were, his words before him.

AGED 32.

SOURCE: François Mignet; included in John Timbs, *A Century of Anecdote, 1760–1860*.

Macaulay was short, stout, and upright, with homely but expressive features, and a fine brow. He was physically clumsy, and, though he took a simple delight in gorgeous waistcoats, never learnt to tie his neckcloth or wield a razor with moderate skill. He never cared for bodily exercises and, when offered a horse at Windsor, said that if he rode it must be on an elephant. He enjoyed pedestrian rambles till his health gave way, but often read as he walked . . .

As an orator, he spoke without grace of voice or manner, but with an impetuosity and fulness of mind, and clearness of language which always dominated his hearers. Members of Parliament were carried away by the rare spectacle of a man of the highest literary fame who yet never soared out of their intellectual ken.

SOURCE: Leslie Stephen, *Dictionary of National Biography*, 1893.

Macaulay made one of those brilliant speeches, his third on the Reform question, which carried the House away in the same whirlwind of mixed passions which seemed to seize himself. Never was a more extraordinary compound of deep philosophy, exalted sentiments, and party bitterness enunciated with a warmth, a vigour, and rapidity inconceivable . . . The public can collect but little of its character from the papers.

SOURCE: E. J. Littleton; A. Aspinall (edit.), *Three Early Nineteenth Century Diaries*, Williams and Norgate, 1952.

McCLINTOCK, SIR FRANCIS LEOPOLD (1819–1907), admiral; commanded expedition in search of Sir John Franklin.

He had a short, slender, but wiry and muscular frame, well fitted for the endurance of long-continued exertion and hardships. Quick in his movements, as in his decisions, he was always quiet and perfectly calm, seeing everything done himself without noise or fuss. While all his orders were carried out promptly and everything was ready and in its place, M'Clintock included in his idea of duty consideration and kindness to everyone on board.

AGED 29.

SOURCE: Sir Clements Markham, *Life of Admiral Sir Leopold M'Clintock*.

MACQUEEN, ROBERT, Lord Braxfield (1722–1799), Scottish judge.

His very name makes people start yet. Strong built, and dark, with rough eyebrows, powerful eyes, threatening lips, and a low, growling voice, he was like a formidable blacksmith. His accent and his dialect were exaggerated Scotch; his language, like his thoughts, short, strong and conclusive.

SOURCE: Henry Cockburn, *Memorials of His Time*, 1856.

MAGEE, WILLIAM CONNOR (1821–1891), Archbishop of York.

Magee was a small, insignificant-looking man until he began to speak. Then all was forgotten except that a born orator was before you. I arrived in the House of Lords after he had been speaking [at the second reading of the Irish Church Bill] about ten minutes. It was an extraordinary sight. The House was packed from the floor to the highest point of the galleries, and in the midst of this magnificent Chamber and this huge audience there was a plain pigmy of a man speaking at a table. But so completely had he already dominated his audience with his tongue that a large proportion of them were unconsciously listening to him with open mouths, expressive of wonder and delight . . .

As he sat down, the staid decorum of the House of Lords vanished, and the House became a pandemonium of enthusiasm, for nearly the whole of the gallery rose up and cheered over and over again, whilst the applause in the House itself was so continuous that Lord Ripon, who followed him, had to wait ten minutes before he could be heard.

SOURCE: Lord George Hamilton, *Parliamentary Reminiscences and Reflections, 1868–1885*, John Murray, 1917.

MAITLAND, JOHN, second Earl and first Duke of Lauderdale (1616–1682), royalist.

He made a very ill appearance. He was too big; his hair red, hanging oddly about him. His tongue was too big for his mouth, which made him bedew all that he talked to; and his whole manner was rough and boisterous, and very unfit for a Court ... He was a man, as the Duke of Buckingham called him to me, of a blundering understanding. He was haughty beyond expression, abject to those he saw he must stoop to, but imperious to all others ... He was the coldest friend and the violentest enemy I ever knew.

SOURCE: Gilbert Burnet, Bishop of Salisbury; *History of My Own Time*, 1723–1724.

This lord was of a most extraordinary composition. He had learning and endowed with a great memory, as disagreeable in his conversation as was his person, his head was towards that of a Saracen fiery face, and his tongue was too big for his mouth, and his pronunciation high Scotch, no highlander like him, uttering bald jests for wit, and repeating good ones of others and ever spoiled them in relating them ... Besides tiring the king with his bald jests, he was continually putting his fingers into the king's snuff-box, which obliged him to order one to be made which he wore with a string on his wrist, and did not open, but the snuff came out by shaking.

SOURCE: *Memoirs of Thomas, Earl of Ailesbury, Written by Himself*, Roxburghe Club, 1890.

MANNERS, JOHN, Marquis of Granby (1721–1770), soldier.

Were there any reality in the idea that noble blood diffuses an air of superior excellence over the outward form, and refines the qualities of the mind; and were that idea not refuted by the majority of examples to the contrary, Lord Granby would have appeared a shining instance of both effects. His large and open countenance, its manly and pure colours glowing with health, his robust and commanding person, and a proportion of florid beauty so great that the baldness of his head, which he carried totally bare, was rather an addition to its comely roundness than a defect, and a singularity more than an affection; all distinguished him without any extrinsic ornament, and pointed out his rank when he walked without attendance, and was mixed with the lowest people, who followed him to beg his charity, or to bless him for it . . . He was dauntless on every occasion, but when it was necessary to surmount his bashfulness. His nerves trembled like a woman's when it was requisite that he should speak in public . . .

His domestic qualities were all of the amiable kind. His only remarkable vice proved fatal to him: his constant excess in wine inflaming his sanguine complexion . . .

AGED 49.

SOURCE: Horace Walpole, *Memoirs*, 1822–1845; for a convenient one-volume edition, see Horace Walpole, *Memoirs and Portraits*, edit. Matthew Hodgart, Batsford, 1963.

MARLBOROUGH, first Duke of (1650–1722). See Churchill, John, first Duke of Marlborough.

MARKHAM, SIR GRIFFIN (1564?–1644?), soldier and conspirator; participated in the 'Bye' Plot of 1603; convicted of high treason, but reprieved by James I when he was on the scaffold.

Sir Griffin Markham hath a large, broad face, of a black complexion, a big nose; one of his hands is maimed by a hurt in his arm, received by the shot of a bullet; he hath thin and little hair upon his beard. All his brethren are tall of stature, young, and without any hair of their faces, of exceeding swarthy and bad complexions, and all have very great noses.

SOURCE: Proclamation for his arrest, July 16, 1603.

MARVELL, ANDREW (1621–1678), poet.

He was of a middling stature, pretty strong set, roundish faced, cherry-cheeked, hazel eye, brown hair. He was in his conversation very modest, and of very few words.

SOURCE: John Aubrey, *Brief Lives*, edit. Andrew Clark, 1898.

MARY I (1516–1558), queen of England.

On the fourth instant [of May], all the ambassadors, with the exception of the Emperor's, were summoned to Greenwich . . . Two of the ambassadors . . . namely the prelate and the soldier, dined with the King, the others dining apart together. On rising from the table they went to the Queen's apartment, where the Princess danced with the French ambassador, the Viscount of Turennes, who considered her very handsome and admirable by reason of her great and uncommon mental endowments, but so thin, spare, and small as to render it impossible for her to be married for the next three years.

SOURCE: Sir Thomas Spinelly, ambassador in Flanders; quoted by
J. S. Brewer in *The Reign of Henry VIII*, edit. James Gairdner, 1884.

She is of low stature, but has no deformity in any part of her person. She is thin and delicate . . . Her features are well-formed and her looks are of a sedate and grave cast. Her eyes are so piercing as to command not only respect but awe from those on whom she casts them. Yet she is very near-sighted, being unable to read, or do anything else, without placing her eyes quite close to the object. Her voice is deep-toned and rather masculine, so that when she speaks she is heard some distance off.

SOURCE: Michiel, Venetian ambassador, *Despatches*, 1554–1557;
quoted in *Dictionary of National Biography*, edit. Sidney Lee, 1893.

She is of low stature, with a red and white complexion, and very thin; her eyes are white and large, and her hair reddish; her face is round, with a nose rather low and wide; and were not her age on decline she might be called handsome rather than the contrary. She is not of strong constitution and of late she suffered from headache and serious affectation of the heart . . . She seems to delight above all in arraying herself elegantly and magnificently . . . She also makes great use of jewels, in which she delights greatly.

AGED 38.

SOURCE: Giacomo Soranzo, Venetian ambassador, 1554.
Venetian Calendar, Public Record Office.

MARY, QUEEN OF SCOTS (1542–1587).

The said Queen of Scots being of stature tall, of body corpulent, round shouldered, her face full and broad, double chinned and hazel eyed and her borrowed hair was of auburn colour. Her attire was thus. On her head she had a dressing of lawn edged on both sides with bone lace, a pomander chain and an Agnus Dei about her neck, a crucifix in her hand and a pair of beads at her girdle with a golden cross at the end of them, a veil of lawn fastened to her caul bowed out with wire, edged round about with bone lace; her gown was of black satin printed, with a train and long sleeves to the ground, set with acorn buttons of jet trimmed with pearl, and short sleeves of black satin cut with a pair of sleeves of purple velvet, whole, under them. Her kirtle, whole of figured black satin; the upper body of her petticoat unlaced in the back which was of crimson satin, and her petticoat skirts of crimson velvet, her shoes of Spanish leather with the rough side outward, a pair of silk garters coloured green, her stockings worsted, coloured, watchet-clocked with silver and edged on the tops with silver, next her legs a pair of Kersey hose, white.

AGED 45.

SOURCE: A transcript, in the hand of Sir Simonds d'Ewes (1602–1650), of Wynkfielde's account of the execution of Mary, in the Essex Record Office; printed in A. C. Edwards, *English History from Essex Sources*, Essex Record Office Publications No. 17, 1952.

MARY OF MODENA (1658–1718), queen of James II.

The princess Mary of Este appeared to be at this time about fourteen years of age; she was tall and admirably shaped, her complexion was of the last degree of fairness, her hair black as jet, so were her eyebrows and her eyes, but the latter so full of light and sweetness as they did dazzle and charm too. There seemed given unto them by nature, sovereign power to kill, and power to save; and in the whole turn of her face, which was of the most graceful oval, there were all the features, all the beauty, and all that could be great and charming in any human creature.

AGED 14.

SOURCE: The Earl of Peterborough; quoted in Carola Oman, *Mary of Modena*, Hodder and Stoughton, 1962.

She hath very good eyes, very good features, and a very good complexion; but she wants the air which should set off all this; and having been bred in a monastery house knows not how to set one foot before another with any gracefulness.

AGED 15.

SOURCE: Lord Conway; quoted in Carola Oman, *Mary of Modena*, Hodder and Stoughton, 1962.

MATILDA (1080–1118), queen of Henry I.

Now it is true that this Matilda was brought up from early childhood in a convent of nuns and grew up there to womanhood, and many believed that she had been dedicated by her parents to God's service as she had been seen walking abroad wearing the veil like the nuns with whom she was living. This circumstance, when, long after she had discarded the veil, the King fell in love with her, set the tongues of many wagging and held back the two from embracing one another as they desired. Accordingly, as all were looking for a sign from Anselm on this question, the girl herself went to him and humbly besought his advice and help in the matter . . .

'But that I did wear the veil,' she said, 'I do not deny. For when I was quite a young girl and went in fear of the rod of my Aunt Christina, whom you knew quite well, she to preserve me from the lust of the Normans which was rampant and at that time ready to assault any woman's honour, used to put a little black hood on my head and, when I threw it off, she would often make me smart with a good slapping and most horrible scolding, as well as treating me as being in disgrace. That hood

I did indeed wear in her presence, chafing at it and fearful; but, as soon as I was able to escape out of her sight, I tore it off and threw it on the ground and trampled on it and in that way, although foolishly, I used to vent my rage and the hatred of it which boiled up in me. In that way, and only in that way, I was veiled, as my conscience bears witness.'

SOURCE: Eadmer, monk of Canterbury; *Historia Novorum in Anglia*, translated by Geoffrey Bosanquet, Cresset Press, 1964.

MATTHEWS, HENRY, Viscount Llandaff (1826–1913), lawyer and home secretary.

It is curious what an inherent dislike the average Englishman has to gesticulation or to what in the boxing ring would be known as 'foot movement' during a public speech. Mr. Henry Matthews (Lord Llandaff) was certainly one of the most eloquent and scholarly Parliamentary speakers of his time; but he gesticulated a great deal with his hands, and he wobbled with his knees. The result was that he never attained in the House of Commons the oratorical fame which his undoubted great powers entitled him to achieve. A lady who was an habituée of the Speaker's Gallery and a good judge of Parliamentary likes and dislikes, once said to me: 'If I could only bandage Mr. Matthews' knees before he made his next big speech, he would become and would be acknowledged to be one of the great orators in the House of Commons.

SOURCE: Lord George Hamilton, *Parliamentary Reminiscences and Reflections, 1862–1885*, John Murray, 1917.

MAXWELL, WILLIAM, fifth Earl of Nithsdale (1676–1744), Jacobite; taken prisoner at Preston and condemned to death; rescued from the Tower by his wife.

The Countess of Nithsdale brought the Earl out of the Tower by an ingenious piece of substitution, involving herself, her friend Mrs. Morgan, and her landlady Mrs. Mills. On the eve of his execution, the Earl was visited by the Countess and Mrs. Morgan, who had concealed about her some woman's garments, which she deposited in the cell. The Countess then escorted her back to the staircase, begging her in a loud voice to send her maid to her to help her dress, since she had to go to Court to present a last petition for her husband's life.

I despatched her safe, and went partly down the stairs to meet Mrs. Mills, who had the precaution to hold her handkerchief to her face, as was very natural for a woman to do when she was going to bid farewell to a friend on the eve of his execution. I had indeed desired her to do it, that my lord might go out in the same manner. Her eyebrows were rather inclined to be sandy, and my lord's were dark and very thick. However, I had prepared some paint of the colour of hers to disguise his with. I also brought an artificial head-dress of the same coloured hair as hers, and I painted his face with white, and his cheeks with rouge, to hide his long beard, which he had not had time to shave. All this provision I had before left in the Tower . . .

I made Mrs. Mills take off her own hood, and put on that which I had brought for her. I then took her by the hand, and led her out of my lord's chamber, and in passing through the next room, in which there were several people, with all the concern imaginable I said, 'My dear Mrs. Catherine, go in all haste and fetch me my waiting maid; she certainly cannot reflect how late it is; she forgets that I am to present a petition tonight, and if I let slip this opportunity I am undone, for tomorrow will be too late. Hasten her as much as possible, for I shall be on thorns till she comes.'

When I had seen her out I returned back to my lord, and finished dressing him. I had taken care Mrs. Mills did not go out crying as she came in, that my lord might the better pass for the lady who came in crying and affected; and the more so because he had the same dress she wore. When I had almost finished dressing my lord in all my petticoats, I perceived that it was growing dark, and was afraid that the light of the candles might betray us; so I resolved to set off. I went out leading him by the hand, and he held his handkerchief to his eyes. I spoke to him in the piteous and most afflicted tone of voice, bewailing bitterly the negligence of Evans, who had vexed me by her delay. Then said I, 'My dear Mrs. Betty, for the love of God run quickly and bring her with you. You know my lodging, and if you ever made despatch in your life, do it at present, I am almost distracted with this disappointment.' The guards opened the doors, and I went downstairs with him, still conjuring him to make all possible despatch.

As soon as he had cleared the door, I made him walk before me, for fear the sentinels should take notice of his walk; but I still continued to press him to make all the despatch he possibly could. At the bottom of the stairs I met my dear Evans, into whose hands I confided him . . .

In the meanwhile, as I had pretended to have sent the young lady on a message, I was obliged to return up stairs, and go back to my lord's room in some feigned anxiety of being too late, so that everybody seemed sincerely to sympathise with my distress. When I was in the room, I talked to him as if he had been really present, and answered my own questions in my lord's voice as nearly as I could imitate it; I walked up and down, as if we were conversing together, till I thought they had time enough thoroughly to clear themselves of the guards. I then thought proper to make off also. I opened the door and stood half in it, that those in the outward chamber might hear what I said; but held it close that they could not look in . . . Then, before I shut the door, I pulled through the string of the latch, so that it could only be opened on the inside. I then shut it with some degree of force, that I might be sure of its being well shut. I said to the servant as I passed by . . . that he need not carry in candles to his master till my lord send for them, as he desired to finish some prayers first. I went downstairs, and called a coach.

SOURCE: Winifred, Countess of Nithsdale; a letter written by the Countess to her sister, Abbess of the Augustine nuns at Bruges.

MAY, PHILIP WILLIAM, known as **PHIL MAY** (1864–1903), comic artist and cartoonist.

In appearance May was very slight and about five feet seven inches in height. His hair was cut straight across his forehead, and he wore very close-fitting garments, giving him somewhat the appearance of a jockey. He had a very observant eye, slightly hooked nose, and an expressive and mobile mouth. His manner was courteous and nearly always deferential; and he would 'suffer fools gladly' to a degree that I do not remember to have seen equalled.

SOURCE: Julian Ashton, *Now Came Still Evening On*, Angus and Robertson, Sydney, 1941; quoted in Birch and Macmillan, *The Sydney Scene, 1788–1960*, Melbourne University Press, 1962.

MELBOURNE, LORD (1779–1848), statesman.

His head was a truly noble one. I think, indeed, he was the finest specimen of manly beauty in the meridian of life I ever saw. Not only were his features eminently handsome, but his expression was in the highest degree intellectual. His laugh was frequent and the most joyous possible, and his voice so deep and musical, that to hear him say the most ordinary things was a pleasure. But his frankness, his freedom from affectation, and his peculiar humour, rendered almost everything he said, though it seemed perfectly natural, yet quite original.

AGED ABOUT 56.

SOURCE: Charles Robert Leslie, R.A., *Autobiographical Recollections*, edit. Tom Taylor, 1860.

... up started Lord Melbourne like an artillery rocket. He began in a fury. His language flowed out like fire. He made such palpable hits that he floored the Duke of Wellington as if he had shot him. But the moment the stimulus was over, his habitual apathy got ahead. He stammered, hemmed and hawed. But it was the most pictorial exhibition of the night. He waved his white hand with the natural grace of Talma; expanded his broad chest, looked right at his adversary, like a handsome lion, and grappled him with the grace of Paris.

AGED 54.

SOURCE: Benjamin Haydon's *Autobiography*.

MELVILLE, LORD (1742–1811). See Dundas, Henry, first Viscount Melville.

M.P.'s IN THE 18th CENTURY.

The Members of the House of Commons have nothing particular in their dress; they even come to the House in their great coats, and with boots and spurs. It is not at all uncommon to see a member lying stretched out on one of the benches, while others are debating. Some crack nuts, others eat oranges, or whatever else is in season.

SOURCE: Carl Philipp Moritz, *Travels, chiefly on foot, through several parts of England in 1782;* edit. P. E. Matheson, Humphrey Milford, 1924. (Reprint of 1795 English translation).

MEREDITH, GEORGE (1828–1909), novelist and poet.

The great man was talking to his dog. He was sitting to one side of the fire, dressed in a soft, quilted jacket, with a rug upon his knees. On a little rickety table by his side stood two candles and one of those old-fashioned eye-screens which flirt out green wings at a touch; a pile of lemon-coloured volumes lay beside it. His face beneath a tousled thatch of grey hair, soft as the finest wood-ash, and combed down into a fringe upon a high round forehead, had a noble, ravaged handsomeness. The vanity and delicacy ... which marks Watts' portrait of him was not discernible; rather a noteworthy boldness. I guessed him to be one of those men who seem bigger seated than when on their legs. At this time he could not rise from his chair. That keen look in profile, as of an upward-pointing arrow, had gone. Old age had blurred his eyelids, and his eyes, once blue, were faded and full of 'the empty untragic sadness of old age'; but that vitality which had inspired many a packed page still vibrated in his powerful voice, and told in the impetuosity of his greeting. His talk was full of flourishes and his enunciation grandiose, as though he loved the sound of his own words. This characteristic at first, I remember, somewhat disconcerted me. It struck me that he talked with a kind of swagger, and I was not prepared for that. Copy-book biographies always insist upon modesty as a sign of true greatness. I had certainly found out that humility was not the invariable accompaniment of power and insight, but I still clung to the idea that great men were always, as biographers say, 'simple'. Now, 'simple' Meredith was not, nor was he 'natural', 'unaffected'. . . . He was almost stone-deaf, which accounted for the exaggerated loudness of his voice, and the continuity of his discourse, which rolled elaborately along; but the eagerness with which he would now and again curve a hand round his ear and stoop forward to catch an interjection, showed that he was not a born monologist, and that he missed the give and take . . .

Had we tired him unconscionably, we asked ourselves anxiously outside the door? As I hoisted on my coat, I heard again that resonant rumble. He was talking to his dog.

SOURCE: Desmond MacCarthy, *Portraits*, Putnam, 1931.

MILL, JOHN STUART (1806–1873), philosopher.

In manner he was quiet and unassuming. His face gave constant evidence of the extent to which in later life, as in his earlier life, his nervous system had been overtaxed; for he had frequent twitchings of some facial muscles. Another trait of expression I can recall: there was a certain habitual setting of the lips implying, as it seemed to me, a conscious self-restraint. Too stern a discipline in his boyhood, and perhaps too serious a view of things in his later years, put, I think, an undue check on the display of pleasurable feelings. I do not remember his laugh; and my impression is that though he appreciated good things he did not laugh heartily.

AGED 59.

SOURCE: Herbert Spencer, *An Autobiography*, 1904.

MILTON, JOHN (1608–1674), poet.

Some people have lately nicknamed me 'the Lady'. But why do I seem to them too little of a man? I suppose because I have never had the strength to drink off a bottle like a prize-fighter; or because my hand has never grown horny with holding a plough handle; or because I was not a farm hand at seven, and so never took a midday nap in the sun—last perhaps because I never showed my virility the way those brothellers do. But I wish they could leave playing the ass as readily as I the woman.

AGED 20.

SOURCE: John Milton, *Vacation Exercise*, 1628.

His eyesight was decaying about 20 years before his death . . . His harmonical and ingenious soul did lodge in a beautiful and well-proportioned body. He was a spare man. He was scarce so tall as I am . . . of middle stature . . . He had auburn hair. His complexion exceeding fair—he was so fair that they called him *the Lady of Christ's College*. Oval face. His eye a dark gray.

He had a delicate tuneable voice and had good skill. Of a very cheerful humour.

SOURCE: John Aubrey, *Brief Lives*, edit. Andrew Clark, 1898.

He was of a moderate stature, and well proportion'd, of a ruddy complexion, light brown hair, and handsome features; save that his eyes were none of the quickest. But his blindness . . . added no further blemish to them. His deportment was sweet and affable; and his gait erect and manly, bespeaking courage and undauntedness . . . On which account he wore a sword while he had his sight, and was skill'd in using it. He had an excellent ear, and could bear a part both in vocal and instrumental music.

SOURCE: John Phillips(?); included by Helen Darbyshire (edit.) in *The Early Lives of Milton*, Constable, 1932; from a MS in the Bodleian.

MITFORD, MARY RUSSELL (1787–1855), writer and conversationalist.

What, indeed, should I do at a dance with my dumpling of a person tumbling about like a cricket-ball on uneven ground, or a bowl rolling among nine-pins—casting off with the grace of a frisky Yorkshire cow, or going down the middle with the majesty of an overloaded hay-waggon passing through a narrow lane. What should I do at a ball?

SOURCE: Mary Russell Mitford, on herself; *Correspondence.*

She enjoyed the sweets of popularity, and a pilgrimage to Three Mile Cross had become something of an institution ... very few ever went away disappointed from the narrow, comfortless presence-chamber of the grey-haired lady, who beamed upon her guests from that wonderful wall of a forehead, and welcomed them most cordially with a most admirable voice ... a very pathetic expression about her mouth and in her large, slowly moving, sad, grey eyes, though they lighted up every now and then with a glancing gleam of the drollest humour.

AGED ABOUT 65.

SOURCE: article in Chamber's *Cyclopaedia of English Literature,* edit. David Patrick, 1901.

MONCK or **MONK, GEORGE,** first Duke of Albemarle (1608–1670), soldier; restored Charles II.

He was of a very comely personage, his countenance very manly and majestic, the whole fabric of his body very strong, his constitution very healthful and fitted for business, before his sickness; he was never known to desire meat or drink till called to it, which was but once a day, and seldom drank but at his meal: he was of a great natural force; his eyes were a little deficient at a distance, but near hand very excellently useful, being able to the last to read the worst handwriting without spectacles; his ears were so quick that it was dangerous to whisper in the room without you would have him privy to your discourse; his judgment was slow but sure, he was very cogitative, and of great natural prudence and cunning in his own affairs ...

His temperance was remarkable ... I have known him fast

N

from eating and drinking above thirty hours many times upon the obligation of necessary and important affairs, and constantly made but one meal a day, and in that was not over curious, having been accustomed to the hardships of a soldier's life in his younger years. He was the most watchful person that you have heard of, four hours sleep was to him sufficient and full satisfaction . . .

All his pleasure was walking and conferring with a trusty friend in a spacious room, but if any the least business invited, he applied to it.

SOURCE: Thomas Gumble, *Life of General Monck, Duke of Albemarle*, 1671.

MONMOUTH, DUKE OF (1649–1685), leader of 1685 rebellion; defeated at Sedgemoor.

His face and the exterior graces of his person were such as nature has, perhaps, never bettered. His countenance was all charm; but it was a man's face and in no way insipid or effeminate. Still, every separate feature had its own attraction and its own particular delicacy. He had a great natural disposition for all kinds of exercise, a winning manner of approach, an air of mightiness; in fact, all the physical advantages spoke on his behalf, though, in this concert, the qualities of his mind were absolutely silent. He entertained no sentiment unless it had first been suggested to him; and those, who began by insinuating themselves into his familiarity, took care to inspire him with none but were pernicious. It was this dazzling exterior which made an impression on his arrival; it put into the shade all the previous good reputations at Court.

SOURCE: Anthony Hamilton, *Memoirs of the Comte de Gramont*, trans. Peter Quennell, George Routledge & Sons, 1930.

MONTAGU, or **MONTAGUE, MRS. ELIZABETH** (1720–1800), writer and leader of society; earned the title of 'blue-stocking', denoting a woman affecting learned or literary tastes, from the type of society that met at Montague House under her leadership.

At the time of which I speak, the 'Gens de Lettres' or 'Blue Stockings', as they were commonly denominated, formed a very numerous, powerful, compact phalanx in the midst of London ... Mrs. Montague, in 1776, verged towards her sixtieth year; but her person, which was thin, spare, and in good preservation, gave her an appearance of less antiquity. From the infirmities often attendant on advanced life, she seemed to be almost wholly exempt. All the lines of her countenance bespoke intelligence, and her eyes were accommodated to her cast of features, which had in them something satirical and severe, rather than amiable or inviting. She possessed great natural cheerfulness, and a flow of animal spirits; loved to talk, and talked well on almost every subject; led the conversation, and was qualified to preside in her circle, whatever subject of discourse was started; but her manner was more dictatorial and sententious, than conciliatory or diffident. There was nothing feminine about her, and though her opinions were usually just, as well as delivered in language suited to give them force, yet the organ which conveyed them was not musical. Destitute of taste in disposing the ornaments of her dress, she nevertheless studied or affected those aids, more than would seem to have become a woman professing a philosophic mind, intent on higher pursuits than the toilet. Even when approaching to fourscore, this female weakness still accompanied her; nor could she relinquish her diamond necklace and bows which ... formed, of evenings, the perpetual ornament of her emaciated person. I used to think that these glittering appendages of opulence sometimes helped to dazzle the disputants whom her arguments might not always convince, or her literary reputation intimidate.

SOURCE: Sir N. William Wraxall, *Historical Memoirs of My Own Life*, 1815.

MONTAGU, LADY MARY WORTLEY (1689–1762), writer and society leader.

Did I tell you that Lady Mary Wortley is here? She laughs at my Lady Walpole, scolds my Lady Pomfret, and is laughed at by the whole town. Her dress, her avarice, and her impudence must amaze any one that never heard her name. She wears a foul mob, that does not cover her greasy black locks, that hang loose, never combed or curled; an old mazarine blue wrapper, that gapes open and discovers a canvas petticoat. Her face swelled violently on one side . . . partly covered with a plaister, and partly with white paint, which for cheapness she has bought so coarse, that you would not use it to wash a chimney.

AGED 51.

SOURCE: Horace Walpole, in Florence; *Letters*.

Note: An attack of smallpox in December, 1715, left her without eyelashes and with a deeply pitted skin.

I found her in a little miserable bedchamber of a ready-furnished house, with two tallow candles, and a bureau covered with pots and pans. On her head . . . she had an old black-laced hood, wrapped entirely round, so as to conceal all hair, or want of hair. No handkerchief, but up to her chin a kind of horseman's riding-coat . . . made of dark-green brocade, with coloured and silver flowers, and lined with furs; bodice laced, a foul dimity petticoat, sprig'd, velvet muffeteens on her arms, grey stockings, and slippers. Her face less changed in twenty years than I could have imagined. I told her so, and she was not so tolerable twenty years ago that she need have taken it for flattery.

AGED 73.

SOURCE: Horace Walpole; quoted by John Timbs, *A Century of Anecdote, 1760–1860*.

MOORE, THOMAS (1779–1852), poet.

Moore's forehead was bony and full of character, with 'bumps' of wit, large and radiant enough to transport a phrenologist; Sterne had such another. His eyes were as dark and fine as you would wish to see under a set of vine-leaves; his mouth generous

and good-humoured, with dimples; and his manner as bright
as his talk, full of the wish to please and be pleased. He sang,
and played with great taste on the pianoforte, as might be
supposed from his musical compositions. His voice, which was a
little hoarse in speaking (at least I used to think so), softened
into a breath, like that of a flute, when singing. In speaking, he
was emphatic in rolling the letter *r*, perhaps out of a despair of
being able to get rid of the national peculiarity.

SOURCE: Leigh Hunt, *Autobiography*.

There is a manly frankness, and perfect ease and good breeding
about him which is delightful . . . Not the least touch of the
poet or the pedant. A little—very little man . . . to be sure, his
person is much stouter than that of M.G.L. ['Monk' Lewis],
his countenance is decidedly plain, but the expression is so
very animated, especially in speaking or singing, that it is far
more interesting than the finest features could have rendered it.

SOURCE: Sir Walter Scott, *Journal*, pub. 1890.

Whatever might be his peculiarities and his demands, however,
they were amply repaid by the brilliancy of his conversation
and the charm of his manners. He would now and then, when
entirely at his ease with well-known friends, give an imitation
of the great Irish orator, Curran, which those who had known
the original pronounced to be perfect, while those who had
never seen him were delighted with the wit and humour that
were introduced; but it was when the dinner was ended, the
drawing-room reached, and a few of his much-loved country-
women present, that the charm of Moore's society was felt.
Almost without an invitation he would unaffectedly sit down to
the pianoforte and warble forth some of those enchanting
melodies which he has given to a grateful nation, accompanying
himself with exquisite taste; his voice was rich in tone, and the
expression he threw into his own words, combined with his
beaming face and genial manner, elicited the admiration
of all.

SOURCE: Captain R. H. Gronow, *Reminiscences*.

MORE, HANNAH (1745–1833), religious writer.

Nothing can be conceived so absurd, extravagant, and fantastical, as the present mode of dressing the head. Simplicity and modesty are things so much exploded, that the very names are no longer remembered. I have just escaped from one of the most fashionable disfigurers; and though I charged him to dress me with the greatest simplicity, and to have only a very distant eye upon the fashion, just enough to avoid the pride of singularity, without running into ridiculous excess; yet in spite of all these sage didactics, I absolutely blush at myself, and turn to the glass with as much caution as a vain beauty, just risen from the smallpox.

AGED 30.

SOURCE: Hannah More, in a letter to her sister.

Elsewhere, Hannah describes a party where the girls present had, between them, on their heads 'an acre and a half of shrubbery, besides slopes, grass-plots, tulip-beds, clumps of peonies, kitchen gardens, and green houses.' Her friend David Garrick ridiculed the fashion, appearing on the stage with a fine crop of vegetables on his head, including 'glass cucumber frames, and a pendent carrot at each ear'.

MORE, SIR THOMAS (1478–1535), lord chancellor and author.

... in height and stature he is not tall, nor again noticeably short, but there is such symmetry in all his limbs as leaves nothing to be desired here. He has a fair skin, his complexion glowing rather than pale, though far from ruddy, but for a very faint rosiness shining through. His hair is of a darkish blond or, if you will, a lightish brown, his beard scanty, his eyes bluish grey with flecks here and there ... His expression corresponds to his character, always shewing a pleasant and friendly gaiety, and rather set in a smiling look.

His right shoulder seems a little higher than the left, particularly when he is walking; this is not natural to him but due to force of habit, like many of the little habits which we pick up. There is nothing to strike one in the rest of his body; only his hands are somewhat clumsy, but only when compared with the rest of his appearance. He has always from a boy been very careless of everything to do with personal adornment ... He likes to dress simply, and does not wear silk or purple or gold chains, excepting when it would not be decent not to wear them.

AGED 41.

SOURCE: Desiderius Erasmus, *Letter to Ulrich von Hutten*, 1519; included in J. Huizinga's *Erasmus of Rotterdam*, trans. Barbara Flower, Phaidon Press.

Then, as he was no tall man, so was he no notable low and little man; all the parts of his body were in as good proportion and congruence as a man would wish. His skin was somewhat white, and the colour of his face drew rather to whiteness than to paleness, far from redness, saving that some little thin red sparkles everywhere appeared. His hair was blackish yellow, or rather yellow blackish, his beard thin, his eyes grey and speckled, which kind of eyes do commonly betoken and signify a very good and sharp wit. And they say that such kind of eyes are least encumbered with diseases and faults. His countenance was conformable to his nature and disposition, pleasant and amiable, somewhat resembling and tending to the fashion of one that would laugh.

His voice was neither too boisterous and big, neither too small and shrill. He spake his words very distinctly ... without any manner of hastiness or stuttering. And albeit he delighted in all kind of melody, yet he seemed not of nature to be apt and meet to sing himself.

He enjoyed the health of his body full well; and though he were not very strong of body, yet was he able to go through with any labour and pain meet and convenient for him for to dispatch his business and affairs. He was very little infested and encumbered with sickness, saving a little before he gave over the office of the Lord Chancellor, and especially afterward, when he was shut up in the Tower.

SOURCE: Nicholas Harpsfield, *Life and Death of Sir Thomas Moore*, Early English Text Society, p. 141, 1932. Original Series No. 186 (reprinted 1963). Reproduced here with modernised spelling. Ed. E. V. Hitchcock and R. W. Chambers.

MORGAN, SIR HENRY (1635–1688), buccaneer; knighted and made lieutenant-governor of Jamaica.

Sir Henry Morgan, aged about 45*, lean, swallow-coloured, his eyes a little yellowish and belly jutting out or prominent, complained to me of want of appetite to victuals; he had a kicking or reaching to vomit every morning and generally a small looseness attending him, and withal was much given to drinking and sitting up late, which I supposed had been the cause of his present indisposition.

SOURCE: Sir Hans Sloane, *Voyage to the West Indies*, 1707; quoted by Kemp and Lloyd in *The Brethren of the Coast*, Heinemann, 1960.

MORGAN, SIR THOMAS (?–1679?), soldier.

Little Sir Thomas Morgan, the great soldier, was of mean parentage in Monmouthshire . . .
Sir John Lenthall told me that at the taking of Dunkirk, Marshall Turenne, and, I think, Cardinal Mazarin too, had a great mind to see this famous warrior. They gave him a visit, and whereas they thought to have found an Achillean or gigantic person, they saw a little man, not many degrees above a dwarf, sitting in a hut of turves, with his fellow soldiers, smoking a pipe about 3 inches (or near so) long . . .

SOURCE: John Aubrey, *Brief Lives*.

MORRIS, JANE (1839–1914), wife of William Morris.

Oh, *ma chère*, such a wife! *Je n'en reviens pas*—she haunts me still. A figure cut out of a missal—out of one of Rossetti's or Hunt's pictures—to say this gives but a faint idea of her, because when such an image puts on flesh and blood, it is an apparition of fearful and wonderful intensity. It's hard to say whether she's a grand synthesis of all the pre-Raphaelite pictures ever made—or they a 'keen analysis' of her—whether she's an original or a copy. In either case she is a wonder.

* Aged 53.

Imagine a tall lean woman in a long dress of some dead purple stuff, guiltless of hoops (or of anything else, I should say) with a mass of crisp black hair heaped into great wavy projections on each of her temples, a thin pale face, a pair of strange, sad, deep, dark, Swinburnian eyes, with great thick black oblique brows, joined in the middle and tucking themselves away under her hair, a mouth like 'Oriana' in our illustrated Tennyson, a long neck, without any collar, and in lieu thereof some dozen strings of outlandish beads.

SOURCE: Henry James, *Letters*.

MORRIS, WILLIAM (1834–1896), artist, writer, printer and craftsman.

He was the manliest fellow that ever tried to pull an effete society together. He had the roughness and the strength of a Norseman together with the tenderness, nay, even shyness, of a woman; a great, big, generous character, though a bit narrow from his thoughts running in a groove.

SOURCE: William Richmond; *The Richmond Papers*, Heinemann, 1926.

I cannot remember who first brought me to the old stable beside Kelmscott House, William Morris's house at Hammersmith, and to the debates held there upon Sunday evenings by the Socialist League ... I was a little disappointed in the house, for Morris was an ageing man content at last to gather beautiful things rather than to arrange a beautiful house ... I took to him because of some little tricks of speech and body that reminded me of my old grandfather in Sligo, but soon discovered his spontaneity and joy and made him my chief of men ... A reproduction of his portrait by Watts hangs over my mantelpiece with Henley's, and those of other friends. His grave, wide-open eyes, like the eyes of some dreaming beast, remind me of the open eyes of Titian's *Ariosto*, while the broad vigorous body suggests a mind that has no need of the intellect to remain sane, though it give itself to every fantasy ... A never idle man of great physical strength and extremely irascible—did he not fling a badly-baked plum-pudding through a window upon Christmas Day?—a man more joyous than any intellectual man of our world, he called himself 'the idle singer of an empty day'.

AGED ABOUT 55.

SOURCE: W. B. Yeats, *Autobiographies*, Macmillan, 1955.

MULGRAVE, LORD (1797–1863). See Phipps, Sir Constantine Henry, second Earl of Mulgrave.

MYTTON, JOHN (1796–1834), sportsman and eccentric.

The biceps muscle of his arm was larger than that of Jackson's, the celebrated pugilist's, and those of every other part of his body were equally exuberant and powerful. Unfortunately, however, for himself, and often so for his companions, he was . . . proud of displaying his strength; but fortunately for mankind he would not . . . be instructed in the art of boxing, or he would have been still more formidable with his fists. As it was, in a 'turn up', he was, what is called, a very awkward customer, and when he could get at him he knocked down his man as if he had been a nine-pin. But he was nearly ignorant of the science of self-defence, and, as I have already observed, never attempted to attain it. His bull-dog courage, however, added to his tremendous blow, enabled him to beat any ordinary man; and so well was his prowess known, that few ventured to encounter him.

He had not a handsome face, but by no means an unpleasing countenance; and, without having practised the graces, the air and character of the gentleman were strongly impressed on his carriage. His shoulders were finely formed, with a very expanded chest—height, about five feet nine inches; weight, varying in the last twelve years of his life from eleven to thirteen stone . . .

Never was constitution so murdered as Mr. Mytton's was;

for, what but one of adamant could have withstood the shocks, independent of wine, to which it was almost daily exposed? His dress alone would have caused the death of nine hundred of a thousand men who passed one part of the day and night in a state of luxury and warmth. We will take him from the sole of his shoe to the crown of his hat. He never wore any but the thinnest and finest silk stockings, with very thin boots or shoes, so that in winter he rarely had dry feet. To flannel he was a stranger, since he left off his petticoats. Even his hunting breeches were without lining; he wore one small waistcoat, always open in the front from about the second of the lower buttons; and about home he was as often without his hat as with one. His winter shooting wear was a light jacket, white linen trousers, without lining or drawers, of which he knew not the use; and in frost and snow he waded through all water that came in his way. Nor is this all. He would sometimes strip to his shirt to follow wild-fowl in hard weather, and once actually laid himself down on the snow in his shirt only to await their arrival at dusk . . .

Neither could any man I ever met in the field walk through the day with him, at his pace. I saw him on his own moor in Merionethshire, completely knock up two keepers (who accompanied him alternately), being the whole day bare-headed under a hot sun . . .

Himself and a friend left London together with eighteen pounds of filbert-nuts in his carriage, and they devoured them all before they arrived at Halston. To use his own words, they sat up to their knees in nut-shells. But it was often alarming to witness the quantity of dry nuts he would eat, with the quantity of port wine which he would drink . . . Among other peculiarities, he never carried a pocket-handkerchief, for he never had occasion for the use of one; he very rarely wore gloves, for his hands were never cold; and although he never wore a watch, he always knew the hour.

SOURCE: Charles James Apperley ('Nimrod'), *Memoirs of the Life of John Mytton.*

Note: Despite the sparsity of the clothing worn by Mytton, he owned plenty. Apperley once counted a hundred and fifty-two pairs of breeches and trousers in his wardrobe, with a corresponding number of coats and waistcoats. Not that, apparently, he ever made any attempt to match his garments, but threw on what ever came to hand 'or as his wild fancy prompted him.'

NASH, JOHN (1752–1835), architect; laid out Regent's Park, etc.

... I have your figure before my eyes, a thin, black shadow standing on the foundation walls of the new arcade, with arms folded, contemplating the mode of laying bricks. Oh that I had leisure for such contemplation, and that some friend could describe my thick, squat, dwarf figure, with round head, snub nose and little eyes, in such an act of contemplation ...

SOURCE: John Nash, in a letter to Sir John Soane, September 1822; quoted by John Summerson, in *John Nash, Architect to George IV*. Allen and Unwin, 1935.

NASH, RICHARD, called 'Beau Nash' (1674–1762), leader of fashion and 'king of Bath'.

Of a black-brown complexion that gives a strength to your looks, suited to the elastic force of your nervous fibres and muscles. You have strength and agility to recommend you to your sex, and great comeliness of person to keep you from being disagreeable to the other.

AGED 49.

SOURCE: Anonymous pamphlet addressed to Nash. The writer of this pamphlet gives Nash's height as five foot eight, to which his 'diameter' is 'exactly proportioned'. The chief feature of Nash's costume was a white, or cream-coloured, tricorne hat, worn well forward and touching his right eyebrow. His coat was a sober brown, unbuttoned to show his flowered waistcoat which, in turn, was unbuttoned to show his shirt. His wig was black, in sharp and deliberate contrast to the white hat.

NEATE, BILL (fl. 1820), prize-fighter.

He rolled along, swathed in his loose great-coat, his knock-knees bending under his huge bulk; and, with a modest cheerful air, threw his hat into the ring ... I saw his teeth clenched together and his brows knit close against the sun. He held out his arms at full length straight before him, like two sledge-hammers, and raised his left an inch or two higher.

SOURCE: William Hazlitt, *New Monthly Magazine*, February 1822. See also entry for Tom Hickman.

NELSON, LADY FRANCES (1768–1831), wife of Admiral Lord Nelson.

Lady Nelson appeared in white, with a violet satin head dress and a small white feather. Her ladyship's person is of a very pleasing description; her features are handsome and exceedingly interesting, and her general appearance is at once prepossessing and elegant.

SOURCE: Lord Minto. Sir Gilbert Elliot, first Earl of Minto, was viceroy of Corsica, 1794–1796, minister plenipotentiary at Vienna and later, governor-general of India.

NELSON, HORATIO, Viscount (1758–1805), vice-admiral.

Captain Nelson appeared to be the merest boy of a captain I have ever beheld. He had on a full-faced uniform; his lank, unpowdered hair was tied in a stiff Hessian tail of extraordinary length; the old-fashioned flaps of his waistcoat added to the quaintness of his figure, and produced an appearance which particularly attracted my notice. There was something irresistibly pleasing in his address and conversation, and an enthusiasm when speaking on professional subjects that showed he was no common being.

AGED 24.

SOURCE: Prince William Henry, afterwards William IV; quoted in Lord Charles Beresford, *Nelson and his Times*, Harmsworth Bros.

I often found myself in the company of this odd pair, and Lady Hamilton never stopped talking, singing, laughing, gesticulating and mimicking, while the favoured son of Neptune appeared to leave her no more than did her shadow, trying to meet with his own small eyes the great orbs of his beloved, and, withal, as motionless and silent as a monument, embarrassed by his poor figure and by all the emblems, cords and crosses with which he was be-decked. In a word, the Lord of the Nile seemed as clumsy and dim on land as he is adroit and notable at sea.

AGED 42.

SOURCE: Franz Collenback (1800); quoted in *A Portrait of Lord Nelson*, Oliver Warner, Chatto and Windus, 1958.

... one of the most insignificant figures I ever saw in my life. His weight cannot be more than seventy pounds, and a more miserable collection of bones and wizened frame I have never yet come across. His bold nose, the steady eye and the solid worth revealed in his whole face betray in some measure the great conqueror. He speaks little, and then only English, and he hardly ever smiles. I have no doubt of his high ability, but cannot look without astonishment at his slender body, although this can, of course, have no immediate connection with a great soul. He was almost covered with orders and stars.

AGED 42.

SOURCE: An onlooker at Dresden (1800); quoted in *A Portrait of Lord Nelson*, Oliver Warner, Chatto and Windus, 1958.

Nelson is covered with stars, ribbons and medals more like a Prince of an Opera than the Conqueror of the Nile. It is really melancholy to see a brave and good man, who has deserved well of his country, cutting so pitiful a figure.

AGED 41.

SOURCE: Sir John Moore, during a visit to Palermo.

He was then very ill, and neither in look nor dress betokened the naval hero, having on a pair of drab green breeches, and high black gaiters, a yellow waistcoat, and a plain blue coat, with a cocked hat, quite square, a large green shade over the eye, and a gold-headed stick in his hand . . .

AGED 47.

SOURCE: Sir John Theophilus Lee, *Memoirs of the Life and Services of Sir John Theophilus Lee of the Elms, Hampshire*, 1836.

NEWCASTLE, DUCHESS OF (1624?–1674). See Cavendish, Margaret, Duchess of Newcastle.

NEWCASTLE, DUKE OF (1592–1676). See Cavendish, William, Duke of Newcastle.

NEWCASTLE, DUKE OF (1693–1768). See Pelham-Holles, Thomas, first Duke of Newcastle.

NEWMAN, JOHN HENRY (1801–1890), cardinal and writer.

His appearance was striking. He was above middle height, slight and spare. His head was large, his face remarkably like that of Julius Caesar. The forehead, the shape of the ears and nose, were almost the same. The lines of the mouth were very peculiar, and I should say exactly the same. I have often thought of the resemblance, and believed that it extended to the temperament.

SOURCE: J. A. Froude, 'The Oxford Counter-Reformation', in *Short Studies on Great Subjects*, 1883.

Had any one met Newman walking in the streets of a large town, he would have passed along without attracting attention. A spare, ascetic-looking man, there was otherwise nothing striking in his appearance. His rooms in Oriel were small and simple, books piled here and there. And yet that unobtrusive figure . . . set afloat a literature and enrolled an army of followers that shook the English Church to an extent not known since the Reformation . . .

He was small and spare, his voice clear, but his delivery a monotone; he never raised his eyes from the manuscript, not the slightest action or gesture, nor was there anything attractive in his style, no rhetorical arts; the language was simply good Saxon English. And yet 800 young men would be listening in rapt attention.

SOURCE: Richard W. Hiley, *Memories of Half a Century*, Longmans, Green & Co., 1899.

I seem to see John Henry Newman, standing (to use a familiar phrase) bolt upright in the pulpit, with spectacles on nose, with arms as it were pinned to his side, never using the slightest action except to turn over the leaves of his sermon, trusting entirely for effect to the modulation of a voice most melodious, but ranging, I believe, through a very limited scale, yet rivetting the attention of his hearers as if they were spellbound . . . We marvelled how so little apparent effort was followed by effects so great and permanent.

SOURCE: Dean H. G. Liddell; Rev. Henry Thompson, *Henry George Liddell, D.D.—A Memoir*, John Murray, 1899.

NEWTON, SIR ISAAC (1642–1727), mathematician and natural philosopher.

His carriage then was very meek, sedate and humble, never seemingly angry, of profound thought, his countenance mild, pleasant and comely. I cannot say I ever saw him laugh but once . . . He always kept close to his studies, very rarely went a-visiting, and had as few visitors . . . I never knew him to take any recreation or pastime either in riding out to take the air, walking, bowling, or any other exercise whatever, thinking all hours lost that was not spent in his studies, to which he kept so close that he seldom left his chamber except at term time, when he read in the schools as being Lucasianus Professor, where so few went to hear him, and fewer that understood him, that oftimes he did in a manner, for want of hearers, read to the walls. So intent, so serious upon his studies, that he ate very sparingly, nay oftimes he has forgot to eat at all . . . of which, when I have reminded him, he would reply—'Have I?', and then making to the table, would eat a bite or two standing, for I cannot say I never saw him sit at table by himself . . . I cannot say I ever saw him drink either wine, ale, or beer, excepting at meals, and then but very sparingly. He very rarely went to dine in hall, except on some public days, and then if he has not been minded, would go very carelessly, with shoes down at heels, stockings untied, surplice on, and his head scarcely combed . . .

At some seldom times when he designed to dine in hall, would turn to the left hand and go out into the street, when making a stop when he found his mistake, would hastily turn back, and then sometimes instead of going into the hall, return to his chamber again . . .

When he was about 30 years of age his grey hairs was very comely, and his smiling countenance made him so much the more graceful.

SOURCE: Humphrey Newton, Letters written in 1728 to John Conduit, Master of the Mint; included in L. T. More's *Isaac Newton*, 1934.

NIGHTINGALE, FLORENCE (1820–1910), nursing reformer.

She is tall; very slight and willowy in figure; thick, shortish rich brown hair; very delicate colouring; grey eyes which are generally pensive and drooping, but which when they choose can be the merriest eyes I ever saw; and perfect teeth, making her smile the sweetest I ever saw. Put a long piece of soft net, say 1¼ yards long and half a yard wide, and tie it round this beautifully shaped head, so as to form a soft white framework for the full oval of her face (for she had the toothache and so wore this little piece of drapery) and dress her up in black silk high up to the long white round throat, and a black shawl on and you may get NEAR an idea of her perfect grace and lovely

o

appearance . . . She has a great deal of fun, and is carried along by that, I think. She mimics most capitally . . .

AGED 34.

SOURCE: Mrs. Gaskell; quoted in Cecil Woodham-Smith, *Florence Nightingale*, Constable, 1950.

The magic of her power over men was felt in the room . . . where operations took place. There perhaps the maimed soldier if not yet resigned to his fate, might be craving death rather than meet the knife of the surgeon, but when such a one looked and saw that the honoured Lady in Chief was patiently standing beside him—and with lips closely set and hands folded—decreeing herself to go through the pain of witnessing pain, he used to fall into the mood of obeying her silent command and—finding strange support in her presence—bring himself to submit and endure.

SOURCE: A. W. Kinglake; quoted in Cecil Woodham-Smith's *Florence Nightingale*, Constable, 1950.

Miss Nightingale was a most impressive person. I used to see much of her at Claydon House where she stayed with Sir Henry Verney and her sister Lady Verney, and it was there that I painted her, and somehow I like that picture of mine because it is quite truthful. Miss Nightingale was not a beautiful woman. She was sad-looking, consumed with an ideal which she could not reach. She had a great mind which, while it saw all round a subject, did not let this cripple conviction and action . . .

Miss Nightingale did inspire awe, not because one felt afraid of her *per se*, but because the very essence of *Truth* seemed to emanate from her, and because of her perfect fearlessness in telling it.

SOURCE: William Richmond; *The Richmond Papers*, Heinemann, 1926.

NITHSDALE, EARL OF (1676–1744). See Maxwell, William, fifth Earl of Nithsdale.

NOLLEKENS, JOSEPH (1737–1823), sculptor.

I must indulge in a comparison between the general appearance of Mr. and Mrs. Nollekens, certainly not cheek-by-jowl, but by the simile of placing a pair of compasses and a short pair of callipers side by side; the first opened at ten degrees, or perhaps not quite so much, the latter at full fifteen ... In the way in which the compasses and callipers will appear, when opened at the above degrees, so Mr. and Mrs. Nollekens' figures may be conceived: the lady with legs tall, thin and straight, the gentleman with limbs short and bowed: thus proportioned, they would slowly move, on a Sunday morning, till they arrived at a certain corner of Mortimer street, where they then parted, the one turning to the right, the other to the left: he to the Roman Catholic chapel, and she to the Protestant church ...

His figure was short, his head big, and it appeared much increased by a large-crowned hat, of which kind he was very fond; but his dress-hat, which he always sported when he went to Court, or to the Academy dinners, was nearly flat, and he brought it from Rome. His neck was short, his shoulders narrow, his body too large, particularly in the front lower part ... he was bow-legged and hook-nosed—indeed, his leg was somewhat like his nose, which resembled the rudder of an Antwerp packet-boat—his lips were rather thin, but between his brows there was great evidence of study. He was very fond of his ruffles, and contined to wear them long after they had become unfashionable; indeed, until they were worn out. A drab was his favourite colour, and his suit was generally made from the same piece; though now and then he would treat himself with a striped Manchester waistcoat, of one of which he was so fond that he sat to Abbot for his portrait in it ... His dress-stockings were also rather remarkable, being ornamented with blue and white stripes ...

SOURCE: John Thomas Smith, *Nollekens and his Times*, 1828.

NORTH, CHRISTOPHER (1785–1854). See Wilson, John.

NORTH, FREDERICK, second Earl of Guilford, usually known
as Lord North (1732–1792), statesman.

Frederick, Lord North, eldest son of the Earl of Guilford, was
now in the thirty-eighth year of his age. Nothing could be more
coarse or clumsy or ungracious than his outside. Two large
prominent eyes that rolled about to no purpose (for he was
utterly short-sighted), a wide mouth, thick lips and inflated
visage, gave him the air of a blind trumpeter. A deep untune-
able voice, which, instead of modulating, he enforced with
unnecessary pomp, a total neglect of his person, and ignorance
of every civil attention, disgusted all who judge by appearance,
or without their approbation till it is courted. But within that
rude casket were enclosed many useful talents. He had much
wit, good humour, strong natural sense, assurance and prompt-
ness . . . What he did, he did without a mask, and was not
delicate in choosing his means.

SOURCE: Horace Walpole, *Memoirs*, 1822–1845.

In his person he was of the middle size, heavy, large, and much
inclined to corpulency. There appeared in the cast and
formation of his countenance, nay, even in his manner, so
strong a resemblance to the royal family that it was difficult
not to perceive it. Like them, he had a fair complexion, regular
features, light hair, with bushy eyebrows, and grey eyes,
rather prominent in his head. His face might indeed be esteemed
a caricature of the King . . .

His tongue being too large for his mouth, rendered his
articulation somewhat thick, though not at all indistinct. He
did not bedew his hearers while addressing them, as Burnet
tells us the Duke of Lauderdale, so well known under Charles
the Second's reign, always did in consequence of the faulty
conformation of his tongue. In Parliament, the deficiency of
Lord North's sight was productive to him of many inconveni-
ences. For, even at the distance of a few feet, he saw very
imperfectly; and, across the House, he was unable to distinguish persons with any degree of accuracy. In speaking, walking,
and every motion, it is not enough to say that he wanted grace:

he was to the last degree awkward. It can hardly obtain belief that, in a full House of Commons, he took off on the point of his sword the wig of Mr. Welbore Ellis, and carried it a considerable way across the floor, without ever suspecting or perceiving it. The fact happened in this manner. Mr. Ellis, who was then Treasurer of the Navy, and well advanced towards his seventieth year, always sat at the lowest corner of the Treasury Bench, a few feet removed from Lord North. The latter having occasion to go down the House, previously laid his hand on his sword, holding the chase of the scabbard forward, nearly in a horizontal direction. Mr. Ellis, stooping at the same instant that the First Minister rose, the point of the scabbard came exactly in contact with the Treasurer of the Navy's wig, which it completely took off and bore away. The accident, however ludicrous, was wholly unseen by Lord North, who received the first intimation of it from the involuntary bursts of laughter that it occasioned in quarter of the House. Mr. Ellis, however, without altering a muscle of his countenance, and preserving the most perfect gravity in the midst of the general convulsion, having received back his wig, readjusted it to his head, and waited patiently till the House had recovered from the effect of so extraordinary, as well as ridiculous, occurrence.

In addition to his defect of sight, Lord North was subject likewise to a constitutional somnolency, which neither the animated declamations of Fox, nor the pathetic invocations of Burke, nor the hoarse menaces of Barré, could always prevent. It attacked him even on the Treasury Bench, sometimes with irresistible force. Nor was he always exempt from its influence in private society.

SOURCE: Sir N. William Wraxall, *Historical Memoirs of My Own Life*, 1815.

NORTH, LORD (1732–1792). See North, Frederick, second Earl of Guilford.

OATES, TITUS (1649–1705), rogue and perjurer; invented the 'Popish Plot'.

He was a low man, of an ill cut, very short neck, and his visage and features were most particular. His mouth was the centre of his face, and a compass there would sweep his nose, forehead and chin within the perimeter.

SOURCE: Roger North, *Examen, or an Inquiry into the Credit and Veracity of a pretended Complete History.*

O'CONNELL, DANIEL (1775–1847), Irish politician.

At twelve I went to O'Connell's, and certainly his appearance is very different from what it is in the House of Commons. It was, on the whole, hilarious and good-natured. But there was a cunning look. He has an eye like a weasel. Light seemed hanging at the bottom, and he looked out with a searching ken . . .

After a few moments O'Connell rolled in in a morning-gown, a loose black handkerchief tied round his neck . . . a wig, and a foraging-cap bordered with gold lace.

AGED 59.

SOURCE: Benjamin Haydon's *Autobiography.*

OLD PRETENDER (1688–1766). See Stuart, James Francis Edward.

OUIDA (pseudonym) (1839–1908). See De La Ramée, Marie Louise.

PALMER, ELEANOR, LADY (1720–1818) Irish beauty, wife of Sir Roger Palmer, M.P.

The celebrated Miss Ambrose, of this kingdom, has, to the much-envied happiness of *one* and the grief of *thousands*, abdicated her maiden empire of beauty, and retreated to the temple of Hymen. Her husband is Roger Palmer, Esq., of Castle Lacken, Co. Mayo, M.P.

AGED 32.

SOURCE: Notice in a Dublin paper, 1752.

The admiration which Lord Chesterfield is known to have entertained for this lady induced me to seek an introduction to her. Although rich, she occupied a small lodging in Henry Street, where she lived, secluded and alone. Over the chimney-piece of the front drawing-room was suspended the picture of her Platonic idolator. It was a half-length portrait, and had, I believe, been given to her by the man of whose adoration she was virtuously vain. I was engaged looking at this picture, while I waited, on the day of my first introduction, for this pristine beauty of the Irish Court . . . I fell into a somewhat imaginative train of thought, and asked myself what sort of woman 'the dangerous Papist' must have been, in whom the master of the Graces had found such enchanting peril. 'What a charm,' I said, 'must she have possessed, upon whose face and form those bright eyes reposed in illuminated sweetness—how soft and magical must have been the voice, on whose whispers those lips have hung so often . . . what an easy dignity of deportment, what elegance of movement, what sweet vivacity of expression, how much polished gaiety and bewitching sentiment, must have been united!'

I had formed to myself an ideal image of the young, the soft, the fresh, the beautiful, and tender girl who had fascinated the magician of so many spells! The picture was complete . . . and I almost saw my Lord Chesterfield conducting Lady Palmer through the movements of a minuet, when the door was slowly opened, and in the midst of a volume of smoke, which, during my phantasmagoric imaginations, had not inappropriately filled the room, I beheld, in her own proper person, the being in whose ideal creation I had indulged in a sort of Pygmalian dream. The opening of the door produced a rush of air, which caused the smoke to spread out in huge wreaths about her, and a weird and withered form stood in the midst of the dispersing vapour. She fixed upon me a wild and sorceress eye, the expression of which was aided by her attitude, her black attire, her elongated neck, her marked and strongly moulded but emaciated features. She leaned with her long arm, and her withered hand of discoloured parchment, upon an ivory-headed cane, while she stretched forth her interrogating face ...

Upon the wrongs of her country, she spoke not only with energy, but with eloquence; and with every pinch of snuff, poured out a sentence of sedition ... as she lifted her figure from the stoop of age, with her eyes flashing with fire, and struck her cane violently on the ground.

AGED 98.

SOURCE: quoted in Sir Bernard Burke's *The Rise of Great Families*, 1873.

PALMER, SAMUEL (1805–1881), landscape painter.

Mr. Palmer regarded all life with a profound seriousness. At Shoreham he affected an eccentricity of dress which was much remarked. He had been endowed by nature with a wide and somewhat broad forehead, and he cultivated a flowing beard, a thing almost unheard of in those days when young men went clean-shaven. He likewise wore a cloak which fell almost to his heels, adding fictitiously to his age, and giving him the appearance of a sage. A fine musician, with a powerful tenor voice, he indulged this in odd moments, and so searching were the notes with which he assailed the empyrean that, while he was singing on one of the highest hills above Shoreham, his voice could be heard ringing in the valley below.

AGED ABOUT 22.

SOURCE: A. M. W. Stirling, *The Richmond Papers*, William Heinemann, 1926.

PARKER, RICHARD (1767?–1797), mutineer; led the mutiny at the Nore, and hanged.

The usual forms being gone through, Parker was put on his trial, being then between thirty and forty years of age, about five feet ten inches in stature, of prominent and manly features, but not expressing any degree of mental faculties or acuteness; his hair and eyes dark, and complexion sallow; his appearance was more that of a rude mechanic than a thorough-bred seaman. He was dressed in a blue coat and trousers, a light coloured waistcoat, white cravat and half-boots. His deportment was more cool than collected; and if that, as well as the tone of his voice, are thought to be indications of his character, he had neither a ferocious nor obdurate disposition.

SOURCE: *An Impartial History of the War, from the Commencement of the Revolution in France* . . ., Manchester, 1811.

PARNELL, CHARLES STEWART (1846–1891), political leader.

From the time he entered the House of Commons in 1876 up to the dissolution in 1880, Parnell made his personality more and more felt. Of all the many distinguished men in politics with whom I came in contact, he was the most inscrutable and original. There was a touch of unreason almost amounting to insanity on both sides of his parentage. He had not a symptom of the attributes usually associated with Irishmen—no geniality, no sense of humour, no idea of give-and-take, and no imagination. He was stern, concentrated, inflexible, and unscrupulous. He won his way by sheer determination and a total disregard of all the amenities and obligations of Parliamentary life . . . He was an aristocrat by instinct, and the stronger he became the more haughty and stand-off was his attitude towards his followers. To those with whom he came in personal political contact he will always be an enigma. He was the very essence of concentration and determination . . .

SOURCE: Lord George Hamilton, *Parliamentary Reminiscences and Reflections, 1868–1885*, John Murray, 1917.

PARSONS, WALTER (fl. 1620), porter to James I; renowned for his enormous height.

Walter Parsons, born in this county [Staffordshire], was first apprenticed to a smith, when he grew so tall in stature that a hole was made for him in the ground, to stand therein up to the knees, so to make him adequate with his fellow-workmen. He afterwards was porter to King James; seeing as gates generally are higher than the rest of the building, so it was sightly that the porter should be taller than other persons. He was proportionable in all parts, and had strength equal to height, valour to his strength, temper to his valour, so that he disdained to do an injury to any single person. He would make nothing to take two of the tallest yeomen of the guard . . . under his arms at once, and order them as he pleased.

SOURCE: Thomas Fuller, *The Worthies of England.*

PATER, WALTER HORATIO (1839–1894), author and critic.

As to Walter Pater, whom some literary folk in London seemed to take quite seriously, he was of little account in Oxford, being regarded a *poseur*, not at all as a leader of thought . . . I always wondered why he seemed to have left more impression in the world outside Oxford than his contemporary Andrew Lang—a much more brilliant and attractive figure . . . Pater I only met once or twice; he talked in a precious style, and absorbed the conversation.

SOURCE: Sir Charles Oman, *Memories of Victorian Oxford*, Methuen, 1941.

Since he abjured affairs and shrank from teaching, he attracted little notice in the University. Moreover, his personal appearance was most misleading. Who would have suspected that the trim figure with heavy military moustache, dressed as for Piccadilly, who from time to time emerged from Brasenose, was the archpriest of aesthetic culture? . . . Withdrawn into his own private world of beauty, Pater was content that the whirling stream of our vulgar life should pass him by.

SOURCE: H. A. L. Fisher, *An Unfinished Autobiography*, O.U.P., 1940.

PECKE, SAMUEL (17th century), journalist.

...a bald-headed buzzard, a tall, thin-faced fellow, with a hawk's nose, a meagre countenance and long runagate legs, constant in nothing but wenching, lying and drinking.

SOURCE: A rival journalist; quoted by C. V. Wedgwood in *The Trial of Charles I* from Frank's *The Beginning of the English Newspaper*, 1962.

PEEL, SIR ROBERT, second baronet (1788–1850), statesman.

Sir Robert Peel was a very good-looking man, who though of latter years he had become portly, had to the last a comely presence. Thirty years ago, when he was young and lithe, with curling brown hair, he had a very radiant expression of countenance. His brow was very distinguished, not so much for its intellectual development, although that was of a very high order, as for its remarkably frank expression, so different from his character in life. The expression of the brow might even be said to amount to beauty. The rest of the features did not, however, sustain this impression. The eye was not good; it was sly, and he had an awkward habit of looking askance. He had the fatal defect of a long upper lip, and his mouth was compressed.

SOURCE: Disraeli, *Life of George Bentinck;* quoted in W. F. Monypenny and G. E. Buckle, *Life of Benjamin Disraeli*, John Murray, 1929.

PELHAM-HOLLES, THOMAS, first Duke of Newcastle (1693–1768), politician.

His person was not naturally despicable; his incapacity, his mean soul, and the general low opinion of him, grew to make it appear ridiculous. A constant hurry in his walk, a restlessness of place, a borrowed importance, and real insignificance, gave him the perpetual air of a solicitor, though he was perpetually solicited; for he never conferred a favour till it was wrested from him, but often omitted doing what he most wished done.

This disquiet and habit of never finishing, which, too, proceeded frequently from his beginning everything twenty times over, gave rise to a famous *bon mot* of Lord Wilmington . . . He said, the Duke of Newcastle always loses half an hour in the morning, which he is running after the rest of the day, without being able to overtake it.

AGED 58.

SOURCE: Horace Walpole, *Memoirs*, published 1822–1845.

PEPYS, SAMUEL (1633–1703), diarist.

Had Sarah to comb my head clean, which I found so foul with powdering and other troubles, that I am resolved to try how I can keep my head dry without powder; and I did also in a sudden fit cut off all my beard, which I had been a great while bringing up, only that I may with my pumice stone do my whole face as I now do my chin, and so save time, which I find a very easy way, and gentle.

AGED 29.

This morning I put on my best black cloth suit, trimmed with scarlet ribbon, very neat, with my cloak lined with velvet, and a new beaver, which altogether is very noble, with my black silk canons I bought a month ago.

AGED 29.

My eyes beginning every day to grow less and less able to bear with long reading and writing, though it be by daylight, which I never observed till now.

AGED 30.

. . . by and by comes Chapman the periwig-maker, and upon my liking it, without more ado I went up, and there he cut off my hair, which went a little to my heart at present to part with it.

AGED 30.

To church, where I found that my coming in a periwig did not prove so strange as I thought it would, for I thought that all the church would presently have cast their eyes all upon me, but I found no such thing.

AGED 30.

... and so to the plaisterer's at Charing Cross that casts heads and bodies in plaister: and there I had my whole face done; but I was vexed first to be forced to daub all my face over with pomatum ... Thus was the mould made; but when it came off there was little pleasure in it. ...

AGED 35

And thus ends all that I doubt I shall ever be able to do with my own eyes in the keeping of my Journal, I being not able to do it any longer, having done now so long as to undo my eyes almost every time that I take a pen in my hand; and, therefore, from this time forward, to have it kept by my own people in longhand ... and so I betake myself to that course ... for which, and all the discomforts that will accompany my being blind, the good God prepare me!

AGED 36.

SOURCE: *Diary.*

PERCY, THOMAS (1560–1605), conspirator; organiser of Gunpowder Plot.

He was about forty-six years of age, though from the whiteness of his head, he appeared older; his figure was tall and handsome; his eyes large and lively, and the expression of his face pleasing, though grave; and, notwithstanding the boldness of his mind, his manners were gentle and quiet.

AGED 45.

SOURCE: Greenway's MS.; quoted in David Jardine's *Criminal Trials,* 1832.

PERROT, SIR JOHN (1527?–1592), lord-deputy of Ireland.

Sir John Perrot was a man in stature very tall and big, exceeding the ordinary stature of men by much, and almost equal to the mightiest men that lived in his time; his body was very compact, and proportionable through all the parts. As he did exceed most men in stature, so did he in strength of body. His hair was auburn, until it grew grey in his elder years. His countenance was full of majesty, his eye marvellous piercing, and carrying a commanding aspect, insomuch that when he was angry, he had a very terrible visage or look; and when he was pleased, or willing to show kindness, he then had as amiable a countenance as any man. All which, as many as knew him can well testify for a truth; in this resembling Augustus Caesar, who, as it is written of him, had so great a majesty in his eye and countenance, piercing like the sun-beams, that a soldier beholding him could not continue, but retired back, saying that he was not able to endure the brightness and majesty of his eyes.

SOURCE: *The History of that Most Eminent Statesman, Sir John Perrott*, published 1728, but written about 1600.

PETTY, SIR WILLIAM (1623–1687), political economist.

He is a proper handsome man, measured six foot high, good head of brown hair, moderately turning up . . . His eyes are a kind of goose-gray, but very short-sighted, and, as to aspect, beautiful, and promise sweetness of nature, and they do not deceive, for he is a marvellous good-natured person . . . Eyebrows thick, dark and straight [horizontal]. His head is very large. He was in his youth very slender, but since these twenty years and more past he grew very plump.

SOURCE: John Aubrey, *Brief Lives*, edit. Andrew Clark, 1898.

PHILIPPA OF HAINAULT (1314–1369), queen of Edward III.

The lady whom we saw has not uncomely hair, betwixt blue-black and brown. Her head is clean-shaped; her forehead high and broad, and standing somewhat forward. Her face narrows between the eyes, and the lower part of her face is still more narrow and slender than her forehead. Her eyes are blackish-brown and deep. Her nose is fairly smooth and even, save that it is somewhat broad at the tip and also flattened, and yet it is no snub-nose. Her nostrils are also broad, her mouth fairly wide. Her lips are somewhat full, and especially the lower lip. Her teeth which have fallen and grown again are white enough, but the rest are not so white. The lower teeth project a little beyond the upper; yet this is little seen. Her ears and chin are comely enough. Her neck, shoulders, and all her body are well set and unmaimed; and naught is amiss so far as a man may see. Moreover, she is brown of skin all over, and much like her father; and in all things she is pleasant enough, as it seems to us. And the damsel will be of the age of nine years on St. John's day next to come, as her mother saith. She is neither too tall nor too short for such an age; she is of fair carriage, and well taught in all that becometh her rank, and highly esteemed and well beloved of her father and mother and of all her meinie, in so far as we could inquire and learn the truth.

AGED 8.

SOURCE: Walter Stapledon, Bishop of Exeter; quoted in G. C. Coulton, *Mediaeval Panorama*, C.U.P., 1958. This remarkable description was written for Edward II, when the young Philippa was being considered as a suitable bride for the future Edward III. The merciless scrutiny of an eight-year-old child was apparently accounted satisfactory and she became the bride of Edward III six years afterwards.

PHIPPS, SIR CONSTANTINE HENRY, second Earl of Mulgrave
 (1797–1863).

Lord Mulgrave . . . was formed on a heavy, colossal scale; and, to distinguish him from his younger brother, the Honourable Charles Phipps, who had likewise a seat in Parliament, the former was denominated 'Ursa Major' . . .

Lord Mulgrave was distinguished by a singularity of physical conformation, having *two distinct voices:* the one, strong and hoarse; the other, weak and querulous; of both of which he occasionally availed himself.

SOURCE: John Timbs, *A Century of Anecdote, 1760–1860*.

PICTON, SIR THOMAS (1758–1815), lieutenant-general; prominent in the Peninsular War; killed leading his brigade at Waterloo.

Sir Thomas Picton was a stern-looking, strongly built man, about the middle height ... He generally wore a blue frock-coat, very tightly buttoned up to the throat; a very large black silk neckcloth, shewing little or no shirt-collar; dark trousers, boots, and a round hat; it was in this very dress that he was attired at Quatre Bras, as he had hurried off to the scene of action before his uniform arrived.

AGED 57.

SOURCE: Captain R. H. Gronow, *Reminiscences*.

PITT, WILLIAM, first Earl of Chatham (1708–1778), statesman.

Pitt, it was expected, would take advantage of illness, and not appear [i.e. at the parliamentary enquiries into the loss of Minorca, 1757]. But he refined on that old finesse; and pretending to waive the care of a broken constitution, when his country demanded his service, and as a pledge of his sincerity in the scrutiny, he came to the discussion in all the studied apparatus of the valetudinarian. The weather was unseasonably warm; yet he was dressed in an old coat and waistcoat of beaver laced with gold; over this, a red surtout, the right arm lined with fur, and appendent with many black ribands, to indicate his inability of drawing it over his right arm, which hung in a crape sling, but which, in the warmth of speaking, he drew out with unlucky activity, and brandished as usual.

AGED 51.

SOURCE: Horace Walpole, *Memoirs*, published 1822–1845.

Pitt was undoubtedly one of the greatest masters of ornamental eloquence. His language was amazingly fine and flowing; his

voice admirable; his action most expressive; his figure genteel
and commanding . . . Out of the House of Commons he was
far from being this shining character. His conversation was
affected and unnatural, his manner not engaging, nor his
talents adapted to a country where Ministers must court, if they
would be courted.

SOURCE: Horace Walpole, *Memoirs*, published 1822–1845.

PITT, WILLIAM (1759–1806), statesman, second son of William
Pitt, Earl of Chatham.

It was in reply to Lord Nugent that Pitt first broke silence, from
under the Gallery on the Opposition side of the House. The
same composure, self-possession, and imposing dignity of
manner, which afterwards so eminently characterised him when
seated on the Treasury Bench, distinguished him in this his
first essay of his powers, though he then wanted three months to
have completed his twenty-second year. The same nervous,
correct, and polished diction, free from any inaccuracy of
language, or embarrassment of deportment, which, as First
Minister, he subsequently displayed, were equally manifested
on this occasion.

AGED 21.

In his manners, Pitt, if not repulsive, was cold, stiff, and
without suavity or amenity. He seemed never to invite approach
or to encourage acquaintance; though, when addressed, he
could be polite, communicative, and occasionally gracious.
Smiles were not natural to him, even when seated on the
Treasury Bench; where, placed at the summit of power, young,
surrounded by followers, admirers and flatterers, he maintained
a more sullen gravity than his antagonist exhibited, who beheld
around him only the companions of his political exile, poverty
and privations. From the instant that Pitt entered the doorway
of the House of Commons, he advanced up the floor with a
quick and firm step, his head erect and thrown back, looking
neither to the right nor to the left; nor favouring with a nod or
glance any of the individuals seated on either side, among

P

whom many who possessed five thousand a year, would have been gratified even by so slight a mark of attention.

SOURCE: Sir N. William Wraxall, *Historical Memoirs of My Own Time*, 1815.

Some years later, I saw Mr. Pitt in a blue coat, buckskin breeches and boots, and a round hat, with powder and pigtail. He was thin and gaunt, with his hat off his forehead, and his nose in the air—that nose on which Hazlitt said 'he suspended the House of Commons'.

SOURCE: Leigh Hunt, *Autobiography*.

. . . I should have said that he had a sort of slovenly or negligent look: and the same when he was in a passion. His passion did not show itself by knitting his brows or pouting his mouth, nor were his words very sharp: but his eyes lighted up in a manner quite surprising. It was something that seemed to dart from within his head, and you might see sparks coming from them. At another time, his eyes had no colour at all.

SOURCE: *Memoirs of the Lady Hester Stanhope as related by herself in Conversations with her Physician, Dr. Meryon*, 2nd. edit., 1846.

I really think Pitt is done: his face is no longer red, but yellow; his looks are dejected; his countenance I think much changed and fallen, and every now and then he gives a hollow cough. Upon my soul, hating him as I do, I am almost moved to pity to see his fallen greatness. I saw this once splendid fellow drive yesterday to the House of Lords in his forlorn, shattered equipage, and I stood near him behind the throne till two o'clock this morning. I saw no expression but melancholy on the fellow's face—princes of the blood passing him without speaking to him, and, as I could fancy, an universal sentiment in those around him that *he was done*.

AGED 44.

SOURCE: Thomas Creevey, *The Creevey Papers*.

Note: Pitt was not, in fact, quite done; but to the great annoyance of Creevey and his friends—'out-jockeyed by the villain'—came back to power the next year.

PLIMPSOLL, SAMUEL (1824–1898), called 'The Sailors' Friend'.

There was then in the House a whimsical Radical—Plimpsoll by name—a curious mixture of philanthropy and self-advertisement. He had for some time been collecting and accumulating evidence as to malpractices of certain shipowners who, he asserted, deliberately sent out ships ill-found, unseaworthy, and risked and not infrequently lost the lives of their employees and made money out of the transaction. The influence of the shipowners in the House of Commons was strong, for the vast majority were upright and honourable men, though, as a body, they were opposed to more severe measures of inspection and loading. Plimpsoll heard that the Merchant Shipping Bill was to be withdrawn, and he seized his opportunity with consummate skill and assurance. As soon as the announcement was made in the House by the Prime Minister, he rushed into the gangway between the two sides of the House, gesticulating and flourishing his fists, and shouting out strong language. In vain the Speaker called him to resume his seat and obey the rules of order. He openly defied the Chair, walked up to the Government Bench, looked as if he was about to assault the Prime Minister, and, finally yielding to the persuasions of his friends, left the House shouting: 'Scoundrels, scoundrels, scoundrels!'

SOURCE: Lord George Hamilton, *Parliamentary Reminiscences and Reflections, 1868–1885,* John Murray, 1917.

POPE, ALEXANDER (1688–1744), poet.

The person of Pope is well-known not to have been formed by the nicest model . . . and is described as protuberant before and behind. He is said to have been beautiful in his infancy; but he was of a constitution originally feeble and weak; and as bodies of a tender frame are easily distorted, his deformity was probably in part the effect of his application. His stature was so low that, to bring him to a level with common tables, it was necessary to raise his seat. But his face was not displeasing, and his eyes were animated and vivid.

Most of what can be told . . . was communicated by a female domestic of the Earl of Oxford, who knew him perhaps after the middle of life. He was then so weak as to stand in perpetual need of female attendance; extremely sensible of cold, so that he wore a kind of fur doublet, under a shirt of very coarse warm linen with fine sleeves. When he rose, he was invested in bodice made by stiff canvas, being scarce able to hold himself erect till they were laced, and he then put on a flannel waistcoat. One side was contracted. His legs were so slender that he enlarged their bulk with three pairs of stockings, which were drawn on and off by the maid; for he was not able to dress or undress himself, and neither went to bed nor rose without help. His weakness made it very difficult for him to be clean.

His hair had fallen almost all away; and he used to dine sometimes with Lord Oxford, privately, in a velvet cap. His dress of ceremony was black, with a tye-wig, and a little sword.

SOURCE: Doctor Samuel Johnson, *Lives of the Poets*, 4 vols., 1781.

. . . about four feet six high; very humpbacked and a little deformed; he wore a black coat, and had in a little sword. He had a large and very fine eye, and a long handsome nose; his mouth had those peculiar marks which always are found in the mouths of crooked persons, and the muscles which run across the cheek were so strongly marked as to appear like small cords. Roubiliac, who made a bust of him from life, observed that his countenance was that of a person who had been much afflicted with headache, and he should have known the fact from the contracted appearance of the skin between his eyebrows.

AGED 52.

SOURCE: Sir Joshua Reynolds; quoted in Prior's *Malone*.

POWELL, FREDERICK YORK (1850–1904), regius professor of modern history at Oxford.

There was at that time, so undergraduates reported, an oracle beyond compare on all matters historical, to be discovered in the Meadow Buildings at Christ Church. He was not a Professor or even a lecturer in Modern History, but he 'knew his stuff'. The undergraduates—a favoured few, for to most men his very existence was unknown—called him 'The Yorker'. His name was Frederick York Powell. He held a lectureship in Law and was reported to be omniscient. He was pointed out to me as he peered into the book-shops in the streets, a burly, bearded, open-air figure dressed in a roomy suit of dark navy blue and, but for his tall hat and pince-nez, looking like a sea captain fresh from his last cruise.

SOURCE: H. A. L. Fisher, *An Unfinished Autobiography*, O.U.P., 1940.

But my father's chief friend was York Powell, a famous Oxford Professor of History, a broad-built, broad-headed, brown-bearded man clothed in heavy blue cloth and looking, but for his glasses and the dim sight of a student, like some captain in the Merchant Service. He cared nothing for philosophy, nothing for economics, nothing for the policy of nations; for history, as he saw it, was a memory of men who were amusing or exciting to think about. He impressed all who met him, seemed to some a man of genius, but had not enough ambition to share his thought, nor enough conviction to give rhythm to his style and remained always a poor writer.

SOURCE: W. B. Yeats, *Autobiographies*, Macmillan, 1955.

PRIMROSE, ARCHIBALD PHILIP, fifth earl of Rosebery (1847–1929), statesman and writer; prime minister.

He was at his best with two or three and on his day; and sometimes in larger company he seemed shy and ill at ease. When he was out of humour, he could cast a chill over all, and did not hesitate to freeze and snub. On these occasions his face became expressionless, almost a slab, and his eyes lost their light and fire. One saw an altogether different person. But after a bit one knew the real man was there all the time, hiding beneath a curtain. And all the more agreeable was it when he came out.
   Hardest of all is it to revive the impression which he produced

upon his hearers when dealing with the greatest affairs. His life was set in an atmosphere of tradition. The Past stood ever at his elbow and was the counsellor upon whom he most relied. He seemed to be attended by Learning and History, and to carry into current events an air of ancient majesty. His voice was melodious and deep and often, when listening, one felt in living contact with the centuries which are gone, and perceived the long continuity of our island tale.

SOURCE: Sir Winston Churchill, *Great Contemporaries*, Thornton Butterworth, 1939.

PRYNNE, WILLIAM (1600–1669), puritan and writer of pamphlets.

His manner of study was thus: he wore a long quilt cap, which came 2 or 3, at least, inches over his eyes, which served him as an umbrella to defend his eyes from the light . . .

Upon the opening of the Parliament . . . he girt on his old long rusty sword (longer than ordinary). Sir William Waller marching behind him (as he went to the House), W. Prynne's long sword ran between Sir William's short legs, and threw him down, which caused laughter.

He was of a strange saturnine complexion. Sir C. W. said once that he had the countenance of a witch.

SOURCE: John Aubrey, *Brief Lives*, edit. Andrew Clarke, 1898.

PUSEY, EDWARD BOUVERIE (1810–1882), professor of Hebrew at Oxford and canon of Christ Church.

It was rather fun to take ritualistic ladies, who had fashioned mental pictures of the great Tractarian, to Evensong in Christ Church, and to watch their dismay as that very unascetic figure, with tumbled surplice and hood awry, toddled to his stall. 'Dear me! Is that Dr. Pusey? Somehow I had fancied quite a different-looking man.'

SOURCE: G. W. E. Russell, *On Looking Back*, Wells Gardner, Darton & Co., 1911.

Pusey was in Oxford during the whole of my time. I remember well the first Sunday it was his turn to preach after the time of his suspension had expired. It was at Christ Church Cathedral, of which he was one of the canons by virtue of his office as Regius Professor of Hebrew. There was an enormous crowd of men, and as soon as the cathedral doors were opened the cathedral was filled in every part. In due time there ascended the rostrum a spare, ascetic-looking man, pale as death, with a piercing eye and an equally piercing voice . . . His countenance, though bearing outward signs of great abstemiousness and habits of fasting, showed him to be a man of studious habits, and he had a very benevolent expression.

SOURCE: Richard W. Hiley, *Memories of Half a Century*, Longmans, Green & Co., 1899.

RAE, SIR DAVID, first baronet, Lord Esgrove (1724?–1804), judge.

But a more ludicrous personage could not exist. When I first knew him he was in the zenith of his absurdity. People seemed to have nothing to do but to tell stories of this one man. To be able to give an anecdote of Esgrove, with a proper imitation of his voice and manner was a sort of fortune in society. Scott in those days was famous for this particularly. Whenever a knot of persons were seen listening in the Outer House to one who was talking slowly, with a low muttering voice and a projecting chin, and then the listeners burst asunder in roars of laughter, nobody thought of asking what the joke was. They were sure it was a successful imitation of Esky; and this was enough. Yet never once did he do or say anything which had the slightest claim to be remembered for any intrinsic merit. The value of all his words and actions consisted in their absurdity.

He seemed, in his old age, to be about the average height, but as he then stooped a good deal, he might have been taller in reality. His face varied, according to the circumstances, from a scurfy red to a scurfy blue; the nose was prodigious; the under lip enormous, and supported on a huge clumsy chin, which moved like the jaw of an exaggerated Dutch toy. He walked with a slow, stealthy step—something between a walk and a hirple, and helped himself on by short movements of his elbows, backwards and forwards, like fins. The voice was low and mumbling, and on the Bench was generally inaudible for some time after the movement of the lips showed that he had begun speaking; after which the first word that was let fairly out was generally the loudest of the whole discourse. It is unfortunate that, without an idea of his voice and manner, mere narrative cannot describe his sayings and doings graphically.

SOURCE: Henry Lord Cockburn, *Memorials of His Time*, 1856.

RALEGH, SIR WALTER (1552?–1618), writer and naval commander.

He was a tall, handsome, and bold man; but his naeve was that he was damnable proud . . . His beard turned up naturally . . . Old Sir Thomas Malett, one of the justices of the King's Bench tempore Caroli I et II, knew Sir Walter; and I have heard him say that, notwithstanding his so great mastership in style and his conversation with the learnedst and politest persons, yet he spake broad Devonshire to his dying day. His voice was small, as likewise were my schoolfellows', his grand-nephews . . .

He had a most remarkable aspect, an exceeding high forehead, long-faced, and sour eye-lidded, a kind of pig-eye . . .

SOURCE: John Aubrey, *Brief Lives*, edit. Andrew Clark, 1898.

RANN, JOHN (?–1774), highwayman; known as 'Sixteen String Jack'.

He was about five feet five inches high, wore his own hair, of a light colour, which combed over his forehead, remarkably clean, and particularly neat in his dress, which in two instances was very singular, that of always having sixteen strings to his breeches knees, always silk (by which means he acquired his fictitious name) and a remarkable hat with strings, and a button on the crown. He was straight, of a genteel carriage, and makes a very handsome appearance.

SOURCE: contemporary account, quoted in P. Pringle's *Stand and Deliver*. Rann had the distinction of being mentioned in almost a complimentary manner by Doctor Johnson, who says, in his account of Thomas Gray, that the poet 'towered above the ordinary run of verse as Sixteen String Jack above the ordinary footpad.'

READE, CHARLES (1814–1884), novelist.

Reade's personal appearance was striking; he was over six feet in height, and was of athletic and vigorous build. His general countenance, boisterous manner, impatience of criticism, and impulsive generosity, all helped to make his personality attractive.

SOURCE: Charles Kent, *Dictionary of National Biography*, 1896.

REYNOLDS, SIR JOSHUA (1723–1792), portrait painter.

To coxcombs averse, yet most civilly steering,
When they judged without skill, he was still hard of hearing;
When they talked of their Raphaels, Correggios and stuff,
He shifted his trumpet, and only took snuff.

SOURCE: epigram by Oliver Goldsmith. A reference to Sir Joshua's inveterate taking of snuff, which he spilled liberally over his waistcoat, and to the ear-trumpet he carried because of his deafness.

Sir Joshua Reynolds, precluded by his deafness from mixing in, or contributing to, general conversation, his trumpet held up to his ear, was gratified by the attention of those who addressed to him their discourse.

SOURCE: Sir N. William Wraxall, *Historical Memoirs of My Own Life*, 1815.

Note: Reynolds was slight in build, of less than middle height, scarred by small-pox and his upper lip disfigured as the result of a fall from his horse.

RICHARD I, called RICHARD CŒUR-DE-LION (1157–1199), king of England.

He was lofty of stature, of shapely build, his hair halfway between red and yellow, his limbs straight and supple. His arms were somewhat long and, therefore, better fitted than those of most folk to draw or wield a sword. He had, moreover, long legs in keeping with the character of his whole frame. His features showed him to be a ruler, while his manners and bearing added not a little to his general presence. He could claim the highest position and the praise, not only by reason of his noble birth, but because of his virtues. He far surpassed other men in courtesy and the greatness of his strength.

SOURCE: Richard, Canon of Holy Trinity in Aldgate; *Itinerarium Peregrinorum et Gestis Regis Ricardi;* and quoted in Nicholas Trevet's *Annales.*

RICHARD II (1367–1400), king of England; called 'of Bordeaux'.

Where he sits on his white horse, they draw back so that the good King himself may be seen by his people. How fresh-coloured his face, crowned with yellow hair, his combed locks shining under the garland; gleaming with gold in the red robe that covers too much his fair body.

SOURCE: Richard de Maidstone, *De concordia inter Ricardum Secundum et civitatem London;* quoted in *Chaucer's World*, Columbia University Press, 1948.

Note: Authentic accounts for the appearance of Richard II are elusive; but he is important in the story of portraiture for the reason given by David Piper in *The English Face:*

'He is the classic point of demonstration that the English

portrait has, at last, arrived, at the turn of the fourteenth to the fifteenth century . . . The copper tomb-effigy in Westminster Abbey was ordered from Nicholas Broker and Godfrey Prest, citizens and coppersmiths of London, in 1395, that is, five years before Richard died. The contract allowed Broker and Prest two years for their work, and the suspicion seems legitimate that Richard took a personal interest in his own image. The resulting face is stylised to a degree, but seems recognisably individual with a most unusual nose, tipped like an arrow-head.'

RICHARD III (1452–1485), king of England.

As far without the certainty of a proof is the pretended deformity of his body, which is controverted by many; some peremptorily asserted he was not deformed, of which opinion was John Stow . . . who in all his enquiry could find no such note of deformity in this King . . . but hath acknowledged . . . that he hath spoke with some ancient men, who from their own sight and knowledge affirmed he was of bodily shape, comely enough, only of low stature, which is all the deformity they proportion so monstrously; neither did John Rouce, who knew him, and writ much in his description, observe any other.

SOURCE: Sir George Buc, *Life of Richard III;* quoted in Caroline Halstead's *Life of Margaret Beaufort,* 1839. The inaccurate but traditional picture of Richard III was established in Sir Thomas More's *History of King Richard III*, written about 1513, where he is described as 'little of stature, ill-featured of limbs, crook backed, his left shoulder much higher than his right, hard favoured of visage . . .' But the weight of contemporary description of the king is against this biassed portrait. Those who saw him and described him make no mention of any physical deformity; only that he was small in stature, thin and frail-looking. A German traveller, for instance, Nicolas de Poppelau, mentioned that he was lean, with 'delicate arms and legs', and a speech delivered in Richard's presence by a Scots envoy flatteringly declared that Nature had never enclosed such remarkable powers within so small a frame.

RICHARDSON, SAMUEL (1689–1761), novelist; author of 'Pamela', 'Clarissa Harlowe', etc.

Short; rather plump than emaciated, notwithstanding his complaints; about five foot five inches, fair wig, lightish cloth suit, all black besides; one hand generally in his bosom, the other a cane in it, which he leans upon under the skirts of his coat usually, that it may imperceptibly serve him as a support, when attacked by sudden tremors or startings, and dizziness, which too frequently attack him, but thank God, not so often as formerly; looking directly foreright, as passers-by would imagine, but observing all that stirs on either hand of him without moving his short neck; hardly ever turning back; of a light-brown complexion; teeth not yet failing him; smoothish faced, and ruddy cheeked; at sometimes looking to be about sixty-five, at other times much younger; a regular even pace, stealing away ground, rather than seeming to ride it; a gray eye, too often over-clouded by mistinesses from the head; by chance lively, very lively it will be, if he have hope of seeing a lady whom he loves and honours.

SOURCE: Samuel Richardson (a self-description); *Letters*.

RICHMOND, DUCHESS OF (1647–1702). See Stuart or Stewart, Frances Theresa.

RICHMOND, GEORGE (1809–1896), portrait painter and Royal Academician.

I have a double-breasted blue coat which belonged to my grandfather, still in fair preservation, which was made by Stultz, the fashionable tailor mentioned by Thackeray, and also one of the famous beaver hats which he wore long after they had been discarded by the rest of the world, and which came from Andre, the hatter in Bond Street. He told me how at last the street urchins used to follow him down the street and shout out: 'Who's yer 'atter?' He was the first to smoke cigarettes, or

'Paper Cigars' as they were called, and used them alternately with snuff.

SOURCE: Recollection by one of his grandsons; quoted in *The Richmond Papers*, Heinemann, 1926.

RIDLEY, NICHOLAS (1500?–1555), bishop and martyr.

Upon the northside of the town, in the ditch over against Balliol College, the place of execution was appointed . . . And when everything was in readiness, the prisoners were brought forth by the mayor and the bailiffs. Master Ridley had a fair black gown, furred, and faced with foins*, such as he was wont to wear being bishop, and a tippet of velvet furred likewise about his neck, a velvet night-cap upon his head, and a corner cap upon the same, going in a pair of slippers to the stake, and going between the mayor and an alderman.

AGED 55.

SOURCE: John Foxe, *Book of Martyrs*, 1563.

ROBERT I of Scotland (1274–1329). See Bruce, Robert.

ROBERTS, CAPTAIN BARTHOLOMEW (1682–1722), pirate.

Roberts himself made a gallant figure [in the action against the man-o'-war *Swallow*, in which he was killed] at the time of the engagement, being dressed in a rich crimson damask waistcoat and breeches, a red feather in his hat, a gold chain round his neck, with a diamond cross hanging to it, a sword in his hand, and two pairs of pistols hanging at the end of a silk sling, slung over his shoulders (according to the fashion of the pirates) . . .

Roberts was a tall, black [i.e. swarthy] man near forty years of age . . . of good natural parts and personal bravery, though

* Foin was a kind of fur, either from the marten or from a ferret or weasel.

he applied them to such wicked parts as made them of no commendation . . .

SOURCE: Captain Charles Johnson, *General History of the Pyrates, from their first Rise and Settlement in the Island of Providence, to the Present Time . . . etc.*, 4th Edit., 1726.

RODNEY, GEORGE BRYDGES, first Baron Rodney (1719–1792), admiral; defeated Spanish off Cape St. Vincent and the French under De Grasse off Dominica.

His person was more elegant than seemed to become his rough profession. There was even something that approached to delicacy and effeminacy in his figure; but no man manifested a more temperate and steady courage in action. I had the honour to live in great personal intimacy with him, and have often heard him declare that superiority to fear was not in him the physical effect of constitution; on the contrary, no man being more sensible by nature to that passion than himself; but that he surmounted it from the considerations of honour and public duty . . . He talked much and freely upon every subject; concealed nothing in the course of conversation, regardless who were present; and dealt his censures, as well as his praises, with imprudent liberality; qualities which procured him many enemies, particularly in his own profession.

SOURCE: Sir N. William Wraxall, *Historical Memoirs of My Own Life*, 1815.

ROLLE, RICHARD, of Hampole (1290?–1349), hermit and writer.

Note: Richard Rolle of Hampole was born in the diocese of York and was sent up to Oxford at the expense of the Archdeacon of Durham. He left at the age of eighteen and turned to a religious life, borrowing white and grey frocks from his sister at the outset to provide himself with an appropriate costume.

When, therefore, he had taken them, he forthwith amputated the sleeves of the grey one, and cut off the buttons from the white one, and sewed together as best he could the sleeves of the white tunic, so that they might be to some extent adapted to his purpose. Then he put off his own garments and put on the white frock next his skin; over which he put the grey frock with the amputated sleeves, thrusting his arms through the holes which this amputation had made; then he drew over all this a rain cloak [with hood] in order that to some extent, after his own fashion, he might shape himself roughly into the likeness of a hermit, so far as was possible at that moment. When his sister saw this she was filled with amazement, and cried: 'My brother is gone mad, my brother is gone mad!'

SOURCE: *Early English Text Society*, Vol. 20; quoted in G. G. Coulton's *Medieval Panorama*, C.U.P., 1938.

ROSE, HUGH HENRY, Baron Strathnairn (1801–1885), field-marshal and hero of the Indian Mutiny.

He was a very odd mixture—in society a dandy with a foolish manner, in action the bravest of the brave. We as boys regarded him as a combination of a joke and a hero. He made his reputation in India during the worst phases of the Mutiny by his celebrated march through Central India, where he achieved a series of astonishing successes against great odds and serious climatic difficulties. He had seven sunstrokes during this march, though none of them were severe enough to incapacitate him for long . . .

In society he was dreamy, inconsequent in his remarks and foppish in his dress—the last individual you would associate with deeds of daring and fortitude . . . One of his aide-de-camps described to me the astonishing change in his whole mien the moment serious work had to be done; all the drawing-room graces disappeared, and in the place of the dandy was a stern, watchful, determined soldier.

SOURCE: Lord George Hamilton, *Parliamentary Reminiscences and Reflections*, John Murray, 1917.

ROSEBERY, LORD (1847–1929). See Primrose, Archibald Philip, fifth Earl of Rosebery.

ROSS, SIR JAMES CLARK (1800–1862), rear-admiral; arctic and antarctic explorer; discovered magnetic pole.

. . . short but powerfully built, and remarkable for his aquiline nose and very piercing black eyes.

SOURCE: Sir Clements Markham; quoted in Rear-Admiral Noel Wright's *Quest for Franklin*, Heinemann, 1959.

ROSSETTI, DANTE GABRIEL (1828–1882), poet.

I should have described Rossetti, at this time, as a man who looked quite ten years older than his actual age, which was fifty-two, of full middle height and inclining to corpulence, with a round face that ought, one thought, to be ruddy but was pale, large grey eyes with a steady introspecting look, surmounted by broad protrusive brows and a clearly-pencilled ridge over the nose, which was well-cut and had large breathing nostrils. The mouth and chin were hidden beneath a heavy moustache and abundant beard, which grew up to the ears, and had been a mixed black-brown and auburn, and were now streaked with grey. The forehead was large, round, without protuberances, and very gently receding to where thin black curls, that had once been redundant, began to tumble down to the ears. The entire configuration of the head and face seemed to me singularly noble, and from the eyes upwards, full of beauty. He wore a pair of spectacles, and, in reading, a second pair over the first, but these took little from the sense of power conveyed by those steady eyes . . . his dress was not conspicuous, being however rather negligent than otherwise, and noticeable, if at all, only for a straight sack-coat buttoned at the throat, descending at least to the knees, and having large pockets cut into it perpendicularly at the sides. This garment was, I afterwards found, one of the articles of various kinds made to the author's own design. When he spoke, even in exchanging the preliminary courtesies of an opening conversation, I thought his voice the richest I had ever known any one to possess.

AGED 52.

SOURCE: T. Hall Caine, *Recollections of Dante Gabriel Rossetti*, 1882.

RUPERT, PRINCE, Count Palatine of Rhine and Duke of Bavaria; Duke of Cumberland and Earl of Holderness (1619–1682); nephew of Charles I and cavalry leader in Civil War; admiral in Dutch Wars.

He was brave and courageous even to rashness, and subject to certain eccentricities of which he would have been sorry to correct himself . . . He was polite even to excess unseasonably; but haughty and even brutal when he should have been gentle and courteous.

He was tall and his appearance was most ungracious. He had a dry, hard-faced visage, even when he sought to soften his expression; and in his fits of bad humour his countenance was truly that of a reprobate.

SOURCE: Anthony Hamilton, *Memoirs of the Comte de Gramont,* edit. Henry Vizetelly, 1859.

RUSKIN, JOHN (1819–1900), author, artist and social reformer.

He was fairly tall but his height was already diminished by a little hunch in the shoulders. His hair was dark, long and thick, his beard iron-grey. His head was of the long type. His forehead sloped, and on each side, between his temples and his ears, there was a noticeable depression. He had heavy eyebrows and the bluest of blue eyes. Their colour was repeated with a differ-ence in his large blue neckties . . . His hands were small and delicate . . . He wore very old-fashioned clothes—trousers and double-breasted waistcoat of home-spun and a long dark coat. Round his neck was a gold chain attached to his watch. His smile was kindness itself, his voice sometimes almost caressing. He could not quite pronounce his r's.

AGED 68.

SOURCE: Sydney Carlyle Cockerell, *Friends of a Lifetime,* 1941.

Ruskin used to come to my father's house to what he called 'high tea'; other friends dropped into this genial meal and spent the evening in conversation, almost always finishing up with music. We children were allowed to sit up and partake of the intellectual as well as emotional feast. How well I remember the gaunt, delicate-looking young man, with a profusion of reddish hair, shaggy brows like a Scotch terrier, under them gleaming eyes which bore within them a strange light, the like of which I have never seen except in his . . . The eyes told of an imaginative fire as well as of penetrating observation, likewise of the kindness and generosity of his nature.

SOURCE: William Richmond; *The Richmond Papers*, Heinemann, 1926.

SACHEVERELL, DOCTOR HENRY (1674–1724), political preacher.

He had a haughty insolent air, which his friends found occasion often to complain of; but it made his presence more graceful in public.

His person was framed well for the purpose, and he dressed well. A good assurance, clean gloves, white handkerchief well-managed, with other suitable accomplishments, moved the hearts of many at his appearance [at his impeachment for seditious libels].

Everybody knows that he was afterwards sent about several counties; where, with his usual grace, he received as his due the homage and adulation of multitudes . . .

SOURCE: Sarah, Duchess of Marlborough; *Private Correspondence of Sarah, Duchess of Marlborough*, 1838.

SACKVILLE, LORD GEORGE (1716–1785). See Germain, George Sackville, first Viscount Sackville.

ST. VINCENT, EARL (1735–1823). See Jervis, John, Earl of St. Vincent.

SALISBURY, CATHERINE, Countess of; wife of William de
Montacute, first Earl of Salisbury (1301–1344).

The countess of Salisbury, who was esteemed one of the most
beautiful and virtuous women in England, was in this castle
[Wark], which belonged to the earl of Salisbury, who had been
taken prisoner, with the earl of Suffolk, near Lisle, and was
still in prison at the Chatelet in Paris . . .

The countess comforted much those within the castle; and
from the sweetness of her looks, and the charm of being
encouraged by such a beautiful lady, one man in time of need
ought to be worth two . . .

That same day that the Scots had decamped from before the
castle of Wark, king Edward, and his whole army, arrived there
about mid-day, and took up their position on the ground which
the Scots had occupied. When he found that they were returned
home, he was much enraged; for he had come there with so
much speed, that both his men and horses were sadly fatigued.

He ordered his men to take up their quarters where they
were, as he wished to go to the castle to see the noble dame
within, whom he had never seen since her marriage . . . and
the king, as soon as he was disarmed, taking ten or twelve
knights with him, went to the castle, to salute the countess of
Salisbury, and to examine what damage the attacks of the
Scots had done, and the manner in which those within had
defended themselves.

The moment the countess heard of the king's approach, she
ordered all the gates to be thrown open, and went to meet him,
most richly dressed; insomuch that no one could look at her but
with wonder and admiration at her noble deportment, great
beauty and affability of behaviour. When she came near the
king, she made her reverence to the ground, and gave him her
thanks for coming to her assistance, and then conducted him
into the castle, to entertain and honour him, as she was very
capable of doing.

Every one was delighted with her: the king could not take
his eyes off her, as he thought he had never before seen so
beautiful or sprightly a lady; so that a spark of fine love struck

upon his heart, which lasted a long time, for he did not believe that the whole world produced any other lady so worthy of being beloved.

Thus they entered the castle, hand in hand; the lady led him first into the hall, then to his chamber, which was richly furnished, as belonging to so fine a lady. The king kept his eyes so continually upon her, that the gentle dame was quite abashed. After he had sufficiently examined his apartment, he retired to a window, and leaning on it, fell into a profound reverie.

SOURCE: Sir John Froissart, *Chronicles*, Thomas Johnes's translation, 1806.

SAMPSON, ABBOT (1135–1211), abbot of St. Edmund's.

Abbot Sampson was below the average height, almost bald; his face was neither round nor oblong; his nose was prominent and his lips thick; his eyes were clear and his glance penetrating; his hearing was excellent; his eyebrows arched, and frequently shaved; and a little cold soon made him hoarse . . . On the day of his election he was forty-seven, and had been a monk for seventeen years . . . In his ruddy beard there were a few grey hairs, and still fewer in his black and curling hair. But in the course of the first fourteen years after his election all his hair became white as snow.

He was an exceedingly temperate man; he possessed great energy and a strong constitution.

SOURCE: *The Chronicle of Jocelin of Brakelond*, translated L. Cecil Jane, Chatto and Windus, 1907.

SAVAGE, RICHARD (1697?–1743), poet.

He was of a middle stature, of a thin habit of body, a long visage, coarse features, and melancholy aspect; of a grave and manly deportment, a solemn dignity of mien; but which upon a nearer acquaintance, softened into an engaging easiness of manners. His walk was slow, and his voice tremulous and mournful. He was easily excited to smiles, but very seldom provoked to laughter.

SOURCE: Doctor Samuel Johnson, *Lives of the Most Eminent English Poets* . . . 1781, Vol. III.

SCOTS SOLDIERS in the reign of Edward III (1328 A.D.).

The Scots are bold, hardy, and much inured to war. When they make their invasions into England, they march from twenty to four-and-twenty leagues without halting, as well by night as day; for they are all on horseback, except the camp followers, who are on foot. The knights and esquires are well mounted on large bay horses, the common people on little galloways. They bring no carriages with them, on account of the mountains they have to pass in Northumberland; neither do they carry with them any provisions of bread or wine; for their habits of sobriety are such, in time of war, that they will live for a long time on flesh half-sodden, without bread, and drink the river-water without wine. They have, therefore, no occasion for pots or pans; for they dress the flesh of their cattle in the skins, after they have taken them off; and, being sure to find plenty of them in the country which they invade, they carry none with them. Under the flaps of his saddle, each man carries a broad plate of metal; behind the saddle, a little bag of oatmeal; when they have eaten too much of the sodden flesh, and their stomachs appear weak and empty, they place this plate over the fire, mix with water their oatmeal, and when the plate is heated, they put a little of the paste upon it, and make a thin cake, like a cracknell or biscuit, which they eat to warm their stomachs; it is no wonder that they perform a longer day's march than other soldiers . . .

Their army consisted of four thousand men at arms, knights and esquires, well mounted; besides twenty thousand men, bold and hardy, armed after the manner of their country, and mounted upon little hackneys, that are never tied up or dressed, but turned, immediately after the day's march, to pasture on the heath or in the fields. This army was commanded by two valiant captains. The king of Scotland himself, who had been very brave, yet being old, and labouring under a leprosy, appointed for one that gallant prince, so renowned in arms, the earl of Moray, who bore upon his banner argent three pillows gules; the other was Sir James Douglas, esteemed the bravest and most enterprising knight in the two kingdoms; he bore for arms argent on a chef argent.

SOURCE: Sir John Froissart, *Chronicles*, Thomas Johnes's translation, 1806.

Note: The Scottish king was Robert the Bruce, who died of leprosy in 1329.

SCOTT, SIR WALTER (1771–1832), novelist and poet.

He quite answered all my expectations of him, and you may suppose they were very high. His manners are those of an amiable and unaffected man, and a polished gentleman . . .

He is tall and well-formed, excepting one of his ankles and foot (I think the right) which is crippled and makes him walk very lamely. He is neither fat nor thin. His face is perfectly Scotch, and though some people think it heavy, it struck me as a very agreeable one. He could never have been handsome. His forehead is very high, his nose short, his upper lip long, and the lower part of his face rather fleshy. His complexion is fresh and clear, his eyes very blue, shrewd and penetrating. I should say the predominant expression of his face is that of strong sense. His hair, which has always been very light (as well as his eyebrows and eyelashes) is now of a silvery whiteness, which makes him look older than he really is (I believe forty-six is his age*). He was dressed in a brown frock coat, blue trousers and had on a black cravat.

SOURCE: Charles Robert Leslie, R.A.; letter to Miss Leslie, in *Autobiographical Recollections by the late Charles Robert Leslie*, 1860.

Of the many portraits of him Chantrey's bust is, to my mind,

* Aged 49.

the most perfect. Lawrence gave him a pomposity of manner which he never assumed; but in Chantrey's bust, the gentle turn of the head, inclined a little forwards and down, and the lurking humour about the eye and the mouth, are Scott's own.

SOURCE: Charles Robert Leslie, R.A.; letter to Miss Leslie, in *Autobiographical Recollections by the late Charles Robert Leslie*, 1860.

He had outgrown the sallowness of early ill health, and had a fresh brilliant complexion. His eyes were clear, open, and well set, with a changeful radiance, to which teeth of the most perfect regularity and whiteness lent their assistance, while the noble expanse and elevation of the brow gave to the whole aspect a dignity far above the charm of mere features. His smile was always delightful . . . His figure, excepting the blemish in one limb, must in those days have been eminently handsome; tall, much above the usual standard . . . the head set on with singular grace, the throat and chest after the truest model of the antique, the hands delicately finished; the whole outline that of extraordinary vigour, without as yet a touch of clumsiness.

SOURCE: John Gibson Lockhart, *Life of Sir Walter Scott*, 1838.

When the table was cleared after dinner, Sir Walter, in the exuberance of his loyalty and hospitality, volunteered to sing his own song—'Carle now the King's come.' The whole company gave the chorus, and their host, regardless alike of his lameness and his dignity, sprang up, and, calling upon everybody to join hands, made his guests dance with him round the table to the measure of their tune. The effect of this latter exercise, indulged in by a set of performers all more or less illustrious in the world's eye—and all, with few exceptions, of intensely anti-saltatory habits—would defy the pen of a Rabelais or the pencil of a Hogarth.

SOURCE: *Memoirs of the Life of William Collins, Esq., R.A.*, 1848.

SELKIRK, ALEXANDER (1676–1721), marooned sailor; prototype of Robinson Crusoe; put ashore on the island of Juan

Fernandez, 1704; rescued 1709 by privateer Captain Woodes Rogers.

Immediately our pinnace returned from the shore [of Juan Fernandez] and brought abundance of crawfish, with a man clothed in goatskins, who looked wilder than the first owners of them. He had been on the island four years and four months, being left there by Capt. Stradling in the *Cinque Ports;* his name was Alexander Selkirk, Scotch man ... When his powder failed he took them [the island goats] by speed of foot, for his way of living and continual exercise of walking and running cleared him of all gross humours, so that he ran with wonderful swiftness through the woods and up the hills and rocks, as we perceived when we employed him to catch goats for us ... He likewise tamed some kids, and to divert himself would now and then sing and dance with them and his cats; so that by the care of Providence and vigour of his youth, being now about thirty years old, he came at last to conquer all the inconvenience of his solitude, and to be very easy.

AGED 33.

SOURCE: Woodes Rogers, *A Cruising Voyage Round the World,* 1712; quoted in Kemp and Lloyd, *The Brethren of the Coast,* Heinemann, 1960.

Note: Woodes Rogers introduced Selkirk to Richard Steele, who gave an account of his strange adventures in *The Englishman* (December 2nd, 1713). It was either this or one of the editions of Rogers's book that caught Defoe's attention and led him to write his best-seller *The Life and Surprising Adventures of Robinson Crusoe of York, Mariner . . . Written by himself* (1719).

SEWARD, ANNA (1747–1809), authoress, known as 'The Swan of Lichfield'.

I cannot endure to see a creature so imperfect as myself, invested with attractions and excellencies to which I have no pretence. Perfectly do I feel the ground on which I stand. I know that I have talents, and some good qualities; that I am ingenuous; that my mind is neither stained nor embittered by envy; that I detest injustice, and am grateful for every proof of affection. I can believe what I am told about my countenance expressing the feelings of my heart; but I have no charms, no grace, no elegance of form or deportment. If, in youth, my complexion was clear, glowing and animated; if my features were agreeable, though not regular, they have been the victims of time . . . I wish to be obliging; yet if my manners are not rustic, there is about me an hereditary absence, which always did, and always must, prevent their taking the polish of perfect good-breeding; and, to balance my tolerable properties, there is a frequent indiscretion from an excess of frankness, and from native and yet unconquered impetuosity of temper.

AGED 53.

SOURCE: Anna Seward, on herself; quoted in Hesketh Pearson's *Extraordinary People*, Heinemann, 1965.

SHELLEY, PERCY BYSSHE (1792–1822), poet.

. . . like a girl in boy's clothing, fighting with open hands, and rolling on the floor when flogged, not from the pain, but from a sense of indignity.

His figure was slight and fragile, and yet his bones and joints were large and strong. He was tall, but he stooped so much that he seemed of a low stature. His clothes were expensive, and made according to the most approved mode of the day; but they were tumbled, rumpled, unbrushed. His gestures were abrupt and sometimes violent, occasionally even awkward, yet more frequently gentle and graceful. His complexion was delicate and almost feminine, of the purest white and red; yet he was tanned and freckled by exposure to the sun . . . His features, his whole face, and particularly his head were, in fact, unusually small; yet the last *appeared* of a remarkable bulk, for his hair was long and bushy . . . He often rubbed it up fiercely with his hands, or passed his fingers through his locks unconsciously, so that it was singularly wild and rough . . . His features . . . breathed an animation, a fire, an enthusiasm, a vivid and preternatural intelligence, that I never met with in any other countenance.

AGED 19.

SOURCE: Thomas Jefferson Hogg, *Life of P. B. Shelley*, 1858.

I went a little after the time, and seated myself in the place kept for me at the table, right opposite Shelley himself, as I was told after, for I did not then know what hectic, spare, weakly, yet intellectual-looking creature it was, carving a bit of broccoli or cabbage on his plate, as if it had been the substantial wing of a chicken.

AGED 24.

SOURCE: Benjamin Haydon's *Autobiography*.

He was a boy of studious and meditative habits, averse to all games and sports, and a great reader of novels and romances. He was a slight, thin lad, with remarkably lustrous eyes, fine hair, and a very peculiar shrill voice and laugh . . .

The last time I saw Shelley was at Genoa, in 1822, sitting on the sea-shore, and, when I came upon him, making a true poet's meal of bread and fruit . . . Shelley was looking careworn and ill; and, as usual, was very carelessly dressed. He had on a large and wide straw hat, his long brown hair, already streaked with gray, flowing in large masses from under it, and presented a wild and strange appearance.

SOURCE: Captain R. H. Gronow, *Reminiscences*.

SHERIDAN, RICHARD BRINSLEY (1751–1816), dramatist, parliamentary orator and confidant of the Prince Regent.

Upon the dissolution of Parliament, Sheridan went down to Stafford; but he found circumstances completely changed; he could not obtain the promise of a single vote from his old friends. In consequence of his continued excesses, he had lost much of the charm of outward appearance that had won him friends at an earlier period, and nothing remained of his once expressive face but the remarkable brilliancy of his eyes; his cheeks were bloated, his nose was of a fiery red, and his general aspect bespoke the self-indulgence of the reckless man . . . One man in the crowd bawled out: 'We won't send you to Parliament, for your nose will set the House of Commons on fire . . .'

SOURCE: Captain R. H. Gronow, *Reminiscences*.

SIDDONS, SARAH (1755–1831), actress.

Though I beheld her from the side wing of the stage (a barn about three yards across) and consequently under almost every disadvantage, I own she made so strong an impression on me that I think she cannot fail to be valuable to Drury Lane. Her figure is remarkably fine . . . Her face (if I could judge from where I saw it) is one of the most strikingly beautiful for stage effect that I ever beheld, but this is nothing to her action and general stage deportment, which are remarkably pleasing.

AGED 20.

SOURCE: The Rev. Bates, to David Garrick.

Before us tottered rather than walked a very pretty, fragile-looking creature, dressed in a most unbecoming manner and uncertain where to fix her eyes or her feet.

AGED 20.

SOURCE: A newspaper critic, after her first appearance at Drury Lane.

She acts Macbeth herself better than either Kemble or Kean. It is extraordinary the awe this wonderful woman inspires. After her first reading the men retired to tea. While we were all eating toast and tingling cups and saucers, she began again. It was like the effect of a mass bell at Madrid. All noise ceased. We slunk to our seats like boors, two or three of the most distinguished men of the day, with the very toast in their mouths, afraid to bite. It was curious to see Lawrence in this predicament, to hear him bite by degrees, and then stop for fear of making too much crackle, his eyes full of water from the constraint; and at the same time to hear Mrs. Siddons' 'eye of newt and toe of frog!' and then to see Lawrence give a sly bite, and then look awed and pretend to be listening.

AGED 66.

SOURCE: Benjamin Haydon's *Autobiography*.

Dammit, madam, there is no end to your nose.

SOURCE: Thomas Gainsborough, while painting her portrait.

SIDNEY, SIR PHILIP (1554–1586), soldier and poet.

Sidney was no pleasant man in countenance, his face being spoiled with pimples and of high blood and long.

SOURCE: Ben Johnson; *Conversations with William Drummond of Hawthornden*. Jonson was only 13 at the time of Sidney's death, and doubts have sometimes been cast on the accuracy of his description. But it should be remembered that Jonson was born, and went to school, near Whitehall and must have been very familiar with the appearance of the chief courtiers. It may be supposed, too, that he would retain particularly accurate memories of the poets and writers, whose ranks he aspired to join. Sidney's poor complexion was probably the result of measles and small-pox.

SKEFFINGTON, SIR LUMLEY ST. GEORGE (1751–1850), playwright and dandy; of Skeffington Hall, Leicestershire.

Another dandy of the day was Sir Lumley Skeffington, who used to paint his face, so that he looked like a French toy; he dressed *à la* Robespierre, and practised other follies, although the consummate old fop was a man of literary attainments, and a great admirer and patron of the drama. Skeffington was remarkable for his politeness and courtly manners; in fact, he was invited everywhere, and was very popular with the ladies. You always knew of his approach by an *avant-courier* of sweet smells; and when he advanced a little nearer, you might suppose yourself in the atmosphere of a perfumer's shop.

SOURCE: Captain R. H. Gronow, *Reminiscences*.

SMITH, SIR SIDNEY (1764–1840), admiral.

I remember him well . . . as he stepped on the quarter-deck of H.M. Frigate *El Carmen*, lying in Aboukir Bay, Egypt, in the latter part of the year 1801. He was then of middling stature, good-looking, with tremendous moustachioes, a pair of penetrating black eyes, an intelligent countenance, with a gentlemanly air, expressive of good nature and kindness of heart . . . Sir Sidney, who shortened his moustachioes daily, according to our run made in the night, fully determined to get rid of them by our arrival in England . . .

SOURCE: Lieutenant G. S. Parsons, *Nelsonian Reminiscences*, 1843: edit. by W. H. Long, Gibbings and Company, 1905.

SMITH, WILLIAM HENRY (1825–1891), statesman.

He was a very remarkable man, quiet, unassuming, with no special power of speech or expression, and handicapped by a weak voice; but he hid under this modest exterior rare capacity, courage and judgment . . . It was these latent qualities—the value of which, in spite of his reluctance to push himself forward, became more and more impressed upon his colleagues —that led to his being forced up in every political crisis to a higher position; and in all these crises this kindly, quiet-mannered man was sent to the post of danger. Ultimately, he became, for a troublous five years, Leader of the House of Commons . . . There was one gesture of his which we all knew and to which there was no denial. When asking you to undertake something you very much disliked, he would, after listening to your objection, put his hand on your shoulder, and say: 'I must ask you to do this.' And so we did.

SOURCE: Lord George Hamilton, *Parliamentary Reminiscences and Reflections, 1868–1885*, John Murray, 1917.

SMOLLETT, TOBIAS GEORGE (1721–1771), novelist.

The person of Dr. Smollett was stout and well proportioned, his countenance engaging, his manner reserved, with a certain air of dignity that seemed to indicate that he was not unconscious of his own powers . . . He lived in a hospitable manner, but he despised that hospitality which is founded on ostentation, which entertains only those whose situation in life flatters the vanity of the entertainer . . .

SOURCE: John Moore, M.D., *Works, with Memoirs of his Life*, 1797.

SOUTHEY, ROBERT (1774–1843), poet and man of letters.

Southey is lean as a harrow; dun as a tobacco-spluchan*, no chin (I mean, the smallest), snubbed Roman nose, vehement brown eyes, huge white head of hair; when he rises—all legs together.

SOURCE: Thomas Carlyle, *Letters*.

SPENCER, HERBERT (1820–1903), philosopher.

I can recall nothing more than a few days' illness from one of the disorders of childhood; and on the whole my vigour, though not great, was considerable. There seemed to be then, and continued thereafter, a constitution distinguished rather by good balance than by great vital activity. No spontaneous overflow of energy was exhibited—no high pressure of steam; and hence a certain reluctance to exertion in the absence of strong motive. Nevertheless there was a large margin of latent power—a good deal of 'bottom', as the sporting people call it. In feats of strength I do not remember any superiority except in running. I was more fleet than any of my school-fellows. This may have been associated with an unusual length of limb, by which in boyhood I was characterised. It seems not improbable

* Pouch.

that this physical trait had something to do with the performance of a great feat in walking during later boyhood.

It can, I think, scarcely be doubted that my system received a detrimental shock. That a boy of 13 should, without any food but bread and water and two or three glasses of beer, and without sleep for two nights, walk 48 miles one day, 47 the next, and some 20 the third, is surprising enough. It is strange that the exertion was borne at all; and it is highly improbable that it was borne without injury ... The cost has to be met somehow; and is met, no doubt, by a falling short of ultimate perfection of structure.

As far back as I can remember there have been signs that the periphery of the vascular system has not been well filled. Except in hot weather, or after walking several miles, the ends of my fingers have been inadequately distended; coldness of the hands has been an ordinary trait; and relative dryness of the skin has also shown deficiency of blood supply at the surface.

Even in the streets my state of abstraction was such that I occasionally talked aloud as I went along: a fact of which I was from time to time made aware by people who turned to look at me ... when out of doors I sometimes passed those living in the same house with me without knowing that I had seen them, though I looked them in the face.

SOURCE: Herbert Spencer, *An Autobiography*, 1904. When he was 13, Spencer paid a visit, with his father and mother, to an uncle at Hinton Charterhouse, near Bath. After about a month, his parents returned to Derby, leaving the boy behind. Overcome by homesickness, he set off to walk home, with two shillings in his pocket. He reached Derby about 3 o'clock on Saturday afternoon, having left Hinton Charterhouse at 6 o'clock on Thursday morning.

Everyone knows his portrait, with the domelike, bald head surrounded by iron-grey hair, the grey whiskers, the firm mouth with the long upper lip, the limp, bulging shirt-front, and the rough, old-fashioned clothes he always wore.

But what can a photograph do? It cannot show the fresh ruddy colour in his cheeks, which made him look so well and so often belied his bad health. It cannot properly show the hazel eyes with the dark rims round the irises and the dark spots in them. It cannot show the wonderful play of expression that came over his features when he spoke, or the merry twinkle that shone in his eye when he was amused.

One very cold, foggy day he made up his mind that we should both go shopping with him. One of us demurred, being liable to catch cold; but he was obdurate, declaring that if sufficiently clad, no harm could come of it, as people did not take cold in the face.

But on her arrival in the hall ready dressed for the drive, he at once remarked, 'You haven't enough on,' and insisted upon her wearing his old Inverness cape over everything else.

What a queer sight it was for the Army and Navy Stores! He himself looked quaint enough in his wideawake hat, woolly gloves—in colour the nearest approach to the inevitable 'impure purple' obtainable in London—and dark brown, old-fashioned Inverness cape. But this was nothing compared to the extraordinary figure which closely followed him of a girl, whose identity was almost lost in an exactly similar garment. The voluminous folds of the two capes entirely filled up the gangways as their wearers walked about together from department to department.

To see Mr. Spencer off on his travels from one of the large London stations was an experience not easily forgotten . . . First of all there was the great man himself to be looked after. Then his carriage in charge of his staid and solemn coachman. Then his carrying chair, his hammock, his rugs, air cushions, and endless small paraphernalia, the most important of which was the MS. of *Beneficence*—we think it was—which he carried himself, and for which he made a most amusing arrangement to insure its complete safety.

He tied a thick piece of string round his waist which could not be seen—one end, however, was left two or three yards long, and this issued like a tail from underneath the back of his coat, and to its end the MS. was attached, made into a brown paper parcel, which he then easily held in his hand ...

Experience had taught him that by travelling in a hammock when going a long journey he avoided the evil consequences which usually followed the shaking of the train. On that occasion he became so absorbed in superintending the slinging of it, that he did not at once observe the numerous inquisitive faces which peered eagerly through the windows at him.

Directly, however, he became conscious of them, out rang in stentorian tones to the porters:

'Draw down those blinds!'

The four men present instantly spring to do his bidding, so the little entertainment for those inquisitive persons came to a sudden end.

When all this was complete the officials were dismissed, and he climbed with some difficulty into his exceedingly unstable resting-place.

SOURCE: *Home Life With Herbert Spencer*, by Two; J. W. Arrowsmith, 1906. 'Two' was the pen-name of two ladies whose home he shared from 1889–1897.

SPENCER, JOHN CHARLES, Viscount Althorp and third Earl Spencer (1782–1845), statesman.

The greatest homage that was ever rendered to character and public virtue was exhibited in his popularity and authority during the four eventful years when he led the Whig Government and party in the House of Commons. Without one showy accomplishment, without wit to amuse or eloquence to persuade with a voice unmelodious and a manner ungraceful, and barely able to speak plain sense in still plainer language, he exercised in the House of Commons an influence and even a dominion greater than any Leader either after or before him.

SOURCE: Charles Greville. *The Greville Memoirs.*

R

SPENSER, EDMUND (1552?–1599), poet.

Mr. Beeston says he was a little man, wore short hair, little band and little cuffs.

SOURCE: John Aubrey, *Brief Lives*, edit. Andrew Clark, Clarendon Press, 1898.

SPOONER, WILLIAM ARCHIBALD (1844–1930), warden of New College, Oxford; gave his name, from his occasional lapses of speech, to the 'spoonerism'.

To this admirable man, who has achieved immortality by giving his name to a common human failing, a life of pleasant pastoral activity among young men provided an ideal frame. An Oxford college was just the right size for Spooner, and Spooner was just the right size for an Oxford college. His sweet temper, keen wit, and ingratiating appearance, all rose and silver, his capacity for dealing humorously with youthful folly, his sanity and Christian charity, and the perennial freshness of his interests and conversation, made him the most valuable kind of member in a society such as ours. Men smiled at him, for he was the subject of endless jests, and loved him. His eyesight, which was so imperfect that he could only read with the aid of powerful glasses, debarred him from making any serious addition to knowledge . . . but nevertheless he was able, despite his grave physical infirmity, not only to teach and examine over a wide field of knowledge, but also to keep up an immense correspondence with undergraduates all over the world . . . He seemed to us all to be the happiest and most fortunate man, happy in his charming wife and family, happy in his College drudgery, and above all happy in his opportunities of gentle influence among the young.

SOURCE: H. A. L. Fisher, *An Unfinished Autobiography*, O.U.P., 1940.

STANHOPE, LADY HESTER LUCY (1776–1839), traveller and eccentric; housekeeper to her uncle, William Pitt.

There sat the Lady Prophetess. She rose from her seat very

formally—spoke to me a few words of welcome, pointed to a chair—one already placed exactly opposite to her sofa at a couple of yards' distance—and remained standing up to the full of her majestic height, perfectly still and motionless, until I had taken my appointed place; she then resumed her seat— not packing herself up according to the mode of the orientals, but allowing her feet to rest on the floor or the foot-stool; at the moment of seating herself she covered her lap with a mass of loose, white drapery. It occurred to me at the time that she did this in order to avoid the awkwardness of sitting in manifest trousers under the eye of a European; but I can hardly fancy now, that, with her wilful nature, she would have brooked such a compromise as this.

The woman before me had exactly the person of a prophetess . . . of a good, business-like, practical prophetess, long used to the exercise of her sacred calling. I have been told by those who knew Lady Hester Stanhope in her youth, that any notion of a resemblance betwixt her and the great Chatham must have been fanciful; but at the time of my seeing her, the large commanding features of the gaunt woman, then sixty years old or more, certainly reminded me of the statesman that lay dying in the House of Lords, according to Copley's picture. Her face was of the most astonishing whiteness; she wore a very large turban made seemingly of pale cashmere shawls, and so disposed as to conceal the hair; her dress from the chin down to the point at which it was concealed by the drapery on her lap, was a mass of white linen loosely folding—an ecclesiastical sort of affair more like a surplice than any of those blessed creations which our souls love under the names of 'dress' and 'frock' and 'bodice' and 'collar' and 'habit-skirt' and sweet 'chemisette'.

SOURCE: A. W. Kinglake, *Eöthen*.

STEPHENSON, GEORGE (1781–1848), inventor and railway pioneer; engineer of Stockton and Darlington railway.

Now for a word or two about the master of all these marvels, with whom I am most horribly in love. He is a man of from fifty to fifty-five years of age; his face is fine, though careworn, and bears an expression of deep thoughtfulness; his mode of explaining his ideas is peculiar and very original, striking and forcible; and although his accent indicates strongly his north country birth, his language has not the slightest touch of vulgarity or coarseness. He has certainly turned my heart.

AGED 51.

SOURCE: Frances Anne Kemble, *Records of a Girlhood*, 1878.

STEVENSON, ROBERT LOUIS (1850–1894), writer.

Mr. Stevenson got up whenever he moved at all, and walked about with his hands in his trouser-pockets and his shoulders high. He wore check trousers, a black velvet coat, and a red tie under a turn-down collar. His face is fascinating in its changes. A slightly Scottish accent, and his eyes rove about a good deal as he speaks. His smile is very frank, genial, and kind, as his whole manner is sympathetic.

AGED 36.

SOURCE: Margaret Burne-Jones; *The Richmond Papers*, Heinemann, 1926.

I can see him now, holding in his beautiful fingers, stained with nicotine, a constantly renewed cigarette, and hear his voice so musical, and his sentences so daintily constructed as he drew picture after picture without restraint or pedantry. It was perfect talk, his was! . . . He was a gay fellow, devoted to his friends, and they to him . . . A gentle, consistent vanity was his, that charming form of an otherwise unattractive quality which, owing to a certain freshness and naïveté, assumes that all goes well, that the estimate is a perfectly true one which grants genius *to* genius!

SOURCE: William Richmond; *The Richmond Papers*, Heinemann, 1926.

In personal appearance, Stevenson was of good stature (about 5 foot 10 inches) and activity, but very slender, his leanness of body and limb (not of face) having been throughout life abnormal. The head was small; the eyes dark hazel, very wide-set, intent, and beaming; the face of a long oval shape; the expression rich and animated. He had a free and picturesque play of gesture and a voice of full and manly fibre, in which his pulmonary weakness was not at all displayed.

SOURCE: Sidney Colvin, *Dictionary of National Biography*, 1898.

STEWART, ROBERT, Viscount Castlereagh (1769–1822), statesman.

He was above six feet high and had a remarkably fine commanding figure, very dark eyes, rather a high nose and a mouth whose smile was sweeter than it is possible to describe. It was impossible to look at him and see the benevolent and amiable expression of his countenance without a disposition to like him, and over his whole person was spread an air of dignity and nobleness such as I have never seen in any other person. His manners were perfect as those of a high-born polished gentleman ...

He had a natural slowness of constitution of which he was himself quite aware, for he has often told me that he required the goading and violence of the House of Commons to rouse him, and that he was determined never to go into the House of Lords as they were too quiet and sleepy for him.

AGED 53.

I was afterwards returning towards King Street, when I was accosted by Lord Castlereagh ... This remarkable man was quietly looking on while his windows were being broken by these ruffians. I can see him before me now, dressed in a blue coat buttoned up to the chin, a blue spenser, kerseymere breeches, long gaiters, shoes covered by galoshes, and a white neck-cloth. He was a particularly handsome man, possessed great pluck and energy, and on this occasion [i.e. during the

Corn Law riots], appeared perfectly calm and unconcerned . . .

SOURCE: *The Journal of Mrs. Arbuthnot*, ed. F. Bamford and Duke of Wellington, Macmillan, 1950.

And what shall I say of Lord Castlereagh—that spouter without beginning, middle, or end—who has not an idea in his head, nor a word to say for himself—who carries the House of Commons by his manner alone—who bows and smiles assent and dissent—who makes a dangling proposition of his person, and is himself a drooping figure of speech—what shall I say of this inanimate automaton? Nothing!

SOURCE: William Hazlitt, *On the Present State of Parliamentary Eloquence*, 1820.

STRATHNAIRN, BARON (1801–1885). See Rose, Hugh Henry, Baron Strathnairn.

STUART, CHARLES EDWARD LOUIS PHILIP CASIMIR (1720–1788), the Young Pretender.

He was a tall slender young man, about five feet ten inches high, of a ruddy complexion, high nosed, large rolling brown eyes, long visaged, red-haired, but at that time wore a pale periwig. He was in Highland habit, had a blue sash, wrought with gold, that came over his shoulder; red velvet breeches, a green velvet bonnet, with a white cockade, and gold lace about it. He had a silver-hilted broad sword, and was shewn great respect by his forces.

AGED 25.

SOURCE: An eye witness, at the capture of Edinburgh, 1745; quoted in Tomasson and Buist, *Battles of the '45*, Batsford, 1962.

I went to the road-side where the Chevalier . . . was standing. He was clad as an ordinary Captain, in a coarse blue plaid and blue bonnet. His boots and knees were much dirtied; he seemed to have fallen into a ditch, which I was told by one of his

Lifeguards he had. He was exceeding merry; speaking of his army he said twice, 'My Highlandmen have lost their plaids.' At which he laughed very heartily ... Then he refreshed himself upon the field and with the utmost composure ate a piece of cold beef, and drank a glass of wine, amidst the deep and piercing groans of the wounded and dying, who had fallen a sacrifice to his ambition.

AGED 25.

SOURCE: Andrew Henderson, after the battle of Prestonpans; quoted in Tomasson and Buist, *Battles of the '45*, Batsford, 1962.

The Pretender is naturally above the middle size, but stoops excessively; he appears bloated and red in the face; his countenance heavy and sleepy, which is attributed to his having given into excess of drinking; but when a young man he must have been esteemed handsome. His complexion is of the fair tint, his eyes blue, his hair light brown, and the contour of his face a long oval; he is by no means thin, has a noble person, and a graceful manner. His dress was scarlet laced with broad gold lace; he wears the blue riband outside of his coat, from which depends a cameo, antique, as large as the palm of my hand; and he wears the same Garter and motto as those of the noble order of St. George of England.

AGED ABOUT 50.

SOURCE: Mrs. Miller, *Letters from Italy by an Englishwoman*, London, 1776.

Charles Edward's complexion was dark, and he manifestly bore the same family resemblance to his grandfather James the Second that His Britannic Majesty's countenance presents to George the First, or to the late King. On the occasion just related he wore, besides the decorations of the Order of the Garter, a velvet great coat, which his infirm health rendered necessary even in summer, on coming out of the theatre; and a cocked hat, the sides of which were half drawn up with gold twist. His whole figure, paralytic and debilitated, presented the appearance of great bodily decay.

The strength of his mind had likewise become extinct at this time; and with the decline of his intellectual powers, the suavity of his temper forsaking him, he became irritable, morose, and intractable, particularly in his family. An unhappy propensity to wine, which he gratified to excess, while it enervated his sytem, rendered him frequently an object of pity or of contempt, when in public; divesting him of that dignity which would otherwise always have accompanied the representative of so many kings.

AGED 57.

SOURCE: Sir N. William Wraxall, *Historical Memoirs of My Own Life*, 1815.

STUART or **STEWART, FRANCES THERESA,** Duchess of Richmond and Lennox (1647–1702), beauty.

But it was the finest sight to me, considering their great beauties and dress, that ever I did see in all my life. But, above all, Mrs. Stewart in this dress, with her hat cocked and a red plume, with her sweet eye, little Roman nose, and excellent taille, is now the greatest beauty I ever saw, I think, in my life; and if ever woman can, do exceed my Lady Castlemaine, at least in this dress.

AGED 16.

... my Lord Brouncker sent to Somerset House to hear how the Duchess of Richmond do; and word brought by him that she is pretty well, but mighty full of the small-pox, by which all do conclude she will be wholly spoiled, which is the greatest instance of the uncertainty of beauty that could be in this age ...

AGED 21.

SOURCE: Samuel Pepys, *Diary*.

Hers was a face with more brilliancy than power to touch the emotions. It would have been difficult to imagine less brain, combined with more beauty. Every feature was perfect and regular, but her shape was not very good. None, the less, she was slender, straightly built and taller than the generality of women. She was graceful, an accomplished dancer, and spoke French better than her native tongue; besides, she was polished and possessed that air of fashion which is always so much run after, and which it is so hard to acquire, except it has been learned in France from very early youth.

SOURCE: Anthony Hamilton, *Memoirs of the Comte de Gramont*, trans. Peter Quennell, George Routledge & Sons, 1930.

STUART, JAMES FRANCIS EDWARD (1688–1766), the Old Pretender; known also as the Chevalier de St. George.

The Chevalier de St. George is tall, meagre, melancholy in his aspect. Enthusiasm and disappointment have stamped a solemnity on his person which rather creates pity than respect ... Without the particular features of any Stuart, the Chevalier has the strong lines and fatality of air peculiar to them all. From the first moment I saw him, I never doubted the legitimacy of his birth.

AGED 64.

SOURCE: Horace Walpole, *Memoirs*, 1822–1845.

His person was tall and thin, seeming to be lean rather than to fill as he grows in years. His countenance was pale, yet he seems to be sanguine in his constitution, and has something of a vivacity in his eye that perhaps would have been more visible, if he had not been under dejected circumstances and surrounded with discouragements, which it must be acknowledged, were sufficient to alter the complexion even of his soul as well as of his body. His speech was grave, and not very clearly expressing his thoughts, nor overmuch to the purpose, but his words were few, and his behaviour and temper seemed always composed ... Neither can I say I ever saw him smile ... We saw nothing in him that looked like spirit. He never appeared with cheerfulness and vigour to animate us. Our men began to despise him; some asked if he could speak. His countenance looked extremely heavy ... I am sure the figure he made dejected us.

SOURCE: *True Account of the Proceedings at Perth*, by a Rebel.

And first for the person of the Chevalier, which you desired to know. He is tall, straight and clean-limbed, slender, yet his bones pretty large. He has a very graceful mien, walks fast; and his gait has great resemblance to his uncle, King Charles II, and the lines of his face grow daily more and more like him ... He is always cheerful but seldom merry, thoughtful but not dejected, and bears his misfortunes with a visible magnanimity of spirit ... He is very affable, and has something strangely engaging in his voice and deportment, that none who ever conversed with him but are charmed with his good sense and sweetness of temper.

SOURCE: *A Letter from Mr. Lesly to a Member of Parliament in London;* quoted in *English Historical Documents*, Eyre and Spottiswoode.

STUART, JOHN, third Earl of Bute (1713–1792).

He has a good person, fine legs, and a theatrical air of the greatest importance. There is an extraordinary appearance of wisdom, both in his look and manner of speaking; for whether the subject be serious or trifling, he is equally pompous, slow and sententious. Not content with being wise, he would be thought a polite scholar, but he has the misfortune never to succeed, except with those who are exceedingly ignorant.

SOURCE: James, Earl Waldegrave; *Memoirs from 1854–1858.*

Lord Bute, when young, possessed a very handsome person, of which advantage he was not insensible; and he used to pass many hours every day, as his enemies asserted, occupied in contemplating the symmetry of his own legs, during his solitary walks by the side of the Thames ... Of a disposition naturally retired and severe, he was not formed for an extensive commerce with mankind, or endowed by Nature with talents for managing popular assemblies. Even in his family he was austere, harsh, difficult of access, and sometimes totally inaccessible to his own children. In the House of Lords he neither displayed eloquence nor graciousness of manners.

SOURCE: Sir N. William Wraxall, *Historical Memoirs of My Own Life*, 1815.

SUCKLING, SIR JOHN (1609–1642), poet.

He was of middle stature and slight strength, brisk round eye, reddish faced and red nose (ill liver), his head not very big, his hair a kind of sand colour; his beard turned up naturally, so that he had a brisk and graceful look.

SOURCE: John Aubrey, *Brief Lives*, edit. Andrew Clark, 1898.

SWIFT, JONATHAN (1667–1745), Dean of St. Patrick's, Dublin, and satirist.

He read the service rather with a strong nervous voice than in a graceful manner; his voice was sharp and high-toned, rather than harmonious . . .

The person of Swift had not many recommendations. He had a kind of muddy complexion, which, though he washed himself with oriental scrupulosity, did not look clear. He had a countenance sour and severe, which he seldom softened by an appearance of gaiety. He stubbornly resisted any tendency to laughter . . . His beneficence was not graced with tenderness or civility.

SOURCE: Doctor Samuel Johnson, *Lives of the Most Eminent English Poets*, 1781, Vol. III.

SWINBURNE, ALGERNON CHARLES (1837–1909), poet.

At dinner Swinburne sat silent, at least he did not join in the general talk and laughter, because of his deafness. He can hear nothing now, unless in *tête-à-tête*, slowly and deliberately.

AGED 41.

Swinburne showed some signs . . . of the smaller dilapidations of age: his hair more dusted with grey, his head less stiffly erect. However, his eye, which Burne-Jones (a trained observer who had seen him often and in every possible light) once called green, looked blue to me, particularly blue and clear for a man of his years tonight. Something very direct in his glance struck me always, when he looked up to question or offer an opinion. His deafness, as usual, made conversation slow at first; but it seemed to affect him less as the evening went on.

AGED 68.

SOURCE (for both the above): Alice E. Bird and Ernest Rhys, an article, *Two Evenings with Swinburne*, in *The Bibliophile*, July 1909.

He was short, with sloping shoulders, from which rose a long and slender neck, surmounted by a very large head. The cranium seemed to be out of all proportion to the rest of the structure. His spine was rigid, and though he often bowed the heaviness of his head . . . he seemed never to bend his neck . . . He required very little sleep, and occasionally when I have parted from him in the evening after saying 'Good-night,' he has simply sat back in the deep sofa in his sitting-room, his little feet close together, his arms against his side, folded in his frock-coat like a grasshopper in its wing-covers, and fallen asleep, apparently for the night, before I could blow out the candles and steal forth from the door. I am speaking, of course, of early days; it was thus about 1875 that I closely observed him . . .

His vast brain seemed to weight down and give solidity to a frame otherwise as light as thistledown, a body almost as immaterial as that of a fairy. In the streets he had the movements of a somnambulist, and often I have seen him passing like a ghost across the traffic of Holborn, or threading the pressure of carts eastwards of Gray's Inn Road, without glancing to the left or the right, like something blown before a wind . . .

His extreme natural politeness was always apparent in his

talk, unless, of course, some unfortunate *contretemps* should rouse a sudden ebullition, when he could be neither just nor kind. But, as a rule, his courtesy shone out of his blue-grey eyes and was lighted up by the halo of his cloud of orange hair as he waved it, gravely or waggishly, at the company.

SOURCE: Edmund Gosse, *Portraits and Sketches*, Heinemann, 1912.

TAYLOR, MICHAEL ANGELO (1757–1834), member of Parliament; one of the managers of the impeachment of Warren Hastings.

Michael Angelo was a member of Parliament for many years, and generally sat in one of the most important committees of the House of Commons; for he was a man of authority and an attractive speaker. In appearance he was one of that sort of persons whom you could not pass in the streets without exclaiming, 'Who can that be?' His face blushed with port wine, the purple tints of which, by contrast, caused his white hair to glitter with silvery brightness; he wore leather breeches, top boots, blue coat, white waistcoat, and an unstarched and exquisitely white neckcloth, the whole surmounted by a very broad-brimmed beaver—such was the dress of the universally-known Michael Angelo Taylor.

SOURCE: Captain R. H. Gronow, *Reminiscences*.

TEACH or **THATCH, EDWARD** (?–1718), pirate; known as Blackbeard.

Captain Teach assumed the cognomen of Blackbeard from that large quantity of hair which, like a frightful meteor, covered his whole face, and frightened America more than any comet that has appeared there a long time.

This beard was black, which he suffered to grow to an extravagant length; as to breadth, it came up to his eyes; he was accustomed to twist it up with ribbons, in small tails, after the manner of our Ramillies wigs, and turn them about his ears. In time of action, he wore a sling over his shoulders, with three braces of pistols, hanging in holsters like bandoliers; and stuck lighted matches under his hat which, appearing on each side of his face, his eyes naturally looking fierce and wild, made him altogether such a figure that imagination cannot form an idea of a Fury from hell to look more frightful . . .

Thus it was they passed their lives, with very little pleasure or satisfaction in the possession of what they violently take away from others, and used to pay for it at last by an ignominious death.

SOURCE: Captain Charles Johnson, *General History of the Pyrates, from their first Rise and Settlement in the Island of Providence, to the Present Time* . . . etc., 4th Edition, 1726.

TEMPLE, SIR WILLIAM (1628–1699), diplomat and writer.

He was rather tall than low; his shape, when young, very exact; his hair a dark brown, and curled naturally, and whilst that was esteemed a beauty nobody had it in greater perfection; his eyes grey, but lively; and his body lean, but extreme active, so that none acquitted themselves better at all sorts of exercise.

He was not without strong aversions, so as to be uneasy at the first sight of some he disliked, and impatient of their conversation; apt to be warm in disputes and expostulations, which made him hate the one, and avoid the other . . . He turn'd his conversation to what was more easy and pleasant, especially at table, where he said ill humour ought never to come . . .

He lived healthful till forty-two, then began to be troubled with rheums upon his teeth and eyes, which he attributed to the air of Holland, and which ended, when he was forty-seven, in the gout, upon which he grew very melancholy, being then ambassador at the Hague; he said he was never good for anything after it, and though he continued in business near three years longer, 'twas always with the design of winding himself out as fast as he could.

SOURCE: Martha, Lady Giffard; *Life and Character of Sir William Temple, Bart.*, 1728.

TENNYSON, ALFRED, first Baron Tennyson (1809–1892), poet.

. . . the most picturesque figure, without affectation, that I ever saw; of middle size, rather slouching, dressed entirely in black, and with nothing white about him except the collar of his shirt, which methought might have been clean the day before. He had on a black wide-awake hat, with round crown and wide irregular brim, beneath which came down his long black hair, looking terribly tangled; he had a long, pointed beard, too, a little browner than the hair, and not so abundant as to incumber any expression of his face. His frock-coat was buttoned across the breast though the afternoon was warm. His face was very dark, and not exactly a smooth face, but worn, and expressing great sensitiveness . . . He seemed as if he did not see the crowd nor think of them, but as if he defended himself from them by ignoring them altogether . . .

He shook hands . . . and shuffled away . . . with short, irregular steps, a very queer gait, as if he were walking in slippers too loose for him. I had observed that he seemed to turn his feet slightly inward, after the fashion of Indians . . .

AGED 46.

SOURCE: Description by Nathaniel Hawthorne, following a sight of the poet in Manchester, 1857. Despite his great regard for Tennyson, Hawthorne did not introduce himself, and the two never met.

It is a proud memory that I was once privileged, as a small schoolboy, to take a walk with the old poet at Faringford. I remember how he came sweeping along in his picturesque slouch hat and long cloak, how as I trotted by his side he recited or intoned choice passages from his poetry, how from time to time he would turn round to me with a childish satisfaction and say, 'Isn't that grand?', and how keenly, despite his near sight, he would descry beauty in a flower and bring it to the notice of his companion . . .

No spoiling could rob Tennyson of his essential greatness and simplicity. In some respects he had retained more of that rough county Lincolnshire than one would gather from his son's filial tribute. He liked strong language and strong drink. Nor do I forget that I was privileged to witness the preparation for the poet's weekly bath, the round shallow tub on the landing, and the tall cans of hot water which it was the office of the coachman to pour over the stalwart frame of the seated Laureate!

SOURCE: H. A. L. Fisher, *An Unfinished Autobiography*, O.U.P., 1940.

He had been considerably weakened by the serious illness which attacked him at the end of 1888 and which the doctors fully expected to prove fatal—indeed, nothing but his extraordinarily strong constitution and powerful will had carried him through. Weakened as he was, however, he will always remain in my memory as the most potent and impressive personality I have ever known. He was over six feet in height and very strongly built, very swarthy in colouring, with grizzled beard, and a tall dome-like skull rising above a thick and rather straggly fringe of dark hair. His nose was powerfully aquiline, his eyes dark and heavy-lidded, with great intensity of expression, his face marked by a deep furrow descending from the corner of each nostril towards the jaw. His hands were large, the fingers long and noticeably square-tipped. Someone said of him in his late middle age that if he had been pointed out to you as the author of the *Iliad* you wouldn't have been at all surprised. Another friend described him as like a Hebrew prophet, and another (owing to his habitual untidiness) as 'a dilapidated Jove'. These various descriptions fit very well the old but still dominating figure which I remember, though that figure was beginning to stoop, and the steps, though still rapid, shuffled a little. My grandfather's impressiveness was increased by his deep and extraordinarily vibrant voice, by the strong North Country vowels, traces of which always marked his speech, and by the singularity of his clothes, which, strange to say, were very much the same as those he had worn in the reign of William the Fourth—a sort of John Bull frock-coat, black in winter and grey in summer, with full skirts and broad 'poacher's' pockets, rather loose trousers of the same material hanging in wrinkles which made his legs look like the hind-legs of an elephant, a sleeveless Spanish cloak, with velvet collar, and a broad black wide-awake hat.

SOURCE: Sir Charles Tennyson, *Stars and Markets*, Chatto and Windus, 1957.

Down the great aisle of elms they came, a white Russian deer-hound flashing like silver through the sun or shade and the central figure of the poet, a note of black in the midst of the vivid green, grand in the folds of his ample cloak, and his face looming grandly from the shadow of the giant hat ... The slight stoop, and the heavier step of age made the youthful figure of the son look all the more what he was, his father's vigorous staff and prop.

AGED 81.

SOURCE: Mrs. G. F. Watts; quoted in Joanna Richardson's *The Pre-Eminent Victorian*, Jonathan Cape, 1962.

TENNYSON, LADY EMILY SARAH (1813–1896), wife of Alfred, Lord Tennyson.

She had for many years been troubled with some weakness of the spine, lying all day upon a sofa in the drawing-room and only leaving it to come into lunch or dinner on the arm of her husband or her son, or to be wheeled about the garden in an invalid chair. Lying or standing, she had a look of extraordinary fragility. Rather below the middle height, she was very slight in figure, her skin was clear, but finely wrinkled and in colour and texture like the faintly withered petals of a pale pink rose. Her large grey eyes were very clear, too, and her pale, silky hair was drawn straight back from her finely-modelled forehead and fastened behind in a knot, under a white lace shawl ... It was characteristic (and perhaps commoner in their generation than is generally realized) that she and my grandfather often used the pronoun 'thou' and 'thee' when talking to one another.

SOURCE: Sir Charles Tennyson, *Stars and Markets*, Chatto and Windus, 1957.

S

TESIMOND, *alias* **GREENWAY, OSWALD** (1563–1635), jesuit.
Also known as 'Philip Beaumont'.

Of a reasonable stature, black hair, a brown beard cut close
on the cheeks and left broad on the chin, somewhat long-
visaged, lean in the face but of a good red complexion, his nose
somewhat long and sharp at the end, his hands slender and long
fingers, his body slender, his legs of a good proportion, his feet
somewhat long and slender.

His apparel of cloth, hose and jerkin much after the Italian
fashion, the jerkin buttoned on the breast, his cloak buttoned
down before with ribbons hanging down on his breast, his hat
narrow-brimmed, with a small band and a broad full crown,
as now the fashion is.

SOURCE: Proclamation for his apprehension.

THACKERAY, WILLIAM MAKEPEACE (1811–1863), novelist.

He was then a rosy-faced boy with dark curling hair, and a
quick, intelligent eye, ever twinkling with humour, and *good*
humour. He was stout and broad-set, and gave no promise of
the stature which he afterwards reached . . .

AGED ABOUT 16.

SOURCE: John Frederick Boyes, *Memorials of Thackeray's School
Days*.

. . . a tall, thin, large-eyed, full and ruddy-faced man with an
eye-glass fixed *en permanence* . . . He had always a flow of
humour and pleasantry, and was made much of by his friends.
At supper parties, though not talkative—rather observant—he
enjoyed the humours of the hour, and sang one or two old songs
with great applause. 'Old King Cole' I well remember to have
heard from him at the supper I gave to celebrate my election as
Scholar. It made me laugh excessively—not from the novelty
of the song, but from the humour with which it was given.

AGED ABOUT 21.

SOURCE: William Hepworth Thompson, Master of Trinity
College, Cambridge.

On calling at the address given me . . . I was asked to enter the front apartment, where a tall, slim individual between thirty and thirty-five years of age, with a pleasant smiling countenance and a bridgeless nose, and clad in a dressing gown of a decided Parisian cut, rose from a small table, standing close to the near window, to receive me. When he stood up, the low pitch of the room caused him to look even taller than he really was, and his actual height was well over six feet.

AGED ABOUT 33.

SOURCE: Henry Viztelly, *Glances Back*.

Note : Thackeray broke his nose twice, once in a fight at school (1822) and once as a result of a fall from a donkey (Montmorency, 1835). It was permanently flattened and is obvious in his portraits. For the early part of his life he was quite short—about five feet six inches when he was 15, then, during an illness in 1828, suddenly grew to his full height of six feet three inches. His weight also varied a good deal. In his middle thirties he weighed between 15 and 18 stone. He took little exercise, was not particularly strong as a result, but he was apparently always prepared to give a good account of himself if a fight threatened.

THOMSON, JAMES (1700–1748), poet.

I shaved him, I believe, seven or eight years or more. He had a face as long as a horse; and he perspired so much that, I remember, after walking one day in summer, I shaved his head without lather, by his own desire. His hair was as soft as a camel's—I hardly ever felt such; and yet it grew so remarkably that, if it was but an inch long, it stood upright on end from his head like a brush . . . he was pretty corpulent, and stooped forward rather when he walked, as though he was full of thought. He was very careless and negligent about his dress, and wore his clothes remarkably plain.

SOURCE: William Taylor, his barber; anecdotes, collected by the Earl of Buchan, included in John Timb's *A Century of Anecdote, 1760–1860*.

His worst appearance was when you saw him walking alone, in a thoughtful mood; but let a friend accost him, and enter into conversation, he would instantly brighten into a most amiable aspect, his features no longer the same, and his eye darting a peculiar animated fire. The case was much alike in company; where, if it was mixed, or very numerous, he made but an indifferent figure, but with a few select friends, he was open, sprightly, and entertaining . . . Such was his extreme sensibility, so perfect the harmony of his organs with the sentiments of his mind, that his looks always announced, and half expressed, what he was about to say.

SOURCE: *Account of his Life and Writings*, prefixed to Murdoch's edit. of Thomson's *Works . . . with his last Corrections and Improvements*, 1762.

THOMPSON, FRANCIS (1860–1907), poet.

. . . an undistinguished, weak little man with nothing about him to show that he is so fine a poet.

AGED 38.

. . . attired in dirty rags, and looking the picture of ruin—a very sad sight.

AGED 43.

. . . very thin, but looking far more like a poet than ever before when I have seen him—like some Spanish ascetic with dark hair and a little thin grey beard.

AGED 47.

He was the greatest enigma I ever encountered. He seemed so insignificant and feeble; I could never imagine how he could have written *The Hound of Heaven*. He was interested in cricket—but he couldn't have hit a ball across this room.

SOURCE: Sir Sydney Carlyle Cockerell; all quoted in Wilfrid Blunt's *Cockerell*, Hamish Hamilton, 1964.

THURLOW, EDWARD, first Baron Thurlow (1731–1806), lord
chancellor.

Nor did Thurlow neglect any of the external circumstances, how
trifling soever, by which attention and deference could be
secured on the part of his audience. Not only were his periods
well rounded, and the connecting matter or continuing phrases
well flung in, but the tongue was so hung as to make the
sonorous voice peal through the hall, and appear to convey
things awful to examine too near, and perilous to question ...
He rose slowly from his seat; he left the woolsack with delibera-
tion; but he went not to the nearest place, like ordinary
chancellors, the sons of mortal men; he drew back a pace or
two, and, standing, as it were, askance, and partly behind the
huge bale he had quitted for a season, he began to pour out,
first in a growl, and then in a clearer and louder roll, the matter
which he had to deliver.

SOURCE: Lord Brougham; quoted in John Timb's *A Century of
Anecdote, 1760–1860.*

Thurlow was always dressed in a full suit of clothes of the old
fashion, great cuffs and massy buttons, great wig, long ruffles,
etc.; the black eyebrows exceeded in size any I have ever seen,
and his voice, tho' by no means devoid of melody, was a kind
of rolling, murmuring thunder.

SOURCE: Thomas Creevey, *The Creevey Papers.*

... bent with age, dressed in an old-fashioned grey coat, with
breeches and gaiters of the same stuff, a brown scratch wig,
tremendous white bushy eyebrows, eyes still sparkling with
intelligence, dreadful crowsfeet around them, very deep lines
in his countenance, and shrivelled complexion of a shallow
hue.

AGED ABOUT 74.

SOURCE: Lord Campbell; quoted in John Timb's *A Century of
Anecdote, 1760–1860.*

TIDDY-DOLL (18th Century), famous London street vendor.

This celebrated vendor of gingerbread, from his eccentricity of character, and extensive dealings in his way, was always hailed as the king of itinerant tradesmen. In his person he was tall, well-made, and his features handsome. He affected to dress like a person of rank; white gold laced suit of clothes, laced ruffle shirt, laced hat and feather, white silk stockings, with the addition of a fine white apron. Among his harangues to gain customers, take this as a specimen:

'Mary, Mary, where are you now, Mary? I live when at home at the second house in Little Ball-street, two steps under ground, with a wiscum, riscum, and a why-not. Walk in, ladies and gentlemen; my shop is on the second-floor backwards, with a brass knocker at the door. Here is your nice gingerbread, your spice gingerbread; it will melt in your mouth like a red-hot brickbat, and rumble in your inside like Punch and his wheelbarrow.'

He always finished his address by singing this fag end of some popular ballad:

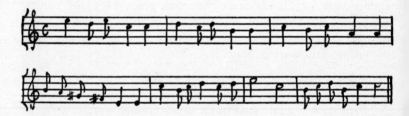

Hence arose his nickname of Tiddy Doll. In Hogarth's print of the execution of the Idle Apprentice at Tyburn, Tiddy Doll is seen holding up a gingerbread cake with his left hand, his right hand being within his coat, and addressing the mob in his usual way.

SOURCE: William Hone, *The Everyday Book and Table Book, or Everlasting Calendar of Popular Amusements*, 1830.

TONSON, JACOB (1656?–1736), publisher; associated with Dryden, Addison, Pope, etc.

> With leering looks, bull-faced, and freckled fair,
> With two left legs, and Judas-colour'd hair,
> And frowsy pores, that taint the ambient air.

SOURCE: John Dryden; included after Dryden's death in *Faction Displayed*, a satirical poem popular with Tories as an attack on the Whigs; quoted by Sir Walter Scott in *The Life of the Author*, accompanying the first collected edition of *Dryden*, London, 1808. The lines were sent to Tonson by Dryden during the course of a quarrel, apparently with the threat that, if necessary, the author could write more in the same vein. It is said that the threat was effective and that Tonson yielded in the dispute.

TOOLE, JOHN LAWRENCE (1830–1906), actor and theatrical manager.

During the last sad years of Toole's life, when he was partially paralysed, he stayed for months together at the 'Old Ship'. He could be seen most evenings in the large smoking-room on the right-hand side of the hall, and he would sit there until the small hours, listening attentively to the conversation that usually turned on theatrical subjects, and occasionally mumbling into the ear of a relative in attendance a correction of some name or date—for his memory to the last was most retentive. Though his voice could rarely rise beyond a whisper, he was the king of a little coterie regular in attendance . . . At the 'Old Ship' smoking room he was treated like royalty. It was rare for any one to leave until he gave the signal for dismissal by his own departure; and when at length he proposed to retire, the whole company would rise, and form a semicircle from his chair to the door. Toole, leaning on a friendly arm, would hobble slowly past, bowing formally to one, nodding to his intimates, shaking hands with new acquaintances, murmuring kind words that only too often could not be distinctly heard . . . an exit of the last of the race of great comedians of bygone days.

AGED ABOUT 75.

SOURCE: Lewis Melville, *Brighton: Its History, Its Follies and Its Fashions*, Chapman & Hall, 1909.

TOWNS[H]END, JOHN (18th Century), Bow Street officer.

Townshend, the famous Bow Street officer, when I knew him, was a little fat man with a flaxen wig, kerseymere breeches, a blue straight-cut coat and a broad-brimmed white hat. To the most daring courage he added great dexterity and cunning; and was said, *in propria persona*, to have taken more thieves than all the other Bow Street officers put together. He frequently accompanied mail coaches when the Government required large sums of money to be conveyed to distant parts of the country . . .

The short corpulent police-officer was, for his daring exploits and general good conduct, selected by the Home Office to attend at drawing rooms, levees and all state occasions; and he became a kind of personage, and was much noticed by the Royal Family and the great people of the day: everyone went up to speak to Townshend. He was eccentric and amusing, and somewhat inclined to take advantage of the familiarity with which he was treated; but he was a sort of privileged person and could say what he liked.

SOURCE: Captain R. H. Gronow, *Reminiscences*.

Note: Townsend's flaxen wig was so well known that a popular song was written about it. It began:

> 'Of all the wigs in Brighton town,
> The black, the grey, the red, the brown,
> So firmly glued upon the crown,
> There's none like Johnny Townsend's;
> Its silken hair and flaxen hue,
> (It is a scratch, and not a queue)
> Whene'er it pops upon the view,
> It's known for Johnny Townsend's!'

A scratch-wig covered a bald part of the head. A queue was a wig with a plaited tail hanging at the back.

TROLLOPE, ANTHONY (1815–1882), novelist.

My college bills had not been paid, and the school tradesmen were told not to extend their credit to me. Boots, waistcoats, and pocket handkerchiefs which, with some slight surveillance, were at the command of other scholars, were closed luxuries to me . . . I had no friend to whom I could pour out my sorrows. I was big, and awkward, and ugly, and, I have no doubt, skulked about in a most unattractive manner. Of course, I was ill-dressed and dirty.

SOURCE: Anthony Trollope, *An Autobiography*. The passage refers to his schooldays at Winchester.

The bell would peal, the knocker begin thundering, the door be burst open, and the next minute the house be filled by the big resonant voice inquiring who was at home. I should say he had a naturally sweet voice, which through eagerness he spoilt by holloing. He was a big man, and the most noticeable thing about his dress was a black handkerchief which he wore *twice* round his neck. A trick of his was to put the end of a silk pocket-handkerchief in his mouth and to keep gnawing at it— often biting it into holes in the excess of his energy; and a favourite attitude was to stand with his thumbs tucked into the armholes of his waistcoat. He was a full-coloured man, and joking and playful when at his ease. Unless with intimates, he rarely laughed, but he had a funny way of putting things, and was usually voted good company.

Trollope was five feet ten, but most people would have thought him taller. He was a stout man, large of limb, and always held himself upright without effort. His manner was bluff, hearty and genial, and he possessed to the full the great charm of giving his undivided attention to the matter in hand. He was always enthusiastic and energetic in whatever he did. He was of an eager disposition, and doing nothing was a pain to him. In early manhood he became bald; in his latter life his full and bushy beard naturally grew to be gray. He had thick eyebrows, and his open nostrils gave a look of determination to his strong capable face. His eyes were grayish-blue but he was rarely seen without spectacles, though of late years he used to take them off whenever he was reading. From a boy he had always been short-sighted.

Standing with his back to the fire, with his hands clasped behind him and his feet planted somewhat apart, the appearance of Anthony Trollope, as I recall him now, was that of a thorough Englishman in a thoroughly English attitude. He was then, perhaps, nearing sixty, and had far more the look of a country gentleman than of a man of letters. Tall, broad-shouldered, and dressed in a careless but not slovenly fashion, it seemed more fitting that he should break into a vivid description of the latest run with the hounds than launch into book-talk . . . Being short-sighted, he had a habit of peering through his glasses, which contracted his brows and gave him the appearance of a perpetual frown, and, indeed, his expression when in repose was decidedly severe. This, however, vanished when he spoke. He talked well, and had generally a great deal to say; but his talk was disjointed, and he but rarely laughed. In manner he was brusque, and one of his striking peculiarities was his voice, which was of an extraordinarily large compass.

AGED ABOUT 60.

SOURCE: Mabel Wotton, *Word Portraits of Famous Writers*, 1887.

Anthony Trollope was very much to the fore, contradicting everybody, subsequently saying kind things to everybody, and occasionally going to sleep on sofas, chairs, or leaning against sideboards, and even somnolent while standing erect on the hearthrug. I never knew a man who could take so many spells of 'forty winks' at unexpected moments, and then turn up quite wakeful, alert, and pugnacious, as the author of *Barchester Towers*, who had nothing of the bear but his skin, but whose ursine envelope was assuredly of the most grisly texture.

SOURCE: George Augustus Sala; a description of the first 'Cornhill' dinner, from an advertising booklet of the Cornhill Merchant Taylors' Co. Ltd.

TURNER, JOSEPH MALLORD WILLIAM (1775–1851), landscape painter.

Turner was short and stout, and he had a sturdy, sailor-like walk. There was, in fact, nothing elegant in his appearance, full of elegance as he was in art; he might be taken for the captain of a river steam-boat at first glance; but a second would find far more in his face than belongs to any ordinary mind. There was that keenness of his expression in his eye that is only seen in men of constant habits of observation. His voice was deep and musical, but he was the most confused and tedious speaker that I ever heard. In careless conversation he often expressed himself happily, and he was very playful; at a dinner table nobody more joyous.

SOURCE: *Autobiographical Recollections by the late Charles Robert Leslie*, 1860.

Lady Simon, wife of Sir John Simon, when young, had to travel by coach to catch the train at Exeter. In the coach seated opposite to her was an elderly gentleman, short and stout, with a red face and a curious prominent nose. The weather was very wild, and by-and-by a violent storm swept over the country, blotting out the sunshine and the blue sky and hanging like a pall over the landscape. The old gentleman seemed strangely excited at this, jumping up to open the window, craning his neck out, and finally calling to her to come and observe a curious effect of light. A train was coming in their direction, through the blackness, over one of Brunel's bridges, and the effect of the locomotive, lit by crimson flame, and seen through the driving rain and whirling tempest, gave a peculiar impression of power, speed, and stress.

Some time afterwards in London she got an invitation to the Private View of the Royal Academy, and in the big room she was struck by the picture 'Rain, Steam and Speed' by Turner. In a flash she realised that the subject of the picture was what she had been called upon to admire out of the window of the coach, and that the eccentric old gentleman could have been none other than Turner himself.

SOURCE: George Richmond; quoted in *The Richmond Papers*, Heinemann, 1926.

TURPIN, DICK (1705–1739), highwayman.

Turpin was born at Thaxted in Essex; is about thirty-five, five feet nine inches high, brown complexion, very much marked with smallpox, his cheek bones broad, his face thinner towards the bottom, his visage short and pretty upright, and broad about the shoulders.

SOURCE: Proclamation for his arrest, 1737; quoted in P. Pringle, *Stand and Deliver*. The proclamation, though it has been followed by a number of writers, was in error in giving Thaxted as Turpin's birthplace. He was born at the Crown Inn at Hempstead, where the registers of St. Andrew's Church contain the entry: 'Richardus Filius Johannis et Maria Turpin bapt. Sept. 25.'

TYNDALE, WILLIAM (d. 1536), translator of the Bible; burned at the stake at Vilvorde.

I believe, right worshipful, that you are not ignorant of what has been determined concerning me; therefore I entreat your lordship, and that by the Lord Jesus, that if I am to remain here during the winter, you will request the Procureur to be kind enough to send me from my goods which he has in his possession, a warmer cap, for I suffer extremely from cold in the head, being afflicted with a perpetual catarrh, which is considerably increased in this cell. A warmer coat also, for that which I have is very thin; also a piece of cloth to patch my leggings; my overcoat is worn out; my shirts are also worn out. He has a woollen shirt of mine, if he will be kind enough to send it. I have also with him leggings of thicker cloth for putting on above; he also has warmer caps for wearing at night. I wish also his permission to have a lamp in the evening, for it is wearisome to sit alone in the dark.

SOURCE: William Tyndale, from his prison at Vilvorde, to the Governor of the castle; reproduced in facsimile, and trans., in Rev. R. Demaus's *William Tyndale*, R.T.S., 1886.

USSHER, DOCTOR JAMES (1581–1656), theologian; archbishop of Armagh.

As for his outward form, he was indifferent tall, and well shaped and went always upright to the last; his hair naturally brown, when young; his complexion sanguine; his countenance expressed gravity, and good nature; his carriage free; a presence that commanded both respect and reverence; and though many pictures were made of him, the air of his face was so hard to hit that I never saw but one that was like him. He was of a strong and healthy constitution, so that he said that, for the most part of his life, he very rarely felt any pain in his head or stomach; in his youth he had been troubled with the *sciatica*, and some years after that, with a long *quartern ague* . . . A little sleep served his turn; and even in his last years, though he went to bed pretty late, yet in the summer he would rise by five, and in the winter by six of the clock in the morning . . . He liked not tedious meals, it was a weariness to him to sit long at table . . .

As for his natural temper, and disposition, he was of a free and easy humour, not morose, proud or imperious, but courteous and affable, and extremely obliging towards all he convers'd with; and though he could be angry, and rebuke sharply when he ought (that is, when religion or virtue were concerned), yet was he not easily provoked to passion.

SOURCE: Richard Parr, *Life of the Most Reverend Father in God, James Usher, Late Lord Archbishop of Armagh* . . . 1686.

VERE, LADY SUSAN (?–1628), wife of Sir Philip Herbert, later Earl of Pembroke and Montgomery.

On St. John's Day we had the marriage of Sir Philip Herbert and the Lady Susan, performed at Whitehall, with all the honour could be done a great favourite. The court was great, and for that day put on the best bravery. The Prince and Duke of Holst led the bride to church; the Queen followed her from thence. The King gave her; and she in her tresses and trinkets brided and bridled it so handsomely, and indeed, became herself so well, that the King said, if he were unmarried, he would not give her, but keep her himself . . . No ceremony was omitted of bride cakes, points, garters, and gloves, which have been ever since the livery of the court; and at night there was sewing into the sheet, casting off the bride's left hose, with many other pretty sorceries.

SOURCE: Sir Dudley Carleton, letter to Sir Ralph Winwood, 1604.

VICTORIA, Queen of Great Britain and Empress of India (1819–1901).

. . . I saw for the first time the ten-year-old Queen of Portugal and our little Victoria . . . Our little Princess is a short, plain-looking child and not near so good-looking as the Portuguese. However, if nature has not done so much for her, fortune is likely to do a great deal more.

AGED 10.

SOURCE: *Greville Memoirs.*

At twelve o'clock the same day, she presided at a Council with as much ease as if she had been doing it all her life; after which she received the archbishops and bishops to who she said nothing, but showed an extreme dignity and gracefulness of manner. This ceremony finished and the duties of the day at an end, she retired with slow stateliness; but forgetful that the door through which she had passed had glass panels which allowed her departure to be seen, she had no sooner left the Chamber than she scampered light-heartedly away like a child released from school.

AGED 17.

SOURCE: Lord Albemarle, describing the young Queen's first Privy Council meeting.

She looked very pretty, and none of the engravings yet published do her anything like justice . . . Her manner is unaffectedly graceful . . . Her hands, by-the-bye, are very pretty, the backs dimpled, and the fingers delicately shaped.

AGED 19.

SOURCE: *Autobiographical Recollections by the late Charles Robert Leslie*, 1860.

You ask about Queen Victoria's visit to Brussels. I saw her for an instant flashing through the Rue Royale in a carriage and six, surrounded by soldiers. She was laughing and talking very gaily. She looked a little, stout, vivacious lady, very plainly dressed, not much dignity or pretension about her. The Belgians like her very well on the whole. They say she enlivened the sombre court of King Leopold, which is usually as gloomy as a conventicle.

AGED 24.

SOURCE: Charlotte Brontë; E. C. Gaskell, *Life of Charlotte Brontë*.

I did not think that the Queen, at the advanced age she has reached, would have possessed such an imposing appearance. There is in her small, rather bent figure a quiet dignity that would single her out at once as a queen, in spite of the extreme simplicity of her dress, as well as of her demeanour, which is that of an elderly woman. The sound of her voice is the same as ever ... The eyes are frank and sincere, and they look at you with an expression of intense truth; but they are imperious, and reveal a character that does not brook contradicting ...

The sight of that aged lady in her simple dress, who represented so much power, so much might, and who bore the burden with such utter lack of affectation, was certainly very impressive, perhaps more so than if she had appeared in her crown and royal robes.

AGED 74.

SOURCE: Princess Catherine Radziwill, *Memories of Forty Years*, Cassell, 1914.

Note: The London Museum has a unique collection of Queen Victoria's dresses, presented by Queen Alexandra and Queen Mary, and specifically identified with the occasions on which they were worn; so that they form not only an intimate record of the Queen's life and tastes, but also reflect general trends in fashion over a period of more than 60 years. Among them are:

1. The dress worn at her first Council, in 1837.

   Blue silk dress, full skirt set on in small pleats, full sleeves caught in François Ier.

2. The robes and vestments worn at her coronation in 1838.

   (i) dalmatic of cloth-of-gold with wide painted sleeves, made without fastenings and edged with gold lace. The design in pale colours is a wavy pattern of leaves, edged with green and enclosing pink roses, purple thistles and green shamrock. Lined throughout with rose-coloured silk;

   (ii) imperial mantle of cloth-of-gold, edged with gold bullion fringe. The design is a branched pattern enclosing red and white Tudor roses, green shamrock, purple and green thistles and silver eaglets. The cloak fastens in front with a gold brooch.

3. Dress worn by the Queen at her wedding on February 10th, 1840.

   White satin dress with pointed and boned bodice. Full skirt set in small pleats all round. Low neck, with deep turnover of lace, small puff sleeves with hanging lace. Square panels of similar lace set low in the front of the skirt. White poke bonnet, trimmed with orange blossom inside and outside the brim, and covered with a lace veil.

4. Dress worn at the ball given at Buckingham Palace on the night of the wedding.

   White silk-faille evening dress, with pointed bodice. Low-cut neck trimmed with silver net, puff sleeves trimmed with similar net and white satin bows. Full skirt set on in small pleats, with a hem flounce of silver net and white satin bows in the front.

5. Two dresses worn at the Great Exhibition of 1851.

   (i) Blue silk dress with separate bodice and skirt. The bodice has long sleeves and is cut in a coat shape with short flaring tassets. An insert bodice of white lace ending in a high lace collar, and decorative buttons at the back. The skirt is full and made with two flounces. The whole dress is trimmed with ruches of silk material.

   (ii) Pink dress of shot silk, woven with silver tissue. Pointed bodice, with low decolletage trimmed in front with a V-shaped bertha of silver lace and gathered pink satin ribbon; short sleeves of silver lace. Full skirt set in small pleats all round, front panel trimmed with rows of silver lace and pink satin bows.

6. Dress worn at the confirmation of the Princess Royal in 1856.
   Mauve silk dress with separate bodice and skirt. The bodice has long sleeves and is cut in a coat shape with short flaring tassels. Inset stomacher of white lace ending in a turn-down collar, skirt very full and made with three flounces. The whole dress is trimmed with gathered mauve ribbon and woven velvet pattern.

7. Dress worn for the State entry into Paris 1855.
   White watered-silk dress with naturalistic shadow pattern. Pointed bodice, laced behind, short sleeves trimmed with white lace. Full skirt set on in small pleats.

8. Costume worn at an inspection of the troops in Hyde Park on their return from the Crimea, 1856.
   Red cloth military jacket, trimmed with gold braid. Round black beaver hat, trimmed with red and white plumes.

9. Dress worn by the Queen for the painting of 'The Four Generations', 1894.
   Black silk dress slightly trimmed crepe and black lace, bodice and skirt separate, bodice buttoned in front. White tulle cap.

10. The last dress worn by the Queen, 1901.
    Black satin dress trimmed with black crepe. Full skirt, long sleeves, V-shape opening at neck.

The descriptions are by Thalassa Cruso, from the London Museum Catalogues: No. 5, *Costume*, 2nd edit., 1935.

VILLIERS, GEORGE, first Duke of Buckingham (1592–1628), court favourite of James I and Charles I; assassinated by John Felton.

His person, from head to foot, could not be charged with any blemish, save that some hypercritics conceived his brows somewhat over-pendulous, a cloud which, in the judgment of others, was by the beams of his eyes sufficiently dispelled.

SOURCE: Thomas Fuller, *The Worthies of England.*

T

VILLIERS, GEORGE, second Duke of Buckingham (1628–1687), member of Charles II's Cabal ministry.

He made up comic ditties, composed old wives' tales ... But his special talent was for catching hold of and imitating in their presence anything that happened to be absurd in other people's behaviour or any peculiarity of speech they had, without letting them notice it. In short, he was apt at counterfeiting so many different parts, and with so much grace and humour, that when he wished to make himself agreeable, it was difficult to dispense with his company ...

He was an exceedingly handsome person, and thought himself a great deal handsomer even than he was. Although very intelligent, his vanity made him appropriate to his personal attractions many civilities which had been evoked only by his talent for buffoonery and repartee.

SOURCE: Anthony Hamilton, *Memoirs of the Comte de Gramont*, trans. Peter Quennell, Routledge & Sons, 1930.

VOLUNTEER REVIEW (Hyde Park 1801).

The largest number of volunteer soldiers ever brigaded together, about 12,000 men, paraded in Hyde Park to be reviewed by George III on his 63rd birthday.

A finer body of men, or of more martial appearance, no country could produce. While they rivalled, in discipline, troops of the line, by the fineness of their clothing, and the great variety of uniform and the richness of appointments, they far exceeded them in splendour. The great number of beautiful standards and colours—the patriotic gifts of the most exalted and distinguished females—and the numerous music, also contributed much to the brilliancy and diversity of the scene.

So early as four o'clock the drums beat to arms in every quarter, and various other music summoned the reviewers and the reviewed to the field. Even then the clouds were surcharged with rain, which soon began to fall; but no unfavourableness of weather could damp the ardour of even the most delicate of the fair. So early as six o'clock, all the avenues were crowded with elegantly dressed women escorted by their beaux; and the assemblage was so great, that when the King entered the Park, it was thought advisable to shut several of the gates to avoid too much pressure. The circumstances of the weather, which, from the personal inconvenience produced, might be considered the most inauspicious of the day, proved in fact the most favourable for a display of beauty, for a variety of scene and number of incidents. From the constant rain and the constant motion, the whole Park could be compared only to a newly-ploughed field. The gates being locked, there was no possibility of retreating, and there was no shelter but an old tree or an umbrella. In this situation you might behold an elegant woman with a neat yellow slipper, delicate ankle, and white silk stocking, stepping up to her garter in the mire with as little dissatisfaction as she would into her coach—there another making the first faux pas, perhaps, she ever did, and seated reluctantly on the moistened clay.

Here is a whole group assembled under the hospitable roof of an umbrella, whilst the exterior circle, for the advantage of having one shoulder dry, is content to receive its dripping contents on the other ... Such was the state of the spectators. That of the troops was still worse—to lay exposed to a pelting rain; their arms had changed their mirror-like brilliancy to a dirty brown; their new clothes lost all their gloss, the smoke of a whole campaign could not have more discoloured them. Where the ground was hard they slipped; where soft, they sunk up to the knee. The water ran out at their cuffs as from a spout, and, filling their half-boots, a squash at every step proclaimed that the Austrian buckets could contain no more.

SOURCE: Contemporary account, included in John Ashton's *The Dawn of the XIXth Century in England*, Fisher Unwin, 1895.

WALKER, TOM (1762–1831), Hambledon cricketer; called 'Old Everlasting' by his fellow-players, owing to his lengthy stays at the wicket.

How strongly are the figures of the men (of Tom's in particular) brought to my mind when they first presented themselves to the club, upon Windmill-down. Tom's hard, ungain, scrag-of-mutton frame; wilted, apple-john face, (he always looked twenty years older than he really was), his long spider legs, as thick at the ankles as at the hips, and perfectly straight all the way down—for the embellishment of a calf in Tom's leg, Dame Nature had considered would be but a wanton superfluity. Tom was the driest and most rigid-limbed chap I ever knew; his skin was like the rind of an old oak, and as sapless. I have seen his knuckles handsomely knocked about from Harris's bowling; but never saw any blood upon his hands—you might just as well attempt to phlebotomize a mummy. This rigidity of muscle (or rather I should say of tendon, for muscle was another ingredient economised in the process of Tom's configuration)—this rigidity, I say, was carried into every motion. He moved like the rude machinery of a steam engine in the infancy of construction, and when he ran, every member seemed ready to fly to the four winds.

SOURCE: John Nyren, *The Young Cricketer's Tutor*, 1833.

WALLER, EDMUND (1606–1687), poet.

He is somewhat above a middle stature, thin body, not at all robust; fine thin skin, his face somewhat of an olivevaster, his hair frizzed, of a brownish colour; oval faced, his forehead high and full of wrinkles; his head but small, brain very hot and apt to be choleric. He is something magisterial . . .

He writes a lamentably bad hand, as bad [as] the scratching of a hen.

SOURCE: John Aubrey, *Brief Lives*, edit. Andrew Clark, 1898.

WALPOLE, HORACE (1717–1797), fourth Earl of Orford, man of letters.

His figure was as has been told, and every one knows, not merely tall, but more properly *long* and slender to excess; his complexion and particularly his hands, of a most unhealthy paleness . . . His eyes were remarkably bright and penetrating, very dark and lively; his voice was not strong, but his tones were extremely pleasant, and if I may say so, highly gentlemanly. I do not remember his common gait; he always entered a room in that style of affected delicacy, which fashion had then made almost natural; *chapeau bras* between his hands as if he wished to compress it, or under his arm—knees bent, and feet on tip-toe, as if afraid of a wet floor.

His dress in visiting was most usually, in summer when I most saw him, a lavender suit, the waistcoat embroidered with a little silver, or of white silk worked in the tabour, partridge silk stockings, and gold buckles, ruffles and frill, generally lace. I remember when a child, thinking him very much under-dressed, if at any time except in mourning, he wore hemmed cambric. In summer, no powder, but his wig combed straight, and showing his very smooth pale forehead, and queued behind—in winter, powder.

SOURCE: Laetitia-Matilda Hawkins, *Anecdotes, Biographical Sketches and Memoirs, 1822–1824.* Quoted in R. W. Ketton-Cremer's *Horace Walpole*, Methuen, 1940.

The person of Horace Walpole was short and slender, but compact and neatly formed. When viewed from behind, he had somewhat of a boyish appearance, owing to the form of his person, and the simplicity of his dress. His features may be seen in many portraits; but none can express the placid goodness of his eyes, which would often sparkle with sudden rays of wit, or dart forth shafts of the most keen and intuitive intelligence. His laugh was forced and uncouth, and even his smile not the most pleasing. His walk was enfeebled by the gout . . . this painful complaint not only affected his feet, but attacked his hands to such a degree that his fingers were always swelled and deformed . . .

SOURCE: John Pinkerton, *Walpoliana*, 1799. There is some divergence of opinion about Walpole's height, but it seems clear that, though he was above middle height, his great leanness made him look taller than he really was. In later years he developed a considerable stoop.

WALPOLE, SIR ROBERT, first Earl of Orford (1676–1745), statesman.

His eloquence, generally plain, perspicuous, and manly, was occasionally brilliant, classical and impassioned . . . The tone of his voice, though he never entirely lost the provincial accent, was highly melodious . . . In his person tall and well proportioned, he was in his youth and opening manhood so comely that he and his wife were called 'the handsome couple'; and in the procession at the installation of the Knights of the Garter in 1725, he was, next to the Duke of Grafton and Lord Townshend, the most distinguished for his appearance. But, in advanced life, he became corpulent and unwieldy. His style of dress was usually plain and simple, his address frank and open, and his manner so fascinating that while he was but adored by his friends, even by his worst virulent opponents he was not hated . . . Affable and gay in his deportment, and in his conversation animated and facetious (occasionally to an unpardonable degree of ribaldry) he was liberal even to prodigality in his expenditure.

SOURCE: Rev. Francis Wrangham, *The British Plutarch*, new edit., 1816.

WATERTON, CHARLES (1782–1865), traveller and naturalist.

He had no idea that he was doing anything out of the general course of things if he asked a visitor to accompany him to the top of a lofty tree to look at a hawk's nest.

SOURCE: Father J. Wood; *Waterton, Essays on Natural History . . . with an Autobiography of the Author*, edit. J. G. Wood, 1878.

His remarkable suppleness of limb and elasticity of muscle, I have seen marvellously and most amazingly displayed in his eighty-first year, by a variety of physical contortions. When Mr. Waterton was seventy-seven years of age, I was witness to his scratching the back part of his head with the big toe of his right foot . . .

I have frequently, in painful suspense and much against my

own inclinations, seen the Squire, when beyond seventy years of age, hop on one leg along the brink of a rock forming the highest terrace in the grotto, whilst the other leg was dangling over the chasm below; and, when thus hopping at a rapid rate, he would return again by hopping back on the contrary leg. On my cautioning him, he would reply: 'Non de ponte cadit qui cum sapienta vadit.'—'He falls not from the bridge who walks with prudence.'

SOURCE: Doctor Richard Hobson, *Life*, 1866.

Note: Edith Sitwell wrote: 'Perhaps as a result of her mother watching the Squire performing these gymnastics, a duck was hatched on the estate with her head reversed, and her bill pointed out, "and, indeed, immediately situated above" the elegant feathers of her tail; so that whenever food was placed upon the ground, she must turn a somersault before seizing it . . . She aroused the liveliest feelings of admiration in the heart of the Squire.'

WATSON, WILLIAM (1559?–1603), priest and conspirator; a leader of the 'Bye' or 'Priest's' Plot, 1603.

William Watson, Priest—a man of the lowest sort, about 36 years of age, his hair betwixt auburn and flaxen; he looketh a-squint, and is very purblind, so as if he read anything, he putteth the paper near to his eyes; he did wear his beard at length, of the same coloured hair as his head; but information is given that now his beard is cut.

SOURCE: Proclamation for his arrest, July 16th, 1603, *Book of Proclamations*.

WATTS, GEORGE FREDERIC (1817–1904), painter and sculptor.

He was on horseback, having ridden from Little Holland House . . . He looked very spendid; his beard was worn long, was very silky, and was blown about in a fascinating fashion first over one shoulder and then the other . . . It is a wonderful instance of the triumph of spirit over matter that he, a frail and delicate man, demonstrated a robustness in his work which exceeded any other English painter.

SOURCE: William Richmond; *The Richmond Papers*, Heinemann, 1926.

WELLESLEY, ARTHUR, first Duke of Wellington (1769–1852), field-marshal and prime minister.

He who rode in front was a thin, well-made man, apparently of middle stature, and not yet past the prime of life. His dress was a plain grey frock, buttoned close to the chin; a cocked hat, covered with oilskin; grey pantaloons, with boots buckled at the side; and a steel-mounted light sabre. Though I knew not who he was, there was a brightness in his eye which bespoke him something more than an aide-de-camp or a general of brigade; nor was I left long in doubt. There were in the ranks many veterans who had served in the Peninsula during some of the earlier campaigns; these instantly recognised their old leader, and the cry of 'Duro, Duro!', the familiar title given by the soldiers to the Duke of Wellington,was raised . . .

As I had never seen the great Captain of the day before, it will readily be imagined that I looked at him on the present occasion with a degree of admiration and respect such as soldier of seventeen years of age, devoted to his profession, is likely to feel for the man whom he regards as its brightest ornament. There was in his general aspect nothing indicative of a life spent in hardships and fatigues; nor any expression of care or anxiety in his countenance. On the contrary, his cheek, though bronzed with frequent exposure to the sun, had on it the ruddy hue of health, while a smile of satisfaction played about his mouth, and told, more plainly than words could have spoken, how perfectly he felt at his ease.

AGED 44.

SOURCE: G. R. Gleig, *The Subaltern*, 1826. Though this was a novel, Gleig was an eye-witness of the occasion described. He later became Chaplain-General of the forces.

Our Commander-in-Chief, as far as I could judge, appeared perfectly composed; but looked very thoughtful and pale. He was dressed in a gray great-coat with a cape, white cravat, leather pantaloons, Hessian boots, and a large cocked hat *à la Russe*.

AGED 46, at the Battle of Waterloo.

SOURCE: Captain R. H. Gronow, *Reminiscences*.

I hit his grand, upright, manly expression. He looked like an eagle of the gods who had put on human shape, and had got silvery with age and service ... Riding hard made him rosy and dozy. His colour was fresh. All the portraits are too pale ... 'Twas a noble head. I saw nothing of that peculiar expression of mouth the sculptors give him, bordering on simpering ...

(The next day). By nine the door opened, and in he walked, looking extremely worn; his skin drawn tight over his face; his eye was watery and aged; his head nodded a little. I put the chair; he mumbled, 'I'd as soon stand'. I thought, 'You will get tired,' but I said nothing; down he sat, how altered from the fresh old man after Saturday's hunting! It affected me. He looked like an aged eagle beginning to totter from his perch.

AGED 70.

SOURCE: Benjamin Haydon's *Autobiography*.

Note: See also entry for Thomas Clarkson.

WELLINGTON, DUKE OF (1769–1852). See Wellesley, Arthur, firstDuke of Wellington.

WESLEY, JOHN (1703–1791), evangelist and methodist leader.

... a lean, elderly man, fresh-coloured, his hair smoothly combed but with a *soupçon* of a curl at the end. Wondrous clean, but evidently an actor as Garrick. He gabbled the early part of his sermon as though he knew it by heart, but towards the end he exalted his voice and acted very ugly enthusiasm.

AGED 63.

SOURCE: Horace Walpole, *Letters*.

I breakfasted with Mr. Whitefield, who seemed to be an old, old man being fairly worn out in his Master's service, though he has hardly seen fifty years and yet it pleases God that I who am now in my sixty-third year, find no disorder, no weakness, no decay, no difference from what I was at five and twenty; only that I have fewer teeth and more grey hairs.

AGED 62.

SOURCE: John Wesley, *Journals*.

I am now an old man decayed from head to foot. My eyes are dim; my right hand shakes much; my mouth is hot and dry every day; my motion is weak and slow. However, blessed be to God, I do not slack my labour; I can preach and write still.

AGED 86.

SOURCE: John Wesley, *Journals*.

WENTWORTH, SIR THOMAS, first Earl of Strafford (1593–1641), statesman; nicknamed 'Black Tom Tyrant'.

In person he was of a tall stature, but stooped much in the neck. His countenance was cloudy whilst he moved or sat thinking, but when he spake, either seriously or facetiously, he had a lightsome and a very pleasant air; and, indeed, whatever he then did he performed very gracefully.

SOURCE: Sir Philip Warwick, *Memoirs of the Reign of Charles I*.

I grow extremely old and full of grey hairs since I came into this kingdom, and should wax exceeding melancholy, were it not for two little girls that come now and then to play by me.

SOURCE: Thomas Wentworth, during his period as lord deputy of Ireland; quoted in John Buchan's *Oliver Cromwell*.

WETHERELL, SIR CHARLES (1770–1846), politician and lawyer.

Sir Charles Wetherell was a tall man, with a considerable stoop and a swing in his gait. His face was intelligent and rather remarkable: the forehead expansive, the eyes not large, but expressive of humour; the nose straight and rather short, or appearing so from the unusual length of the upper lip and chin; his voice was good, but not musical, and his manner was sometimes calm and impressive; but, for the greatest part, his efforts, even upon the most important occasions, were attended with a whimsicality, which was the most distinguished feature of his manners as an advocate...

When he went forth into the street he was even more strange than in Court. He wore clothes that seemed to have been suddenly 'grabbed' from some shop window in Monmouth Street, without any consideration as to the fit. He scorned the appendages of suspenders, and only sometimes wore a waistcoat long enough to meet the other garment, which, for the lack of the appendages aforesaid, was wont to sink below the ordinary level. His inside coat was old, his outside one of great antiquity, and commonly flew behind him in the breeze, while he strode along muttering to himself, with his hands lodged deep in the recesses of his breeches pockets; his cravat seemed as if it had not been folded, but rolled up and tied on in the dark, by hands not of the cleanest; he wore large shoes tied with great black tapes, or what would have been black except that, like his hat, the vicissitudes of time had turned them to a hue of brown.

SOURCE: John Timbs, *A Century of Anecdote, 1760–1860*.

WHIP CLUB, later called the **FOUR IN HAND CLUB,** 1808.

A description of one of the gentlemen's clubs, formed at the beginning of the 19th Century to emulate the professional coachmen:

The WHIP CLUB met on Monday morning in Park Lane, and proceeded from thence to dine at Harrow-on-the-Hill.

There were fifteen barouche landaus with four horses to each; the drivers were all men of known skill in the science of charioteering. Lord Hawke, Mr. Buxton, and the Hon. Lincoln Stanhope were among the leaders.

The following was the style of the set out: Yellow-bodied carriages, with whip springs and dickey boxes; cattle of a bright bay colour, with plain silver ornaments on the harness, and rosettes to the ears. Costume of the drivers: a light drab colour cloth coat made full, single breast, with three tiers of pockets, the skirts reaching to the ankles; a mother of pearl button of the size of a crown piece. Waistcoat, blue and yellow stripe, each stripe an inch in depth. Small cloths corded with silk plush, made to button over the calf of the leg, with sixteen strings and rosettes to each knee. The boots very short, and finished with very broad straps, which hung over the tops and down to the ankle. A hat three inches and a half deep in the crown only, and the same depth in the brim exactly. Each wore a large bouquet at the breast, thus resembling the coachmen of our nobility, who, on the natal day of our beloved sovereign, appear in that respect so peculiarly distinguished. The party moved along the road at a smart trot; the first whip gave some specimens of superiority at the outset by 'cutting a fly off a leader's ear'.

SOURCE: *Morning Post*, June 9, 1808; included in John Ashton's *The Dawn of the XIXth Century in England*, Fisher Unwin, 1895.

WHISTLER, JAMES ABBOT McNEILL (1834–1903), painter.

I dined with Mr. Whistler at Mrs. Joseph Pennell's in London . . . Whistler arrived very late, and kept us waiting for him at every course. He had a moustache and small imperial, his lower jaw protruded, and his white lock was noticeable. His eyes were grey, sharp and bloodshot.

He was profoundly conscious of being the only thing in the world worth attention, so, as there was no critical influence present, he genially expanded. He mumbled, and gave parts of half a dozen sentences instead of one clear sentence, in a piercing treble voice.

AGED 68.

SOURCE: Mrs. Harrison Morris, *The Whistler Journal*.

WHITE, GILBERT (1720–1793), naturalist; author of *The Natural History and Antiquities of Selbourne*.

You are a man, as I have long known, so very much master of your passion, and so guarded in your behaviour, and even in your expressions, that when I see an ebullition, I guess there is a considerable fire underneath.

SOURCE: John Mulso, in a letter to White; quoted in Walter Johnson's *Gilbert White*, 1928.

Note: Considering his great place in English literature, surprisingly few details of Gilbert White's appearance have survived. Apparently, in an age when few escaped it, no portrait was ever painted of him, though a well-authenticated, if crude, little pen and ink sketch occurs on the fly-leaf of one of his books. Apart from that, there are a few scattered clues in the *Natural History*, and in letters. He seems to have been small—perhaps five feet three inches, with stumpy legs and an upright carriage.

WHITEFIELD, GEORGE (1714–1770), Methodist leader and preacher.

He had indeed many natural advantages. He was something above the middle stature, well proportioned, though at that time slender, and remarkable for native gracefulness of manner. His complexion was very fair, his features regular, his eyes small and lively, of a dark blue colour; in recovering from the measles he had contracted a squint with one of them; but this peculiarity rather rendered the expression of his countenance more rememberable than any degree lessened the effect of its uncommon sweetness. His voice excelled both in melody and compass, and its fine modulations were happily accompanied by that grace of action which he possessed in an eminent degree, and which has been said to be the chief requisite of an orator.

SOURCE: John Timbs, *A Century of Anecdote, 1760–1860.*

Note: See also entry for John Wesley.

WILBERFORCE, SAMUEL (1805–1873), bishop; nicknamed 'Soapy Sam'.

Samuel Wilberforce had an attractive manner and a charming expression—an expression of mingled benevolence, intelligence and humour, and there was also an impressive dignity in his bearing . . . Though the lines of beauty were entirely wanting in the Bishop's features, and the contour of his face was not such as to redeem or even soften their defects, this proved no drawback to Richmond's production of a pleasing and most attractive portrait . . .

It must be conceded that Samuel Wilberforce's countenance was of those that change perceptibly with the thoughts and feelings which impress and animate the man. He was a fascinating conversationalist, and his mobile features were to a wonderful degree influenced by what was passing in his mind.

SOURCE: Mrs. Pitt Byrne; quoted in *The Richmond Papers,* Heinemann, 1923.

Let the whole truth, however, be stated: for we may be thought to have been drawing an ideal picture. It is for a reader to inquire—The man's gifts and graces being such have described, and the ends to which he directed them so admirable, are we to understand that we have before us a character without a flaw? Nothing of the sort! His very excellencies were a snare to him; his very gifts and graces proved his most effectual hindrances. He was *too* clever, *too* self-reliant . . . *too* persuasive, *too* fascinating in his manner, *too* fertile in expedients; and he furnished not a few with pleas for suspecting him of insincerity . . . He was—(one can but repeat it)—too fond of being 'all things to all men . . .'

SOURCE: J. W. Burgon, *Lives of Twelve Good Men.* 1888.

WILBERFORCE, WILLIAM (1759–1833), philanthropist; parliamentary leader of the slavery abolition movement.

Limbs, scarcely stouter than that of Asmodeus, sustaining a torso as unlike as possible to that of Theseus, carried him along with the agility of an antelope, though under the weight of two coat pockets protuberant as the bags by which some learned brother of the coif announces and secures his rank as leader of his circuit. Grasping a pocket volume in one hand, he wielded in the other a spud caught up in his progress through the garden. At one instant a staff, on which he leant and listened to the projector at his elbow developing his plan for the better coppering of ships' bottoms, at the next it became a wand pointing out to a portly constituent from the Cloth Hall at Leeds some rich effect of the sunset; then a truncheon, beating time to the poetical reminiscences of a gentleman of the Wesleyan persuasion, looking painfully conscious of his best clothes and of his best behaviour, and ere the sacred cadence had reached its close, a cutlass raised in mimic mutiny against the robust form of William Smith, who as Commodore of this ill-assorted squadron, was endeavouring to convey it to port.

SOURCE: Sir James Stephen.

The scene at prayers is a most curious one. There is a bell which rings when Mr. W. begins to dress; another when he finishes dressing; upon which Mr. Barningham (the tutor) begins to play a hymn on the organ and to sing a solo, and by degrees the family come down to the entrance hall, where the psalmody goes on; first one joins in, and then another; Lizzy calling out: 'Don't go near dear Mama, she sings so dreadfully out of tune, dear!' and William: 'Don't look at Papa, he does make such dreadful faces.' So he does, waving his arms about, and occasionally pulling the leaves off the geraniums and smelling them, singing out louder and louder in a tone of hilarity . . .

SOURCE: Marianne Thornton (in a letter to her sister); *The Richmond Papers*, Heinemann, 1923.

At this date, Wilberforce, seventy-four years of age, frail and slight, was become almost a cripple, so one day his nephews, who adored him, gently forced him into a chair, and then lifted him, chair and all, on to the dining-room table, for he stooped so much that only in an elevated position was it possible to get a good view of his features. They then rushed off to find Mr. Richmond, shouting: 'Come, Mr. Richmond, and paint uncle!'

Now, Mr. Wilberforce had a peculiar mannerism which was well-known to all with whom he was acquainted. He kept two watches, one in each side pocket, and he had a trick of taking these out and comparing the time indicated by each. If he found them exactly the same, he would, as though bored by this discovery, push on the hands of one a little, then replace both in his pockets, next take out the first one again, and finding it now, of course, a little slower than its fellow, he would push on its hands to correspond with the other. This curious trick he would continue absently repeating at intervals; and Mr. Richmond, catching him in the moment when he was indulging in it, sketched him thus in a most characteristic attitude.

AGED 74.

SOURCE: A. M. W. Stirling, *The Richmond Papers*, Heinemann, 1923.

WILKES, JOHN (1727–1797), politician.

... his forehead low and short, his nose shorter and lower, his upper lip long and projecting, his eyes sunken and horribly squinting ...

SOURCE: Sir Joshua Reynolds.

Unrestrained either in his conduct or conversation, he was allowed to have more wit than in truth he possessed; and, living with rakes and second-hand authors, he had acquired fame, such as it was, in the middling sphere of life, before his name was so much as known to the public. His appearance as an orator had by no means conspired to make him more noticed. He spoke coldly and insipidly, though with impertinence; his manner was poor, and his countenance horrid.

AGED 35.

SOURCE: Horace Walpole, *Memoirs, 1822–1845*.

... his dress, for he was a celebrated *beau*, was usually either a scarlet or green suit edged with gold ... Even at this distant period, Mr. Wilkes had lost many of his teeth and it required particular attention to understand him, so imperfect was his articulation.

SOURCE: *Reminiscences of Henry Angelo*, 1830.

WILKIE, SIR DAVID (1785–1841), painter; R.A. and court painter to William IV.

He was tall, pale, quiet, with a fine eye, short nose, vulgar humorous mouth, but great energy of expression.

AGED 20.

With the weakness of our poor nature, Wilkie became visibly affected by his fame—talked very grandly—bought new coats—dressed like a dandy, but in vain tried to look like one. While we were at Bell's his pale, anxious look, his evident poverty and struggle, his broad Scotch accent, had all excited the humour of those students who were better off.

AGED 21.

SOURCE: Benjamin Haydon's *Autobiography*.

WILLIAM I, the Conqueror (1027–1087), king of England.

He was of just stature, extraordinary corpulence, fierce countenance; his forehead bare of hair; of such great strength of arm that it was often matter of surprise that no one was able to draw his bow, which himself could bend when his horse was at full gallop. He was majestic, whether sitting or standing, although the protuberance of his belly deformed his royal person.

SOURCE: William of Malmesbury, *Gesta Regum Anglorum*.

U

King William was of reasonable stature, too great and fat of body, and stern of face, bare of forehead, great of strength in brawn and arms, so that scarcely any man might bend his bow.

SOURCE: Ranulf Higden, *Polychronicon*.

WILLIAM II (1057?–1100), king of England.

He was, when abroad and in public assemblies, of supercilious look, darking his threatening eye on the by-stander; and with assumed severity and ferocious voice, assailing such as conversed with him . . .

Should any one be desirous, however, to know the make of this person, he is to understand that he was well set; his complexion florid, his hair yellow, of open countenance; different-coloured eyes, varying with certain glittering specks; of astonishing strength, though not very tall, and his belly rather projecting; of no eloquence, but remarkable for a hesitation of speech, especially when angry.

SOURCE: William of Malmesbury, *Gesta Regum Anglorum*, edit. J. A. Giles, 1847.

WILLIAM II's COURT.

Now at this time it was the fashion for nearly all the young men of the Court to grow their hair long like girls; then, with locks well-combed, glancing about them and winking in ungodly fashion, they would daily walk abroad with delicate steps and mincing gait. Accordingly Father Anselm made these things the subject of his sermon delivered at the beginning of Lent . . . By so doing he brought a number of them to repentance, with the result that they cut their hair short and adopted again such bearing as becomes a man.

SOURCE: Eadmer, monk of Canterbury, *Historia Novorum in Anglia*, trans. by Geoffrey Bosanquet, Cresset Press, 1964.

Note: Anselm's remonstrations apparently had little permanent effect, despite the fact that he went to the length of excommunicating those who kept to their long hair; for after Anselm's death in 1109, Eadmer laments that 'they now so abound and so boastingly pride themselves on the shameful girlish length of their locks that anyone who is not long-haired is branded with some opprobious name, called "country bumpkin" or "priest".'

WILLIAM III (1650–1702), king of England.

He had a thin and weak body, was brown-haired, and of a clear and delicate constitution. He had a Roman eagle nose, bright and sparkling eyes, a large front, and a countenance composed to gravity and authority. All his senses were critical and exquisite. He was always asthmatical; and the dregs of the small-pox falling on his lungs, he had a constant deep cough. His behaviour was solemn and serious, seldom cheerful, and but with a few. He spoke little and very slowly, and most commonly with a disgusting dryness, which was his character at all times, except in a day of battle; for then he was all fire, though without passion.

SOURCE: Gilbert Burnet, Bishop of Salisbury, *History of my Own Time*.

WILLIAM IV (1765–1837), king of Great Britain.

The King is a little, old, red-nosed, weather-beaten, jolly-looking person.

SOURCE: quoted in Mary Hopkirk's *Queen Adelaide*, John Murray, 1946.

His life had been hitherto passed in obscurity and neglect, in miserable poverty . . . without consideration or friends, and he was ridiculous from his grotesque ways and little meddling curiosities. Nobody even invited him into their house, or thought it necessary to honour him with any mark of attention or respect; and so he went on for forty years, till Canning brought him into notice by making him High Admiral at the time of his great Ministerial schism. In that post he distinguished himself by making ridiculous speeches, by a morbid official activity, and a general wildness which was thought to indicate incipient insanity . . .

A few days after my return I was sworn in, all the Ministers and some present. His Majesty presided very decently, and looked like a respectable old Admiral. The Duke told me he was delighted with him . . .

He was in no hurry to take upon himself the dignity of King, nor to throw off the habits and manners of a country gentleman . . . Altogether, he seems a kind-hearted, well-meaning, not stupid, burlesque, bustling old fellow, and if he doesn't go mad may make a very decent King, but he exhibits oddities . . .

July 20th—Yesterday was a very busy day with H. Majesty, who is going much too fast, and begins to alarm his Ministers and astonish the world. In the morning he inspected the Coldstreams, dressed (for the first time in his life) in a military uniform and with a great pair of gold spurs half-way up his leg like a game-cock, although he was not to ride . . .

AGED 65.

SOURCE: *The Greville Memoirs.*

WILLIAM FREDERICK, second Duke of Gloucester (1776–1834), field-marshal.

. . . they breakfasted and then went away, the Duke of Gloucester bowing to the company while nobody was taking any notice of him or thinking about him. Nature must have been very merry when she made this Prince, and in the sort of mood that certain great Artists used to exhibit in their comical caricatures; I never saw a countenance which that line in M'Flecknoe would so well describe—*And lambent dullness plays around his face.*

AGED 54.

SOURCE: *The Greville Memoirs.*

WILSON, JOHN (1785–1854), author; the 'Christopher North' of Blackwood's; professor of moral philosophy at Edinburgh.

Wilson looked like a fine Sandwich Islander who had been educated in the Highlands. His light hair, deep sea-blue eye, tall athletic figure, and hearty hand-grasp, his eagerness in debate, his violent passions, great genius, and irregular habits, rendered him a formidable partisan, a furious enemy, and an ardent friend.

AGED 35.

SOURCE: Benjamin Haydon's *Autobiography*.

Larger and taller men we have seen, figures more artistically framed we have seen, faces more chastely chiselled, and 'sicklied o'er with the pale cast of thought' are not uncommon; but the power and peculiarity of Wilson's body lay in the combination of all those qualities that go to form a model man. There was his stature, about six feet two inches. There was his erect port and stately tread. There was his broad and brawny chest. There was a brow—lofty, round and broad. There were his eyes, literally flames of fire when roused. There were a nose, mouth, and chin, expressing, by turns, firmest determination, exquisite feeling, humour of the drollest sort, and fiery rage. And flowing round his temples, but not 'beneath his shoulders broad,' were locks of the truest Celtic yellow . . . Yet there was a want of polish and finish about his look, his hair, his dress, and gesture, that seemed *outré* and savage, and which made some hyper-critics talk of him as a splendid beast—a cross between the man, the eagle, and the lion . . .

We enter the classroom, and take, we shall suppose, the most remote seat in the sloping array of benches . . . At last you hear a certain bustle, and immediately after, there comes rushing along from the left-hand side a tall, yellow-haired man, in a gown, who steps up to the platform, and turns towards your eyes, a brow, a cheek, a chin, a chest, and a port, which instantly stamp him a Titan among the children of men. His hair rolls down his temples like a cataract of gold; his eyes are light-blue, sparkling, and at times so fierce, that they seem two loopholes opening into a brain of fire; his cheek is flushed by exercise and air into a rich manly red . . . He begins his lecture. For a little you are disappointed. His voice is deep, but seems monotonous; his utterance is slow; his pronunciation is peculiar; his gesture uncouth; what he says is a rather confused and embarrassed repetition of a past lecture; and you are resigning yourself to a mere passive and wondering gaze at the *personnel* of the man, expecting nothing from his mouth, when the progress of his discussion compels him to quote a few lines of poetry, and then his enthusiasm appears, not rapidly bursting, but slowly defiling like a great army into view, his eyes kindle, enlarge, and seem to embrace the whole of his audience in one glance, his chest heaves, his arms vibrate, sometimes his clenched fist smites the desk before him, and his tones deepen down and down into abysses of pathos and melody, as if searching for the very soul of sound, to bring it into upper air. And, after thus having arrested you, he never for an instant loses his grasp, but, by successive shock after shock of electric power, roll after roll of slow thunder, he does with you what he wills, as with his own, and leaves you in precisely the state in which you feel yourself when awakening from some deep, delightful dream.

SOURCE: George Gillfillan, *A Third Gallery of Literary Portraits*, 1854.

WINTER, THOMAS (1572–1606), Gunpowder Plot conspirator.

He was about forty-six years of age, though from the whiteness of his head, he appeared to be older; his figure was tall and handsome; his eyes large and lively, and the expression of his face pleasing, though grave; and notwithstanding the boldness of his mind, his manners were gentle and quiet.

SOURCE: Father Oswald Greenway, from Greenway's MS; quoted in David Jardine's *Criminal Trials*, 1832.

WOLFE, JAMES (1727–1759), major-general.

It is not easy to describe myself in my present state. If I say

I'm thinner, you'll imagine me a shadow, or a skeleton in motion. In short, I'm everything but what the surgeons call a subject for anatomy; as far as muscles, bones, and the larger vessels can serve their purpose, they have a clear view of them in me, distinct from fat or fleshy impediment.

SOURCE: James Wolfe, letter to his mother, 1749; quoted in Beckles Willson's *Life and Letters of James Wolfe*, Heinemann, 1909.

Folks are surprised to see the meagre, consumptive, decaying figure of the son, when the father and mother preserve such good looks; and people are not easily persuaded that I am one of the family. The campaigns of 1743, '4, '5, '6 and '7, stripped me of my bloom, and the winters in Scotland and at Dover have brought me to old age and infirmity, and this without any remarkable intemperance.

SOURCE: James Wolfe, letter to his mother, 1749; quoted in Beckles Willson's *Life and Letters of James Wolfe*, Heinemann, 1909.

. . . you shall laugh at my short red hair as much as you please.

SOURCE: James Wolfe, letter to his mother, 1749; quoted in Beckles Willson's *Life and Letters to James Wolfe*, Heinemann, 1909.

Mr. Pitt had him to dinner with no other person present but Lord Temple (Mr. Greville's Uncle). After dinner Wolfe got greatly excited, drew his sword, flourished it about, and boasted of the great things he would do with it in a wonderfully braggart style.

SOURCE: *Greville Memoirs*. An occurrence on the eve of Wolfe's departure to take command in North America.

WOLSEY, THOMAS (1475?-1530), statesman and cardinal.

Now will I declare unto you his order in going to Westminster Hall daily in the term season. First, before his coming out of his privy chamber, he heard most commonly every day two masses in his privy closet; and there then said his daily service with his chaplain ... And after mass he would return in his privy chamber again, and being advertised of the furniture of his chambers without, with noblemen and gentlemen, and other persons, would issue out into them, apparelled all in red, in the habit of a cardinal; which was either of fine scarlet, or else of crimson satin, taffety, damask, or caffa, the best he could get for money; and upon his head a round pillion, with a neck of black velvet set to the same in the inner side; he had also a tippet of fine sables about his neck; holding in his hand a very fair orange, whereof the meat or substance within was taken out, and filled up again with the part of a sponge, wherein was vinegar, and other confections against the pestilent airs; to the which he most commonly smelt unto, passing among the press, or else when he was pestered with many suitors. ... There was also borne before him first, the great seal of England, and then his cardinal's hat, by a nobleman or some worthy gentleman, right solemnly, bareheaded. And as soon as he was entered into his chamber of presence, where was attending his coming to wait upon him to Westminster Hall, as well noblemen and other worthy gentlemen, as noblemen and gentlemen of his own family; thus passing forth with two great crosses of silver before him; with also two great pillars of silver, and his pursuivant at arms with a great mace of silver gilt. Then his gentleman ushers cried, and said: 'On my lords and masters; make way for my Lord's Grace!'

Thus passed he down from his chambers through the hall; and when he came to the hall door, there was attendant for him, his mule, trapped all together in crimson velvet, and gilt stirrups. When he was mounted, with his cross bearers, and pillar bearers, also upon great horses trapped with red scarlet, then marched he forward, with his train and furniture in manner as I have declared, having about him four footmen, with silver pollaxes in their hands; and thus he went until he came to Westminster Hall door.

SOURCE: George Cavendish, *The Life and Death of Thomas Wolsey*. Cavendish was for many years in constant attendance on Wolsey as usher.

WOOD, ABRAHAM (fl. 1805), celebrated pedestrian.

On Thursday, the 16th of April, Abraham Wood, the noted Lancashire pedestrian, ran forty miles over Newmarket Heath in four hours and fifty-six minutes, being four minutes within the time allowed . . . he ran the first eight miles in forty-eight minutes, and the first twenty miles in two hours and seven minutes.

He is a remarkably fine, tall, well-made man. He ran without shoes or stockings, and had only a pair of flannel drawers and a jacket upon him, and at no time appeared fatigued or overcome by this extraordinary exertion . . . he is supposed to have sprung nearly two yards at every step; the wind was so very high as to occasion him considerable inconvenience. His arms kept nearly equal motion with his legs.

SOURCE: A contemporary magazine, 1807; included in Andrew W. Tuer's *The Follies and Fashions of our Grandfathers*, 1886–1887.

WORDSWORTH, DOROTHY (1771–1858), William Wordsworth's sister.

Immediately behind her [Mrs. Wordsworth] moved a lady, shorter, slighter, and perhaps, in all other respects, as different from her in personal characteristics as could have been wished for the most effective contrast. 'Her face was of Egyptian brown'; rarely, in a woman of English birth, had I seen a more determinate gipsy tan. Her eyes were not soft, as Mrs. Wordsworth's, nor were they fierce or bold; but they were wild and startling, and hurried in motion. Her manner was warm and even ardent; her sensibility seemed constitutionally deep; and some subtle fire of impassioned intellect apparently burned within her, which, being alternately pushed forward into a conspicuous expression by the irrepressible instincts of her temperament, and then immediately checked, in obedience to the decorum of her sex and age, and her maidenly condition, gave to her whole demeanour, and to her conversation, an air of embarrassment, and even of self-conflict, that was almost distressing to witness. At times, the self-counteraction and self-

baffling of her feelings caused her even to stammer, and so deter-
minately to stammer that a stranger who should have seen her
and quitted her in that state of feeling would have certainly
set her down for one plagued with that infirmity of speech as
distressingly as Charles Lamb himself . . . The greatest deduc-
tion from Miss Wordsworth's attractions . . . were the glancing
quickness of her motions, and other circumstances in her
deportment (such as her stooping attitude when walking),
which gave an ungraceful, and even unsexual character to her
appearance when out of doors. She did not cultivate the graces
which preside over the person and its carriage. But, on the
other hand, she was a person of very remarkable endowments
intellectually . . . She was content to be ignorant of many
things; but what she knew and had really mastered lay where
it could not be disturbed—in the temple of her own most
fervid heart.

SOURCE: Thomas De Quincey, *Reminiscences of the English Lakes
and the Lake Poets*, contributed to Tait's *Edinburgh Magazine*.

WORDSWORTH, MARY (1770–1859), wife of William Wordsworth.

. . . a tallish young woman, with the most winning expression
of benignity upon her features, advanced to me, presenting her
hand with so frank an air that all embarrassment must have
fled in a moment before the native goodness of her manner.
This was Mrs. Wordsworth, cousin of the poet, and, for the last
five years or more, his wife. She was now mother of two
children, a son and a daughter; and she furnished a remarkable
proof how possible it is for a woman neither handsome nor even
comely according to the rigour of criticism—nay, generally
pronounced very plain—to exercise all the practical fascination
of beauty, through the mere compensatory charms of sweetness
all but angelic, of simplicity the most entire, womanly self-
respect and purity of heart speaking through all her looks, acts
and movements . . . Her figure was tolerably good. In complexion she was fair, and there was something peculiarly

pleasing even in this accident of the skin, for it was accompanied by an animated expression of health, a blessing which, in fact, she possesses uninterruptedly. Her eyes, the reader may already know, were

> Like stars of twilight fair;
> Like twilight, too, her dark brown hair;
> But all things else about her drawn
> From May-time and the cheerful dawn.

Yet strange it is to tell that, in those eyes of vesper gentleness, there was a considerable obliquity of vision; and much beyond that slight obliquity which is often supposed to be an attractive foible in the countenance: this *ought* to have been displeasing or repulsive; yet, in fact, it was *not*. Indeed all faults, had they been ten times more and greater, would have been neutralised by that supreme expression of her features to the unity of which every lineament in the fixed parts, and every undulation in the moving parts, of her countenance, concurred, viz. a sunny benignity—a radiant graciousness such as in this world I never saw surpassed.

SOURCE: Thomas De Quincey, *Reminiscences of the English Lakes and the Lake Poets*, contributed to Tait's *Edinburgh Magazine*. Mary Wordsworth, according to the poet's statement, was the subject of one of her husband's best-known poems, beginning:—

> She was a phantom of delight
> When first she gleam'd upon my sight.

WORDSWORTH, WILLIAM (1770–1850), poet.

He was quaintly dressed (according to the costume of that unconstrained period) in a brown fustian jacket and striped pantaloons. There was something of a roll, a lounge in his gait, not unlike his own Peter Bell. There was a severe, worn pressure of thought about his temples, a fire in his eye (as if he saw something in objects more than the outward appearance), an intense high narrow forehead, a Roman nose, cheeks furrowed by strong purpose and feeling, and a convulsive inclination to laughter about the mouth, a good deal at variance with the solemn, stately expression of the rest of his face. Chantry's bust wants the marking traits; but he was teased into making it regular and heavy; Haydon's head of him, introduced into the *Entrance of Christ into Jerusalem*, is most like his drooping weight of thought and expression. He sat down and talked very naturally and freely, with a mixture of clear, gushing accents in his voice, a deep guttural intonation, and a strong tincture of the northern burr, like the crust on wine. He instantly began to make havoc of the half of a Cheshire cheese on the table.

AGED 28.

SOURCE: William Hazlitt, *My First Acquaintance with Poets*, The Liberal, April, 1823.

I had a cast made yesterday of Wordsworth's face. He bore it like a philosopher. John Scott was to meet him at breakfast, and just as he came in the plaster was put on. Wordsworth was sitting in the other room in my dressing-gown, with his hands folded, sedate, solemn and still. I stepped in to Scott and told him as a curiosity to take a peep, so that he might say the first sight he had ever had of so great a poet was in this stage towards immortality. I opened the door slowly, and there he sat, innocent and unconscious of our plot, in mysterious stillness and silence . . .

In phrenological development he is without constructiveness, while imagination is as big as an egg.

AGED 45.

It is singular how success and the want of it operate on two extraordinary men—Walter Scott and Wordsworth. Scott enters a room and sits at table with the coolness and self-possession of conscious fame: Wordsworth with a mortified elevation of the head, as if fearful he was not estimated as he deserved . . . Wordsworth must always be eloquent and profound, because he knows that he is considered childish and puerile. Scott seems to wish to appear less than he really is, while Wordsworth struggles to be thought, at the moment, greater than he is suspected to be.

AGED 51.

SOURCE: Benjamin Haydon's *Autobiography*.

Note: Haydon measured Wordworth's height and found he was 'eight heads high' or 5 feet $9\frac{7}{8}$ inches.

One evening, riding near Rydal, I saw Wordsworth sauntering towards me wearing a shade over his eyes, which were weak, and crooning out aloud some lines of a poem which he was composing ... Wordsworth was a very remarkable looking man. He looked like an old shepherd, with rough, rugged, weather-beaten face, but his features were fine and high cut. He was a grand man.

SOURCE: C. Venables, in Kilvert's *Diary*.

His face bore the marks of much not always peaceful meditation; the look of it not bland or benevolent, so much as close, impregnable and hard ... The eyes were not very brilliant, but they had a quiet clearness; there was enough of brow, and well shaped; rather too much of cheek ('horse-face' I have heard satirists say), face of squarish shape and decidedly longish ... He was large-boned, lean, but still firm-knit, tall and strong-looking when he stood; a right good old steel-gray figure, with a fine rustic simplicity and dignity about him, and a veracious *strength* looking through him which might have suited one of those old steel-gray *Markgrafs* ... whom Henry the Fowler set up to ward the marches, and do battle with the intrusive Heathen, in a stalwart and judicious manner ...

Still more memorable is an ocular glimpse I had in one of those Wordsworthian lion-dinners, very symbols to me of his general deportment there, and far clearer than the little feature of opposite sort, ambiguously given above ... Dinner was large, luminous, sumptuous; I sat a long way from Wordsworth ... I looked upwards, leftwards, the coast luckily being for a moment clear: there, far off, beautifully screened in the shadow of his vertical green circle, which was on the farther side of him, sat

Wordsworth, silent, in rock-like indifference, slowly but steadily gnawing some portion of what I judged to be raisins, with his eye and attention placidly fixed on these and these alone.

AGED 70.

SOURCE: Thomas Carlyle, *Reminiscences*, 1887 edit.

Note: The 'vertical green circle' refers to the sort of 'skeleton brass candle-stick' which Wordsworth carried in his pocket. He was in the habit of setting it on the table between him and the chief lights and releasing a vertical green shade, which threw his eyes into shadow.

WREN, SIR CHRISTOPHER (1632–1723), architect; surveyor general and principal architect for rebuilding London after the Great Fire.

He was in his person low and thin; but by temperance and skilful management, for he was proficient in anatomy and physic, he enjoyed a good state of health and prolonged his life to an unusual length. For this, however, he might probably be indebted to his remarkable cheerfulness and equanimity.

SOURCE: Rev. Francis Wrangham, The *British Plutarch*, new edit., 1810.

YORK, DUCHESS OF (1637–1671). See Hyde Anne, Duchess of York.

YORK, DUKE OF (1763–1827). See Frederick Augustus, Duke of York.

YOUNG PRETENDER (1720–1788). See Stuart, Charles Edward Louis Philip Casimir.